P9-BHR-822

BATMAN

ARCHIVES ▾ VOLUME 1

BOB KANE

ARCHIVE  EDITIONS

THE BATMAN ARCHIVES
VOLUME ONE

PUBLISHED BY DC COMICS INC.

DC COMICS INC.
666 FIFTH AVENUE, NEW YORK, NY 10103
A WARNER BROS. INC. COMPANY

PRINTED IN CANADA. FIRST PRINTING.

THE DC ARCHIVE EDITIONS

SPECIAL THANKS TO GREG
THEAKSTON, MARK WAID, AND
JOSEPH MANNARIO

COLOR RECONSTRUCTION BY
BOB LE ROSE AND DANIEL VOZZO

JACKET AND TEXT DESIGN BY
ALEX JAY/STUDIO J

FOREWORD

He came out of nowhere, yet he came out of a rich tradition.

He came out of the shadows.

There was no one like him, but soon there were many like him—or so their creators wished and dreamed and strained.

He was The Dark Knight, and he was a bright vision.

The format of the comic book—and the genre of super-hero adventure stories—was brand-new, and setting American youth on its ear, when the Batman made his debut. The year was 1939; Superman was a national sensation; and the company that introduced the Man of Steel was bidding for another success. Hardly could anyone involved with this new character—publishers, editors, creators, not even readers—have known what this new hero represented.

For the Batman became more than a classic character. Longevity is a mighty testament all by itself, but those publishers, editors, creators and readers *sensed* what we can now see in retrospect—and examine in these pages: The Batman represented a new type of hero in comic books. He was both a distillation of types and a departure. He inspired a whole school of premise and character development and writing. He did not just chase bad guys, or move through scenes, or solve mysteries.

What made the Batman unique (and, significantly, this happened at the instant of his creation; other elements evolved and matured, but not this aspect) was the *mood* he manifested. He embodied the darker elements of the city through which he stalked; his motives seemed to be as much revenge as justice; and hence the world in which his creators placed him was not a setting but a home. The Batman is a type more than a character, and his adventures were to be chapters in an unfolding epic—variations on themes he was destined to play over and over again—not random episodes of adventures and thrills.

So readers seized on this new character because he was different, because his world was so unified (and so frightening), because he *fit* in that world in ways readers could sense and not just see, from elements like his costume to the manner in which he was drawn against those compelling, bizarre cityscapes. He was intriguing because readers were treated to glimpses of his private life and real identity—yet when he was the Batman, he could be as remote and idiosyncratic to them as to the criminals and cops who knew nothing, absolutely nothing, about his essence.

Did he reveal himself? Well, there were the countless platitudes like Sunday-school lessons or Fourth of July speeches about justice, but there was also "It says 'no admittance'—but that doesn't mean *us*, Robin!" He was called by his creators not just a menace to criminals but a "weird menace to all crime." The holy moment where he consecrates his life to fighting criminals is yet called by his creators a "curious and strange scene." He is completely vulnerable to harm, yet he "trains his body to physical perfection." An enigma? You bet! Let's keep reading those comic-book stories—who *is* this guy? We know his origin, his motivations, his dual identity, his limitations and talents, but we don't know *him*. Wow.

All this in comic books?

Finally, yes. There was a rich tradition from which the Batman emerged. What immediately seemed different was that he did private eyes one better—he was not merely private but secret. More, he was a super-hero without super powers.

But in a sense, one of the distinguishing characteristics of the Batman was not his uniqueness but his noble lineage, how much he resembled other crimefighters. There were costumed avengers all through legend and literature, from Robin Hood to the Scarlet Pimpernel to the Lone Ranger (whose family had also been murdered). In the movies, Zorro and the Lone Wolf donned costumes to do their justice-work. In newspaper comic strips Lee Falk's Phantom relied heavily on his costume to preserve his aura and accomplish his just deeds. On radio there was the Green Hornet. In pulp magazines there was the Gray Seal (who, when out of costume, was a bored millionaire) and the Shadow—mysterious even to readers, a figure of the dark, all costume and threats of terrible justice.

Sherlock Holmes has influenced every crime novelist since his original appearances, and the Batman's creators cited a marriage of the brilliant Holmes and the flashy, acrobatic Douglas Fairbanks of the movies in their conception of the Batman persona. Robin was meant to evoke Robin Hood in young readers' minds.

Not bad company.

So the *different* character of the day was Superman, whose invulnerability made his own costume and dual identity more like props than essential elements. Yet Batman seemed, and seems still, revolutionary. What was it?

The answer lies in the Batman's environment. His moody, urban, terror-filled backdrop, courtesy of his creators' skills, was brilliant and compelling. But mainly the Batman's success was due to his paper environment: living in a comic book.

What the Batman did was to live the best of the lives of his predecessors from epics, sagas, legends, literature, movies, strips, stories, and radio in a totally new environment. A costumed, mysterious, avenging, obsessed, schizophrenic justice-seeker was perfect for a comic-book format; and the comics were crying out for such a character.

But someone had to put him there.

Robin was not the first Boy Wonder associated with the Batman.

There were New York city kids before him. There was Bob Kane, 22 years old in May of 1939, and Bill Finger, a year younger, the two of whom had been collaborating on comic-book features during the dawning Golden Age. Kane produced the art—crude, halting, humorously inclined, but art nevertheless; and Finger wrote the scripts. Kane's credits, even then, made him a veteran of sorts in the nascent comic-book industry, having drawn features with names like Peter Pupp for outfits like the Jerry Iger and Fiction House shops. Bill Finger was one of those rare, gifted souls whose singular talent blesses an emergent art form or format: he was a writer who thought in visual terms. This was just the touch the comic book needed at this moment, when Superman's impact promised an explosion of titles.

Writers had to plot longer stories than newspaper comic strips; they had to manage the action in a way similar to the movies; they had to bring the vivid characterizations that were the pulps' hallmarks to the comic book pages; and they had to weave all these requirements into coherent stories that were supposed to make readers turn the page . . . and buy the succeeding issue. Bill Finger—seemingly instinctively—had all these abilities.

DC editor Vincent Sullivan's request for a new hero to capitalize on Superman's popularity was a suggestion, not a prescription. And Kane's initial conception foreshadowed the arresting themes and preoccupations to come. In later years Kane cited such disparate models for his hero as Leonardo's studies of bats, and a Mary Roberts Rinehart play, *The Bat*, in which the title character was actually a villain. But the recipe changed while the pot was boiling. Finger suggested some changes in the character's appearance and costume (pointed ears, a cape that would resemble bat-wings when the protagonist jumped through the air), and he plotted the first story. His immediate model was the Shadow (as Finger later recalled); villains would resemble the bizarre rogues gallery of *Dick Tracy*; the artwork's composition would draw on innovative camera angles in the work of filmmakers like Orson Welles.

But "swipes" were not afoot. The tried-and-true formulas were refreshingly new—and startlingly innovative—when transferred to the comic-book format. Similarly, the Batman team, who bought so many tickets to watch *Citizen Kane* (no relation) that they could recite dialogue while sitting at their drawing boards, were happily stunned to learn years later that filmmakers they admired credited comics with inspiring their own pacing and composition and direction!

So Kane and Finger fashioned something old, something new in the Batman. Their showcase was to be in DETECTIVE COMICS, so, obviously, there had to be mysteries to solve. The mixture of genres Kane and Finger loved resulted in the Batman living in the best of all worlds (besides that city which, incidentally, was New York before being changed to Gotham)—a traditional detective mystery could be combined with an exotic costumed-hero tale; the protagonist could be cerebral as well as an action-figure; plotting could be sophisticated (to a comic-book point) but also could have—*should* have—some violence and visual verve. To solve a mystery with brains and catch the bad guys with brawn bids fair to satisfy almost every reader.

If the City—that backdrop which was sometimes a mood-setting frieze, sometimes an enveloping or even choking atmosphere that mirrored the twisted preoccupations of villains—could mesmerize readers in Batman stories, so could the origin tale provide an irresistible tug. As explained for the first time in DETECTIVE COMICS #33 (and now part of American folklore) young Bruce Wayne witnessed his parents' wanton murder and vows to devote his life to the apprehension of criminals (not necessarily the eradication of crime, which could be the subject of the introduction to the Compleat Analyst's Archives of the Batman someday). All he needs thenceforth are his maniacal compulsion and his family inheritance to fulfill that vow.

What's left? Once again, the touch of Kane and Finger. The artwork, clunky at first as the stories in this book will display, somehow served the premise well. A drawing style too realistic might have seemed sterile, or boring. A cartoony feel lent an air of unreality to the increasingly believable ambiance. The unreality—strange props (a favorite device of Finger), distorted perspective, flailing shadows—was reminiscent of the Surrealist German movie *The Cabinet of Dr. Caligari* . . . and could be just as nightmarish. The best newspaper comic strips of the day dealing with crime and melodrama and action were, respectively, *Dick Tracy*, *Little Orphan Annie*, and *Captain Easy*—none of them drawn in an ultra-realistic style, and all of them classically effective at their jobs.

Finger's plotting featured something rather new in comic books, an aspect that can almost be called movies on paper. The early Batman stories have heavy doses of action, and the motion of characters is as thoroughly, almost lovingly, dissected as in motion-picture direction or editing. Leaps are visually dispersed and delineated in their several component parts. Fights are graphically depicted from various angles and with a reporter's attention to changing fortunes therein. Captions abound, but seldom is one used as a "crutch" to bridge a scene . . . when Batman's speeding car can be shown or a jumping Batman can be revealed. These are comics, folks, and the groping, experimenting team of Kane and Finger are having fun. In cartooning that virtually always means the readers will have fun, too.

The final puzzle pieces that insured Batman's success—his definitive persona, a more sophisticated design, an overall richness of characterization—came with the arrival of Jerry Robinson just three issues into the Batman's run, and later, the contributions of writer Gardner Fox. In 1939 Robinson was 17, and beginning college at the Columbia School of Journalism; side-work in comics was to be a part-time means of supporting his education. In a way, Robinson was almost an amalgam of Kane and Finger, for he had sense of both design and structure. A better artist than Kane, he was able to make the Batman's adventures look more professional—anatomy was corrected, and a handsome patina covered the renderings—but he was wise enough to preserve the slightly surreal appearance of the feature. He recognized that an important component of Finger's scripts and Kane's initial artwork was that deliberate unreality, and his work merely codified that aspect in a handsome way: Robinson polished a gem.

Gardner Fox was already a veteran scripter for the fledgling DC group when the Batman came along, but his work on the early stories brought a maturity of plotting and structure. Fox's specialty was an underpinning of plausible gimmicks and effects combined with a certain comic-book believability that interestingly was juxtaposed with the fantastic basis of the Batman books. Fox had a career in the "real world"—writing more than 100 books of fiction in various categories—and he brought a wide range of storytelling experience to the table.

It may seem incredible today in retrospect, but before Robin, the Boy Wonder, there really were no major boy-sidekicks to major heroes. In text fiction the device worked, as well as, occasionally, in newspaper strips (Milton Caniff's Dickie Dare and Terry each had heroic, adult buddies, as did Mel Graff's Patsy), but it seemed natural to pitch an appeal to the kids who comprised a bulk of the readership. No matter that most young readers probably were vicarious Batmen and not young Robins—if you're going to engage in transference and fantasy, why not shoot for the name above the lights?—because Robin formed a great counterpoint to the Batman. Robin was even more vulnerable; he had to be even more resourceful; and, maybe best of all, even if not by intention, Robin provided a sounding-board. No longer did Batman have to reveal himself to readers through thought-balloons or awkward soliloquies: he plotted with Robin, and began to engage in the humorous banter that has become a trademark of the series. The first boy-sidekick was responsible for more than just *being* there.

Some incredible talents maintained the Batman episodes through the years (including, but not confined to, such greats as Mort Weisinger, Dick Sprang, Bill Woolfolk, Julius Schwartz, Dennis O'Neil, Neal Adams, Frank Robbins, Dick Giordano, Steve Englehart, Marshall Rogers, Frank Miller, and Alan Moore), and the Batman has visited other showcases like newspaper strips, television series, and motion pictures. Whether he triumphed in these areas or survived them is an open question—but ultimately an irrelevant question in the context of considering the essence of the Batman.

What you have here in this book is the classic character as he was born, as he grew, and as he was standardized—quickly—in conception. It's what everything else was built on. And it's all anyone has needed.

According to the Old Testament it was Abraham's sons Isaac and Ishmael who founded the two great nations of the Jews and the Arabs. Well, it was two super-heroes born within a year of each other (Superman's debut was in June 1938 and the Batman's in May 1939) who were also progenitors: it can be said that virtually every super-hero who has followed has been in the mold of one or the other (or, at the most innovative limit, borrowing characteristics of each).

Comic-book super-heroes have a universal appeal, and for some reason their universality has appealed more to Americans than to readers elsewhere around the world. But there is something, it seems, in the American psyche that is receptive to costumed crimefighters with amazing physical skills and incredible prowess. No doubt there is a lot of vicarious transference—"You'll Believe a Man Can Fly" proved to be one of the great descriptions of a Superman's appeal.

Speaking personally (and for a legion of superfans, too), if I have to identify with a hero, and my only choice is dreaming of having bullets bounce off my chest or living like a playboy while inventing toys to foil criminals—the choice is easy.

Basically it is the Batman's ultimate vulnerability, not invulnerability, that seizes our attention, affection, and loyalty. We could be him, if. . . . And we can share his contempt for the rotten sorts who lurk in the shadows, and we would share others' fear . . . if we knew he was not there to protect us. The Batman—for all his mystery—is one of us. He's a type, and he's our type. Get to know him again in these pages, see how he was born and how he grew, and share the enthusiasm of the young creators who grew with him.

RICK MARSCHALL

RICK MARSCHALL is a noted author and lecturer on American popular culture. He has written more than 17 books, most on comics and cartoons, as well as many articles on the topic. He has organized exhibits abroad and spoken on behalf of the U.S. Information Service on the subject of comics; and is the editor of *Nemo: The Classic Comics Library* (a quarterly magazine about comics). A former editor of Marvel Comics, he is currently president of Cartoon Inc, which organizes comics exhibitions, and Remco Worldservice Books, which packages reprints of classic strips like *Little Nemo* and *Krazy Kat*.

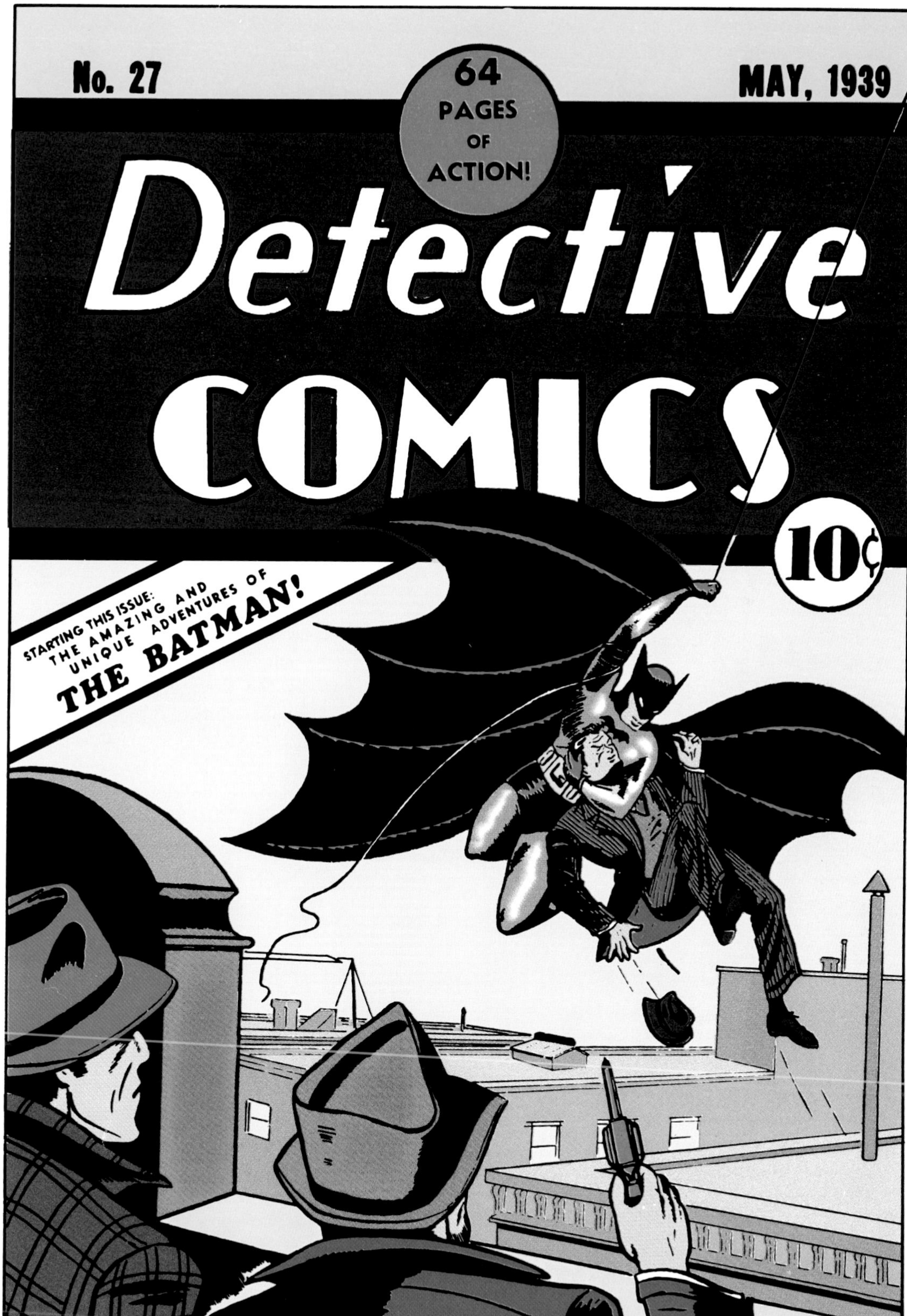

No. 27
64 PAGES OF ACTION!
MAY, 1939
Detective
COMICS
10¢
STARTING THIS ISSUE:
THE AMAZING AND UNIQUE ADVENTURES OF
THE BATMAN!

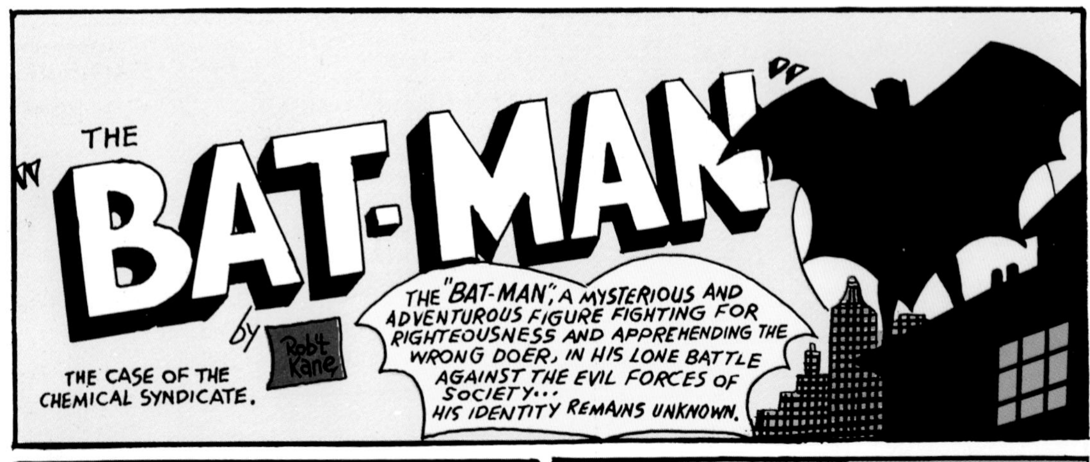
THE "BAT-MAN"
by Rob't Kane
THE CASE OF THE CHEMICAL SYNDICATE.
THE "BAT-MAN", A MYSTERIOUS AND ADVENTUROUS FIGURE FIGHTING FOR RIGHTEOUSNESS AND APPREHENDING THE WRONG DOER, IN HIS LONE BATTLE AGAINST THE EVIL FORCES OF SOCIETY... HIS IDENTITY REMAINS UNKNOWN.

THE HOME OF COMMISSIONER GORDON, WHO AT THE MOMENT IS ENTERTAINING HIS YOUNG SOCIALITE FRIEND, BRUCE WAYNE.
WELL, COMMISSIONER, ANYTHING EXCITING HAPPENING THESE DAYS?
-NO-O- EXCEPT THIS FELLOW THEY CALL THE "BAT-MAN" PUZZLES ME!
RING!

HELLO... WHAT'S THAT? LAMBERT, THE CHEMICAL KING... STABBED TO DEATH? HIS SON'S FINGER PRINTS ON THE KNIFE?... I'LL BE RIGHT OVER!

--TALK ABOUT SOMETHING EXCITING... OLD LAMBERT HAS BEEN MURDERED AT HIS MANSION.., I'M GOING THERE NOW. LIKE TO COME ALONG?
OH WELL, NOTHING ELSE TO DO, MIGHT AS WELL.

THE COMMISSIONER AND BRUCE WAYNE SPEED TOWARD THE LAMBERT RESIDENCE...

HELLO, SERGEANT, EVERYTHING UNDER CONTROL?
YES SIR, WE'VE GOT YOUNG LAMBERT IN THE BACK ROOM!

... AND AFTER A THOROUGH EXAMINATION OF THE SCENE OF THE CRIME, THE ROOM BECOMES BUSY WITH THE USUAL POLICE ROUTINE...
WELL I'M FINISHED IN HERE. LET ME TALK TO YOUNG LAMBERT.

HELLO, LAMBERT, THEY SAY YOU KILLED YOUR FATHER!
I DIDN'T DO IT! COMMISSIONER, BELIEVE ME, I DIDN'T DO IT!!!

CALM YOURSELF, MY BOY, AND TELL ME ALL ABOUT IT!
...WELL SIR... TONIGHT I CAME HOME EARLY, AND AS I WAS PASSING THE LIBRARY I HEARD A GROAN... I RUSHED IN AND THERE WAS MY FATHER LYING ON THE FLOOR, WITH A KNIFE IN HIM!

... AND AS I RUSHED IN, I GOT THE IMPRESSION OF SOMETHING LEAPING OUT OF THE WINDOW... I ALSO NOTICED THAT FATHER'S SAFE WAS OPENED...

...I PULLED THE KNIFE OUT OF MY FATHER'S BODY, AND TURNED HIM TOWARD ME JUST IN TIME TO HEAR HIM SAY...
...CONTRACT... CONTRACT... OHHHH!

...AND THEN HE DIED. THAT'S HOW I GOT MY FINGER PRINTS ON THE KNIFE... THAT'S THE TRUTH, COMMISSIONER!
HMM! DID YOUR DAD HAVE ANY ENEMIES OR PEOPLE WHO HAD AN INTEREST IN HIS BUSINESS ACTIVITIES?

...NOT THAT I KNOW OF, EXCEPT HIS THREE FORMER BUSINESS PARTNERS... LET'S SEE, THEY WERE STEVEN CRANE, PAUL ROGERS AND ALFRED STRYKER
COMMISSIONER, THERE'S A MAN NAMED STEVE CRANE WHO WANTS TO SPEAK TO OLD LAMBERT... WHEN I TOLD HIM THAT OLD LAMBERT WAS MURDERED HE GOT VERY EXCITED AND WANTED TO SPEAK TO YOU!

THIS IS COMMISSIONER GORDON. WHAT'S THE TROUBLE?
YESTERDAY, MR. LAMBERT CALLED AND TOLD ME HE RECEIVED AN ANONYMOUS THREAT ON HIS LIFE... TODAY I RECEIVED THE SAME... THAT'S WHY I CALLED UP... AND I'M AFRAID I'LL BE NEXT... WHAT SHALL I DO?

WAIT... AND DO NOT LET ANYBODY IN-- WE'LL BE OVER SOON AS WE CAN-- WHAT'S THAT, BRUCE?
HO HUM! I'LL LEAVE YOU HERE TO FINISH YOUR WORK... I'M GOING HOME.
CLICK!
2

...MEANWHILE STEVEN CRANE SITS IN HIS LIBRARY WITH A FEELING OF IMPENDING DANGER... WHEN SUDDENLY...
AHHHHH!

...THERE IS A SICKENING SHOT... CRANE SLUMPS IN HIS CHAIR... DEAD! THE MURDERER RUSHES TO THE SAFE AND SECURES A PAPER...

DID YOU GET THE PAPER?
YEAH!

...AS THE TWO MEN LEER OVER THEIR CONQUEST, THEY DO NOT NOTICE A THIRD MENACING FIGURE STANDING BEHIND THEM... IT IS THE "BAT-MAN!"
THE BAT-MAN !!!

THE "BAT-MAN" LASHES OUT WITH A TERRIFIC RIGHT...

...HE GRABS HIS SECOND ADVERSARY IN A DEADLY HEADLOCK... AND WITH A MIGHTY HEAVE...

SENDS THE BURLY CRIMINAL FLYING THROUGH SPACE...

THE "BAT-MAN" SWIFTLY PICKS UP THE PAPER THAT THE MURDERER STOLE FROM STEVEN CRANE'S SAFE...

...MEANWHILE THE COMMISSIONER DRAWS UP IN HIS CAR...
IT'S THE BAT-MAN! GET HIM!

MR. CRANE HAS BEEN MURDERED, SIR-- IT'S HORRIBLE!
THAT'S TWO DEAD PARTNERS OUT OF THE FOUR THAT HAVE RECEIVED THREATENING NOTES. THE OTHER TWO MUST HAVE RECEIVED THEM TOO...LET'S GO TO ROGERS NEXT!

THE "BAT-MAN" READS THE PAPER HE SNATCHED FROM THE KILLERS AND A GRIM SMILE COMES TO HIS LIPS...

... HE SPEEDS HIS CAR FORWARD TO AN UNKNOWN DESTINATION...
3

...MEANWHILE ROGERS, WHO HAS LEARNED OF LAMBERT'S DEATH BY NEWS BROADCAST, HAS ALREADY GONE TO THE NEIGHBORING LABORATORY OF HIS ERSTWHILE PARTNER, ALFRED STRYKER...
HELLO, JENNINGS. I MUST SEE STRYKER QUICKLY.
WON'T YOU COME IN?

SOCK!

JENNINGS, STRYKER'S ASSISTANT, CARRIES ROGERS TO THE BASEMENT OF HIS LABORATORY...
HEH! HEH! ONE MORE OUT OF THE WAY-- SOON I'LL CONTROL EVERYTHING!

THIS IS THE GAS-CHAMBER I USE TO KILL GUINEA PIGS, TO EXPERIMENT WITH-- BUT NOW YOU ARE MY GUINEA PIG ! HEH-HEH !! WHEN THIS GLASS LID COVERS YOU ENTIRELY, GAS WILL COME THROUGH THE JET AND KILL YOU (HEH-HEH)!
YOU FIEND!

JENNINGS PULLS A BRAKE WHICH STARTS THE GLASS DOWN OVER ROGERS AND CERTAIN DOOM...
I'M GOING DOWN NOW TO TURN THE GAS ON... SLEEP WELL... HEH-HEH!

...AT THAT MOMENT THE "BAT-MAN" LEAPS THROUGH AN OPEN TRANSOM...

...THE "BAT-MAN" SEIZES A WRENCH FROM A TABLE AND LEAPS FOR THE GAS-CHAMBER...

THE "BAT-MAN" QUICKLY PLUGS THE GAS-JET WITH A HANDKERCHIEF, AS THE GAS CHAMBER DESCENDS ENTIRELY OVER THEM...
SISSSS

...HE THEN UNTIES ROGERS, AND WITH A POWERFUL SWING...
CRASH
4

JENNINGS RETURNS AND IS STARTLED BY THE BAT-MAN... HE REACHES FOR HIS GUN...
WHAT TH--?

...THE "BAT-MAN" GREETS JENNINGS WITH A FLYING TACKLE...

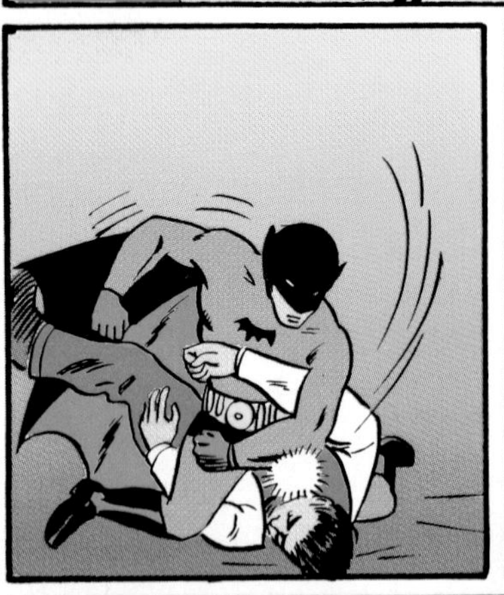

MEANWHILE, ALFRED STRYKER HAS HEARD THE CRASH OF THE GAS-CHAMBER... AS HE ENTERS THE LABORATORY...
ROGERS? WHAT HAPPENED?
YOUR ASSISTANT, JENNINGS, TRIED TO KILL ME!

HOWEVER, STRYKER HAS NOT NOTICED THE "BAT-MAN" WHO HAS SECLUDED HIMSELF IN THE SHADOWS...
SO HE DIDN'T GET YOU AFTER ALL... WELL, I'LL FINISH YOU AND THEN THROW YOUR BODY IN THE ACID TANK BELOW.
YOU?

OHHH! MY HAND~

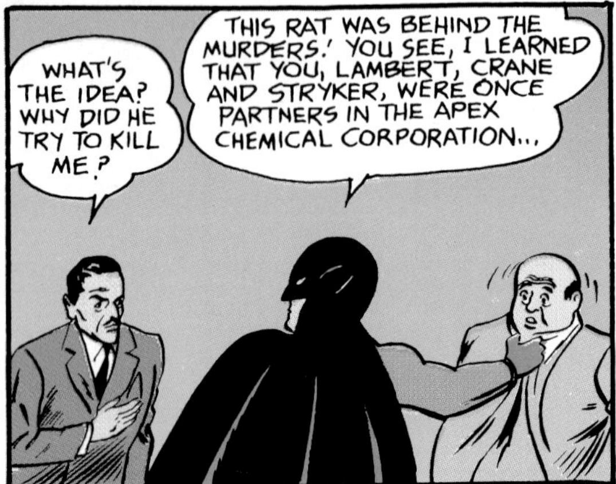
WHAT'S THE IDEA? WHY DID HE TRY TO KILL ME?
THIS RAT WAS BEHIND THE MURDERS! YOU SEE, I LEARNED THAT YOU, LAMBERT, CRANE AND STRYKER, WERE ONCE PARTNERS IN THE APEX CHEMICAL CORPORATION...

...STRYKER, WHO WISHED TO BE SOLE OWNER, BUT HAVING NO READY CASH, MADE SECRET CONTRACTS WITH YOU, TO PAY A CERTAIN SUM OF MONEY EACH YEAR UNTIL HE OWNED THE BUSINESS. HE FIGURED BY KILLING YOU AND STEALING THE CONTRACTS, HE WOULDN'T HAVE TO PAY THIS MONEY.
5

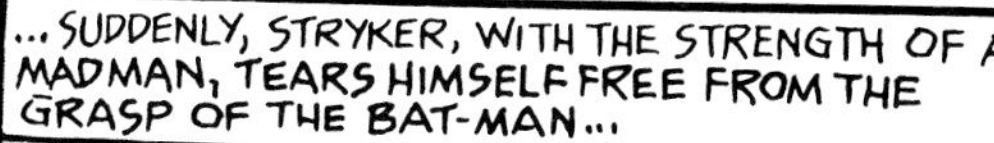

THE NEXT DAY, YOUNG BRUCE WAYNE IS AGAIN A VISITOR AT THE COMMISSIONER'S HOUSE... WHO HAS JUST FINISHED TELLING BRUCE THE LATEST EXPLOITS OF THE "BAT-MAN"!

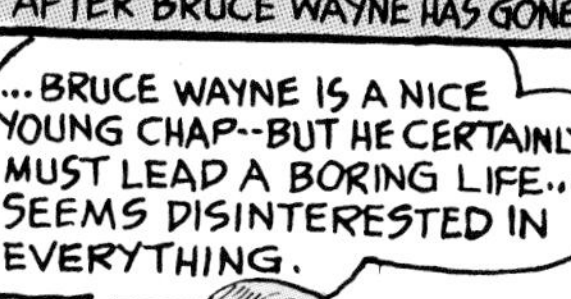

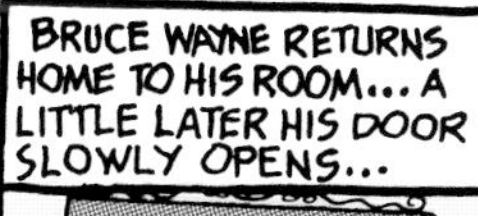

...AND REVEALS ITS OCCUPANT... IF THE COMMISSIONER COULD SEE HIS YOUNG FRIEND NOW... HE'D BE AMAZED TO LEARN THAT HE IS THE "BAT-MAN!"

WATCH FOR A NEW THRILLING "BAT-MAN" STORY

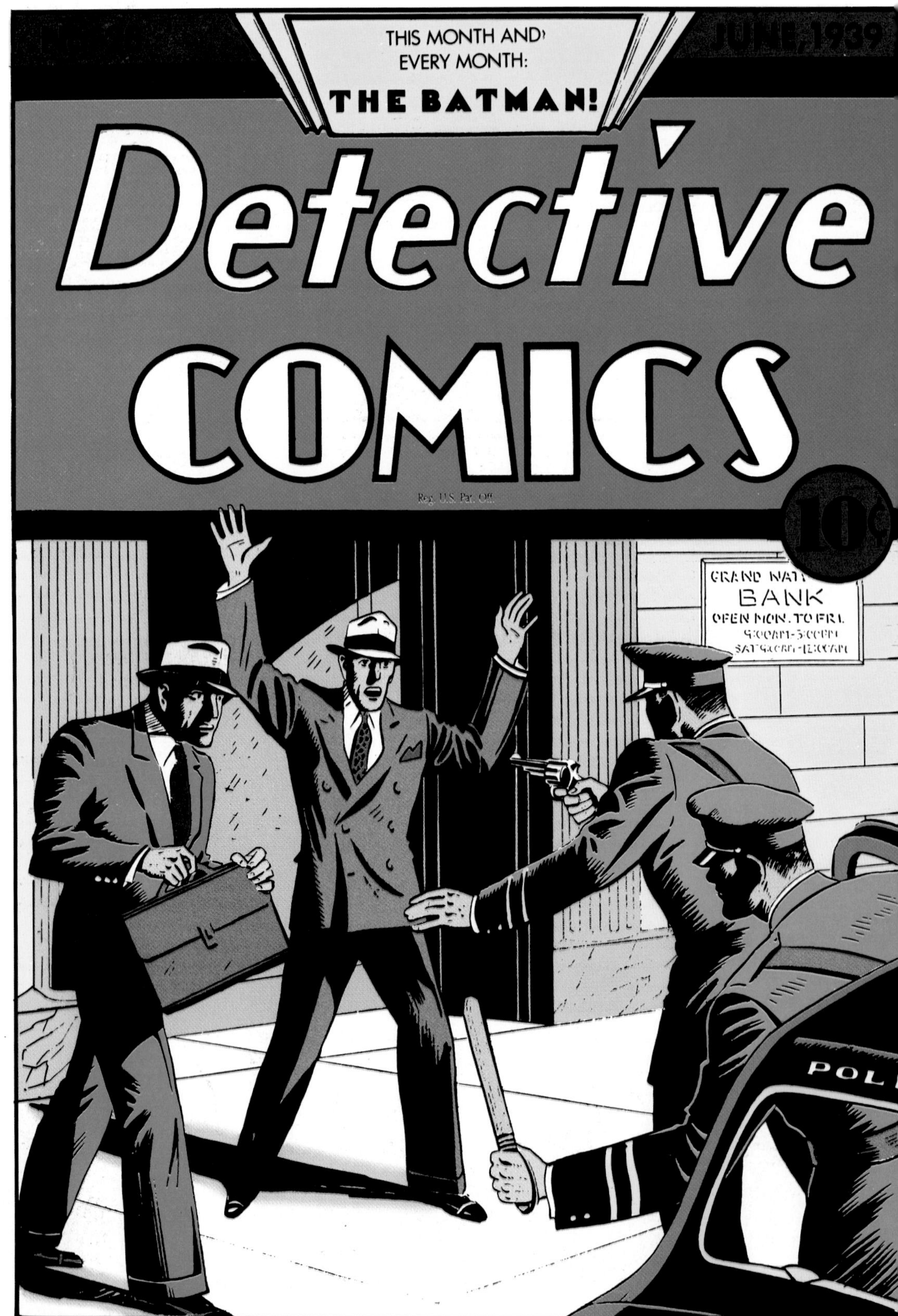
JUNE, 1939
THIS MONTH AND EVERY MONTH:
THE BATMAN!
Detective COMICS
Reg. U.S. Pat. Off.
10¢
BANK
OPEN MON. TO FRI.

THAT NIGHT, BRUCE WAYNE, THE "BAT-MAN" DIALS A NUMBER AND THEN DISGUISING HIS VOICE, SPEAKS...

HELLO GIMPY-THIS IS COMMISSIONER GORDON. DID YOU GET THAT INFORMATION ABOUT THE JEWEL GANG? IF YOU DID YOU'D BETTER SPILL IT-OR ELSE YOU'LL BE BACK IN THE PEN TO STAY-WELL?

GIMPY, IS A "STOOL PIGEON IN THE EMPLOY OF THE POLICE DEPARTMENT, HAVING A CRIMINAL RECORD, HE HAS ACESS TO THE HAUNTS OF THE UNDERWORLD.

LOOK CHIEF - FRENCHY BLAKE IS BEHIND THE GANG AND THEY'RE GOING TO PULL A JOB TONIGHT AT THE APARTMENT OF THE VANDERSMITHS. IT'S THE TRUTH, S'HELP ME!

THE "BAT-MAN" REACHES DOWN FOR THE BAG OF STOLEN JEWELS—AND DOES A CURIOUS THING—HE STOPS-HE "SEEMS" TO BE WAITING...

THE BODY OF THE MAN THAT WENT OVER THE ROOF HAS ATTRACTED THE POLICE. THEY "SEEM" TO "SURPRISE" THE "BAT-MAN" WHO "DROPS" THE BAG OF JEWELS...
IT'S THE "BAT-MAN"!

SO SORRY, GENTLEMEN, BUT I'M AFRAID I HAVE TO GO NOW... GOOD NIGHT!

TO THE HORRIFIED EYES OF THE POLICE, THE "BAT-MAN" DIVES OFF THE ROOF..

.. HE TURNS A COMPLETE SOMERSAULT IN MID-AIR AND..

... LANDS ON HIS FEET ON THE PENTHOUSE ROOF BELOW!

HE QUICKLY DRAWS A TOUGH SILK ROPE FROM HIS BELT AND TWIRLS IT ABOVE HIS HEAD

. LASSOING A FLAGPOLE JUTTING OUT ON A NEARBY BUILDING

THE "BAT-MAN" SWINGS OUT INTO SPACE...!

AND DROPS SAFELY ON TO THE ROOF OF A LOWER BUILDING

HE GOT AWAY ALL RIGHT.
-AND HOW HE GOT AWAY... WHEW!

WELL AT LEAST WE GOT THE JEWELS AND THE OTHER GUYS -
AND WE KNOW THAT THE "BAT-MAN" IS ONE OF THEM, MAYBE THE HEAD OF THE GANG - SAY, I WONDER WHAT THEY FOUGHT OVER, THOUGH?
THIS IS EXACTLY WHAT THE "BAT-MAN" WANTS THEM TO THINK- WE'LL SEE WHY IN A MOMENT

NEXT DAY..
The Tribune
"BAT-MAN" HEAD OF JEWEL GAN
ELUDES CAPTURE BY SPECTACULAR LEAP

THAT "BAT-MAN" CERTAINLY FIXED US. "RICKY" IS DEAD AND "GLOVES" IS IN THE PEN. I'D LIKE TO GET MY HANDS ON THAT GUY... ONE GOOD THING THOUGH, THE COPS THINK THE "BAT-MAN" IS IN ON IT..

.. NOW THAT MEANS THEY'LL BE WATCHING FOR HIM AND THAT LEAVES US FREE TO CONTINUE OUR WORK — NOW TONIGHT, I WANT YOU BOYS TO...
THIS IS WHY THE "BAT-MAN" WANTED TO BE CON - NECTED WITH THE ROBBERIES... SO THAT THE JEWEL THIEVES WOULD THINK THEY WEREN'T BEING WATCHED.

..AND WOULD CONTINUE, GIVING THE "BAT-MAN" THE OPPORTUNITY OF THEIR CAPTURE
HOWEVER, OUTSIDE, THE "BAT-MAN" LISTENS.

THAT NIGHT, FRENCHY'S MEN ARE AT WORK-
SOME HAUL, EH, "SLICK"-IT'S A GOOD THING THE "BAT-MAN" ISN'T HERE, TONIGHT
JUST LET HIM COME- WE'RE READY FOR HIM THIS TIME!

THE "BAT-MAN" TIES THE MEN UP, THEN CROSSES THE ROOM AND "PHONES"

THE APARTMENT OF FRENCHY BLAKE.
KNOCK!
KNOCK!

IS THAT YOU, BOYS?
YEAH LET US IN

YOU!

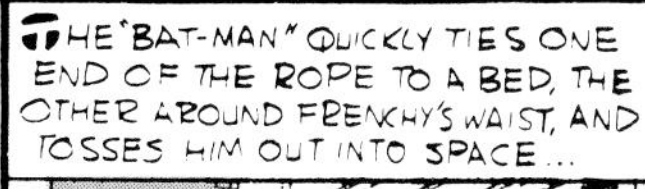
THE "BAT-MAN" QUICKLY TIES ONE END OF THE ROPE TO A BED, THE OTHER AROUND FRENCHY'S WAIST, AND TOSSES HIM OUT INTO SPACE...

KEEP QUIET AND LISTEN - I WANT A COMPLETE WRITTEN CONFESSION FROM YOU ABOUT THOSE JEWEL ROBBERIES, OR ELSE I'LL CUT THIS ROPE...

ALL RIGHT! ALL RIGHT! PULL ME UP- I'LL CONFESS- PULL ME UP...
5

THE "BAT-MAN" PULLS HIM IN AND FRENCHY WRITES AND SIGNS A COMPLETE CONFESSION ...
- THAT SHOULD INTEREST THE POLICE, FRENCHY!

SUDDENLY....

THE "BAT-MAN" MEETS FRENCHY'S JAW AND SENDS HIM FLYING BACK OVER THE TABLE.

DON'T HIT ME LIKE THAT AGAIN, PLEASE. DON'T HIT ME, DON'T ..

THE "BAT-MAN" TIES FRENCHY UP AND CARRIES HIM TO HIS CAR.

THAT EVENING A CAR PULLS UP IN FRONT OF POLICE HEADQUARTERS, DUMPS AN UNCONSCIOUS BODY ON THE SIDEWALK - BLOWS ITS HORN AND SPEEDS AWAY..
HONK! HONK!

COME ON, KELLY- DID YOU SEE THAT?

HMM- LOOKS LIKE THE ONCE DAPPER FRENCHY BLAKE.. HE WAS SURE MESSED UP!
LOOK! THIS LETTER IS FOR THE COMMISSIONER- WAS PINNED TO HIS BACK. THERE'S ALSO A BRIEF CASE

A FEW MINUTES LATER THE COMMISSIONER READS THE MESSAGE.
DEAR COMMISSIONER— I THOUGHT YOU MIGHT LIKE TO HAVE THE LEADER OF THE JEWEL GANG AM ALSO LEAVING HIS CONFESSION AND STOLEN JEWELS TILL WE MEET AGAIN- I REMAIN- THE
Rob't Kane
Finis

DON'T MISS THE FURTHER INTRIGUING ADVENTURES OF THE
"BAT-MAN"
NEXT MONTH IN DETECTIVE COMICS

No. 29
64 PAGES OF Thrill-Packed ACTION!
JULY, 1939
Detective COMICS
Reg. U.S. Pat. Off.
10¢
Another thrilling episode of
THE BATMAN
in this issue
BOB KANE

The
BAT-MAN
BY BOB KANE
"THE BATMAN MEETS DOCTOR DEATH"

THE BAT MAN, EERIE FIGURE OF THE NIGHT, HAS BECOME A LEGENDARY FIGURE IN THE LIFE OF THE TEEMING METROPOLIS, RIGHTING WRONGS AND BRINGING JUSTICE WHERE IT HAS NEVER BEEN BEFORE...

IN THE STUDY OF DOCTOR KARL HELLFERN, LATER TO BE MORE WIDELY KNOWN AS DOCTOR DEATH!
JABAH, COME HERE!

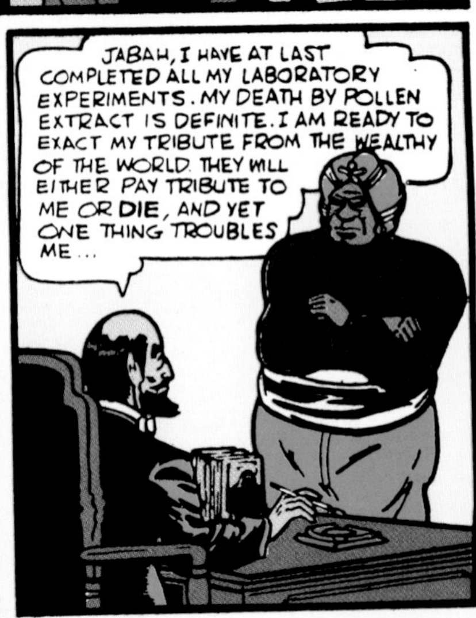
JABAH, I HAVE AT LAST COMPLETED ALL MY LABORATORY EXPERIMENTS. MY DEATH BY POLLEN EXTRACT IS DEFINITE. I AM READY TO EXACT MY TRIBUTE FROM THE WEALTHY OF THE WORLD. THEY WILL EITHER PAY TRIBUTE TO ME OR DIE, AND YET ONE THING TROUBLES ME...

...THIS MAN THEY CALL THE BAT MAN — A CRIME SUCH AS OURS IS SURE TO ATTRACT HIS ATTENTION. HE MUST BE DONE AWAY WITH! IF I KNEW WHO HE IS—BUT. NO ONE DOES. I MUST TRAP HIM!

—PERHAPS WE CAN CONTACT HIM THROUGH THE PERSONAL NOTICE COLUMN IN THE DAILY NEWSPAPERS...

ACROSS THE CITY, BRUCE WAYNE, IN REALITY THE BAT MAN, READS THE DAILY PAPER, THE NEXT MORNING...
HMM! WHAT'S THIS?

PUBLIC NOTICES
Batman:
If you will go to General Post Office and ask for a letter addressed to John Jones you will find a message of vital Importance.

HAVE YOU A LETTER ADDRESSED TO JOHN JONES?
U.S POST OFFICE

BRUCE WAYNE OPENS THE LETTER
Batman -
At 10 P.M. tonight at suite B on the 14th floor of the Beverly Apts I will commit a murder and I defy you without the aid of the police to stop me..

BRUCE RETURNS HOME. HE KNEELS BEFORE A SMALL CHEST AND TAKES OUT HIS BAT-LIKE MANTLE...

HALF AN HOUR TO CHANGE AND HALF AN HOUR TO GET TO THE PENTHOUSE

THESE GLASS PELLETS OF CHOKING GAS MIGHT COME IN HANDY TONIGHT.. IF THIS IS WHAT I THINK IT IS.

LIKEWISE THESE SUCTION GLOVES AND KNEE PADS. THE PENT-HOUSE WILL REQUIRE A BIT OF CLIMBING.

IN PLACE OF BRUCE WAYNE, THE WEALTHY SOCIAL FIGURE - THE BATMAN!

THE BATMAN GLANCES AT THE DASHBOARD CLOCK.
8:30 EXACTLY. I'M OFF!

A FEW MINUTES BEFORE NINE, A CAR SLIDES TO A STOP NEAR THE DESIGNATED BUILDING.

QUITE A CLIMB TO THE PENTHOUSE. I THINK I'LL WANT MORE PRIVACY FOR MY CAR. THAT VACANT LOT FOR INSTANCE.

THE BATMAN PARKS HIS CAR IN THE VACANT LOT WHERE SOME CONSTRUCTION WORK HAS BEEN GOING ON -
CON

A WEIRD FIGURE RACES THROUGH THE NIGHT.
CONST
DANG

THE BATMAN THROWS HIS LASSO UP TO CATCH A JUTTING WINDOW SILL.

I THINK MY SUCTION PADS WILL COME IN HANDY HERE

HE PUTS THEM ON AND STARTS UP THE SIDE OF THE BUILDING.
NOW FOR THE PENTHOUSE.

LIKE A GIGANTIC BAT..HE MOVES UP THE SHEER FACE OF THE BUILDING.

THE BATMAN STANDS ON TOP OF THE PENTHOUSE GARDEN ROOF

FOR A QUICK GETAWAY THE BATMAN HAS HIS ROPE HANDY.

THE BATMAN SURVEYS HIS GROUND CAUTIOUSLY...

UNSEEN BY THE BATMAN. ARE THE GUNMEN PLACED TO TRAP HIM BY DOCTOR DEATH.
HE BIT FOR IT! SHALL I GIVE IT TO HIM?
NO. THE DOCTOR SAID TO KILL HIM INSIDE SO'S THE POLICE WILL FIND HIM IN HERE. WAIT. HE'S COMING IN!

THE LIGHTS BLAZE ON. AND THE BATMAN IS CAUGHT IN A TRAP.

PUT'EM UP, BATMAN! WE'VE GOT YOU AT LAST!

BUT THE GUNMEN RECKON WITHOUT THE GREAT SPEED AND AGILITY OF THE BATMAN
BANG
BANG!

-AND THE HIRED KILLERS GO DOWN...

QUICK AS A PANTHER, THE BATMAN IS UPON THE GUNMEN, LASHING OUT WITH BOTH FISTS...

...AND WHO SENT YOU, MAY I ASK?
WE CAN'T TELL YOU. HE'D KILL US!

5.
YOUR CHOICE, GENTLEMEN! TELL ME! OR I'LL KILL YOU!

-GOOD EVENING, BATMAN. DOCTOR DEATH SENDS HIS GREETINGS...

JABAH FIRES!

THE BATMAN IS HIT!

THE WOUNDED BATMAN EJECTS A GLASS PELLET FROM HIS BELT.

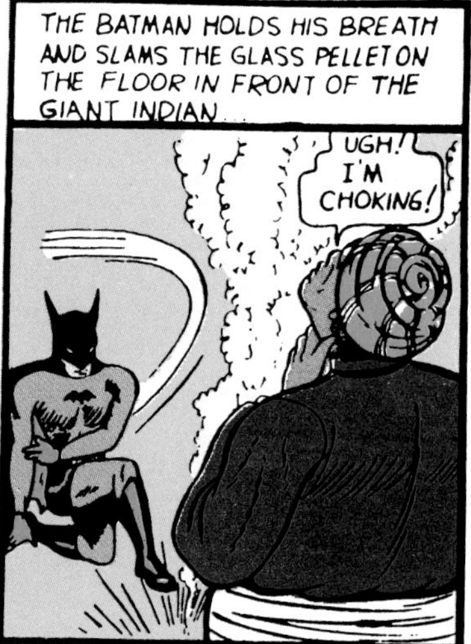
THE BATMAN HOLDS HIS BREATH AND SLAMS THE GLASS PELLET ON THE FLOOR IN FRONT OF THE GIANT INDIAN...
UGH! I'M CHOKING!

THE ROOM BECOMES FILLED WITH A DEADLY GAS. THE WOUNDED BATMAN LEAPS FOR THE GLASS WINDOWS LEADING TO THE PENTHOUSE ROOF.

GAWD! HE'S JUMPED OFF!

BUT WHAT THE GUNMEN OF DOCTOR DEATH FAIL TO SEE

THE BATMAN SWINGS ONTO A PROJECTING CORNICE OF THE ROOF

THE BLOOD STILL SEEPING FROM HIS WOUND, HE SLIPS ON HIS SUCTION GLOVES AND KNEE PADS.

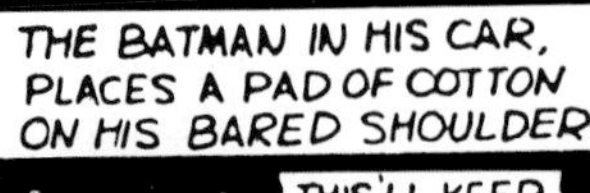
THE BATMAN IN HIS CAR, PLACES A PAD OF COTTON ON HIS BARED SHOULDER.

THIS'LL KEEP UNTIL I GET TO A PHONE BOOTH.

DRESSED IN CIVILIAN CLOTHES ONCE MORE, BRUCE WAYNE, THE BATMAN, ENTERS A PHONE BOOTH...

DAILY GLOBE? I WANT THIS INSERTED IN YOUR PUBLIC NOTICE COLUMN: "I ACCEPT YOUR CHALLENGE, DOCTOR DEATH. THE BATMAN."

I GUESS I'D BETTER SEE THE FAMILY DOCTOR AT ONCE. THIS SHOULDER IS BEGINNING TO ACHE.

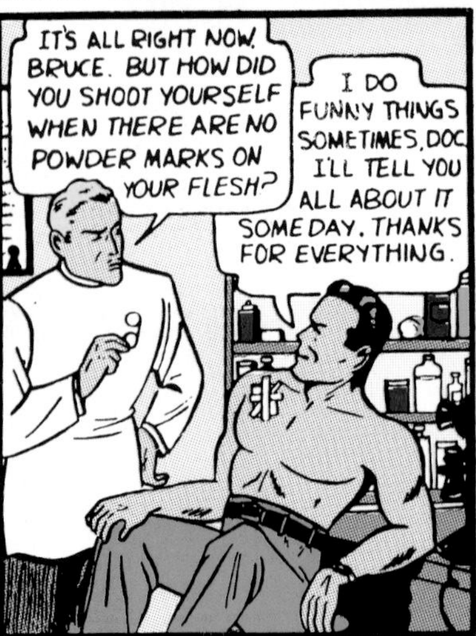
IT'S ALL RIGHT NOW, BRUCE. BUT HOW DID YOU SHOOT YOURSELF WHEN THERE ARE NO POWDER MARKS ON YOUR FLESH?
I DO FUNNY THINGS SOMETIMES, DOC. I'LL TELL YOU ALL ABOUT IT SOME DAY. THANKS FOR EVERYTHING.

THE NEXT MORNING IN DOCTOR DEATH'S STUDY.
YOU FOOLS! YOU BUNGLERS! HE WALKS INTO A TRAP AND YOU LET HIM GO. IF YOU MISS THE NEXT TIME... FOLLOW ME, JABAH!

HERE IS A PICTURE OF JOHN P. VAN SMITH. HE REFUSES TO PAY TRIBUTE TO ME. HE MUST DIE! I HAVE IMMUNIZED YOU WITH MY SERUM FROM THIS POLLEN, WHICH YOU WILL BLOW AT YOUR VICTIM AS HE COMES FROM HIS CLUB TONIGHT.
DOOMED
7

JABAH GOES ON HIS ERRAND OF DEATH...

MY WOULD-BE KILLER OF LAST NIGHT! I THINK I'LL FOLLOW HIM.

AS THE UNSUSPECTING VICTIM STEPS FROM HIS CLUB...

HIS ERRAND FULFILLED, JABAH FLEES.. BUT HE HAS NOT RECKONED UPON THE PRESENCE OF BRUCE WAYNE, THE BATMAN.
DON'T BREATHE OR YOU'RE DEAD!

I HAVEN'T TIME FOR QUESTIONS BUT I'VE A HUNCH THAT IF YOU HAD BREATHED IN WHAT THAT MAN BLEW, IT WOULD BE CURTAINS FOR YOU. I'VE GOT TO TRAIL HIM. ADIEU!

PREPARE FOR A VISIT TONIGHT, DOCTOR DEATH. FROM THE BATMAN.

THAT NIGHT, ON THE SIDEWALK BEHIND DOCTOR DEATH'S HOUSE

ON HIS ROPE, THE BATMAN CLIMBS TO THE SECOND STORY OF THE HOUSE.
ONLY A FEW MINUTES MORE, DOCTOR DEATH. WE HAVE A SCORE TO EVEN.

A CREAK OF A GLASS CUTTER AND THE BATMAN ENTERS...

THE BATMAN FINDS DOCTOR DEATH AND HIS GIANT SERVANT JABAH IN THE LABORATORY
IT WON'T BE LONG, DOCTOR.

A SNAP OF A LASSO AND JABAH IS JERKED FROM THE TABLE.
THE BATMAN!

GOOD EVENING, DOCTOR - BUT IT WON'T BE ... AFTER I'M THROUGH WITH YOU!
YOU FOOL

DOCTOR DEATH PRESSES A BUTTON AND DROPS INTO A SECRET CHUTE.
I CAN JUST MAKE IT BEFORE IT CLOSES-I HOPE!

INTO THE UNKNOWN, AFTER DOCTOR DEATH, PLUNGES THE BATMAN...

...WHO LANDS ON A MAT AND SEES DOCTOR DEATH DISAPPEARING DOWN THE HALL...

THE BATMAN PURSUES DOCTOR DEATH RELENTLESSLY.

DOCTOR DEATH RETURNS TO THE LABORATORY IN A LAST DESPERATE ATTEMPT TO ELUDE THE BATMAN.
THERE IS YET TIME.

THE BATMAN SEIZES A FIRE EXTINGUISHER ON THE WALL AND..
YOU ARE JUST TOO LATE, MY FOE. WATCH! THE FIERY DEATH_

FLINGS IT AT DOCTOR DEATH, KNOCKING THE DEADLY TUBE TO THE FLOOR WHERE IT SWIFTLY IGNITES INTO A BLAZING INFERNO!!!

HA! HA! OH.. HA-HA-HA.. YOU.. YOU FOOL!

YOU ARE THE POOR FOOL! HE HAS GONE MAD.

DEATH...TO DOCTOR DEATH!
BOB KANE
...BUT IS IT DEATH TO THIS ARCH CRIMINAL? FOLLOW THE FURTHER AMAZING AND UNIQUE ADVENTURES OF THE
BAT-MAN
IN
Next Month's
DETECTIVE COMICS

No. 30

64 PAGES OF Thrill-Packed ACTION!

AUGUST, 1939

Detective COMICS

Reg. U.S. Pat. Off.

10¢

GUARDINER

Another thrilling episode of THE BATMAN in this issue

The BAT-MAN
BY BOB KANE
... IN THE STRANGE LIVES OF THOSE DENIZENS OF THE HIDDEN WORLD OF CRIME, THE BATMAN. WINGED FIGURE OF VENGEANCE HAS BECOME A MENACE...
LESS THAN A WEEK AGO, THE BATMAN SAW HIS SWORN ENEMY. THE GRIM DOCTOR DEATH, BURNED TO ASHES IN A FIRE THAT WRECKED AN ENTIRE HOUSE...
AND YET IN THE MORNING PAPER AN ITEM APPEARS -
WHAT'S THIS ?
... strange death overcomes man. Victim of queer disease turns purple Doctors baffled.
ONLY DOCTOR DEATH COULD BE AT THE BOTTOM OF THIS. YET HE IS DEAD. I WONDER... IT'S STRANGE, THIS HUNCH OF MINE THAT HE IS STILL ALIVE, ALMOST A CERTAINTY
ONE HOUR LATER BRUCE WAYNE PAYS A VISIT TO THE DEAD MAN'S HOME.
I'M A REPORTER. I'D LIKE TO SPEAK TO MRS. JONES.
JUST A MOMENT, M'SIEU.
YES, MY HUSBAND RECEIVED A THREATENING NOTE THAT UNLESS HE PAID HALF A MILLION DOLLARS TO A DOCTOR DEATH HE WOULD DIE.
I WAS RIGHT. HE IS STILL ALIVE!

WE HAVE NO MORE MONEY. JOHN LOST IT IN THE DEPRESSION. BUT WE HAVE SOME DIAMONDS. IT WAS JOHN'S HOBBY TO COLLECT THEM. I HAVEN'T SEEN THEM FOR YEARS. I MUST GET THEM OUT, FOR I NEED SOME MONEY
I'D ADVISE YOU TO HAVE THOSE DIAMONDS REMOVED TO A SAFE PLACE, MRS. JONES.
9

NEARLY SIX. I THINK I'LL EAT, THEN RETURN TO MRS. JONES' LIVING ROOM. I'M AFRAID DOCTOR DEATH KNOWS OF THOSE DIAMONDS.
10

AT THE WAYNE MANSION THAT EVENING...
11

-THE BATMAN PREPARES TO MEET DOCTOR DEATH AGAIN.
THESE GAS VIALS MAY BE NEEDED TONIGHT.

TOWARD THE JONES HOME DRIVES THE BATMAN IN HIS SPECIALLY BUILT HIGH-POWERED AUTO.
13

14
ONE BLOCK AWAY FOR SAFETY. THE CAR HANDY IF NEEDED. AN APPROACH FROM THE REAR WILL BE BEST.

15

THE BATMAN EASILY CLEARS THE HIGH WALL..
16

THESE WINDOWS ARE BARRED. I'LL TRY THE UPPER ONES.
17

18

19

THAT WAS EASY! NOW FOR THOSE DIAMONDS.
20

THERE SHOULD BE A WALL SAFE BEHIND ONE OF THESE PICTURES. I'LL TRY THAT ONE.
21

WELL, HERE IT IS. NOW LET'S SEE.. 13..24..5....
22

MEANWHILE DOCTOR DEATH STILL LIVES!
THAT BATMAN..HE BROUGHT ME TO THIS! ONLY BY A SECRET DOOR DID I ESCAPE FROM THAT FIRE. AND NOW MIKHAIL, I NEED FUNDS TO REESTABLISH MYSELF. THAT FOOL JONES WAS NEARER BANK-RUPTCY THAN I SUSPECTED. BUT..
23

HIS WIDOW HAS A FORTUNE IN DIAMONDS ABOUT THEIR HOUSE. BREAK IN TONIGHT AND GET THEM. BRING THEM TO HERD THE FENCE IN THE BOWERY.
24

THE BATMAN SEEKS TO STALL DOCTOR DEATH.
THOSE DIAMONDS ARE AS GOOD AS IN MY HANDS NOW!
25

A MUFFLED FOOTFALL REACHES THE BATMAN!
26

27

28
WHAT A BREAK - SAFE'S OPEN!

29
ONE OF DOCTOR DEATH'S COSSACKS, SUCH AS JABAH. I'LL FOLLOW HIM TO DOCTOR DEATH.

WHILE ON THE FLOOR ABOVE.
DEAR ME, I CAN'T SLEEP. PER-HAPS A GLASS OF HOT MILK WOULD HELP ME.
30

OH! A LIGHT. WHO...
31

OOH! HE...

THE BATMAN ACTS WITH THE SPEED OF THOUGHT!
34

35

HE NEEDS THESE TO LEAD ME WHERE HE'S GOING.
36

THIS SEEMS FOOLISH, BUT I'VE GOT TO FIND DOCTOR DEATH. THE ONLY WAY I CAN FOLLOW HIS COSSACK IS BY GIVING HIM THE JEWELS HE CAME AFTER.
37

JUST FAINTED. A DAMP RAG WILL REVIVE HER.
38

-AND NOW FOR MY COSSACK THIEF!

40

HE'LL COME TO IN A MOMENT.
41

WHATEVER HAPPENED UP THERE, I'M GLAD I CLUNG ONTO THIS BAG!
42

THE BATMAN TRAILS HIS QUARRY
43

IVAN HERD'S, EH? SO HE'S THE 'FENCE' FOR DEATH'S DIAMONDS.
IVAN HERD
PAWN S
44

THE BATMAN WATCHES AS THE COSSACK MIKHAIL DEPARTS FROM THE PAWN SHOP.
45

ONCE MORE THE CHASE IS RESUMED...
46

QUEER THAT DOCTOR DEATH SHOULD LIVE HERE. BUT THAT FIRE MAY HAVE TAKEN AWAY ALL HIS MONEY. ANYHOW, I'LL GIVE IT A TRY.
Rooms
47

THEY MIGHT EXPECT A VISITOR FROM THE FRONT DOOR, BUT NOT FROM THE ROOF.
48

NOW, FOR THE RIGHT APARTMENT.
49

50
THE BATMAN LEAPS THROUGH THE SKYLIGHT!

THAT'S LUCK! THIS IS IT–
51

THE MASKED FIGURE EJECTS A CAPSULE FROM HIS BELT.
HE WOULDN'T BE ASLEEP YET SO TO BE SURE.
52

THE VIAL OF GLASS SHATTERS.
53

THAT... OH, I'M CHOKING
54

AFTER ALLOWING THE GAS FUMES TO DISSIPATE. THE BATMAN IS IN THE ROOM WHERE MIKHAIL IS STRETCHED OUT ON THE BED UNCONSCIOUS. HE SEARCHES THE DRESSER, RUFFLING PAPERS.
55

NOT A HINT! A PRETTY POOR NIGHT'S WORK. I...

YOU WAITED TOO LONG TO SEARCH, BATMAN. I RECOVERED FROM THAT GAS OF YOURS AND NOW YOU DIE!
57

BUT THE BATMAN WHEELS AND...
58

CATCHES HIS SILKEN ROPE!
59

BAH! MISSED AT THAT DISTANCE. HE IS LIKE A JACK-IN-THE-BOX, THAT BATMAN! BUT I'LL GET HIM FROM THE WINDOW.
60

BUT AS MIKHAIL PUTS HIS HEAD THROUGH THE WINDOW..
61

THERE IS A SICKENING SNAP AS THE COSSACK'S NECK BREAKS UNDER THE MIGHTY PRESSURE OF THE BATMAN'S FOOT.
SNAP!

FIRST JABAH, NOW YOU.. AND YET DOCTOR DEATH LIVES ON!

A PHONE CALL TO THE POLICE WILL SERVE MY PURPOSE-JUST BEFORE I VISIT 'IVAN HERD' FOR THE JONES' DIAMONDS.
65

YES, THE JONES' DIAMONDS, I TELL YOU-AT IVAN HERD'S.. NEVER MIND WHO THIS IS...
66

A WEIRD FIGURE APPEARS ON TOP OF THE BUILDING NEXT TO THE SHOP OF THE PAWNBROKER, ONE MINUTE LATER...
67

THIS WILL AFFORD ME AN ENTRANCE-AND PERHAPS AN EXIT IN NEED.
68

69

70

WHAT!

YOU'RE IVAN HERD, EH? I WANT THESE DIAMONDS-THEY BELONG TO AN OLD LADY WHO NEEDS THEM FAR MORE THAN YOU DO!
72

I KNOW YOU-
THE BATMAN!

AND NOW MAYBE YOU'LL TALK- WHERE IS THE MAN WHO ORDERED THESE DIAMONDS BROUGHT TO YOU? YOU MAY KNOW HIM BY HIS NAME OF DOCTOR DEATH!
74

NO YOU..
75

LIKE LIGHTNING, THE BATMAN BRINGS FORTH ANOTHER SILKEN LASSO. AND FLIPS THE OPEN-THROATED CORD STRAIGHT FOR THE OLD MAN.
76

WHAT'S THE MATTER WITH YOUR HAIR? I DO BELIEVE IT'S A WIG-

-AND A SKIN MASK, TOO!

DOCTOR DEATH! BUT... YOUR FACE?
HA! HA! YES, MY FACE! IT WAS DESTROYED IN THE FIRE YOU- YOU DID IT! HOW I WANTED TO GET MY REVENGE!

THE BATMAN DEPARTS, LEAVING THE BOUND FORM OF DR. DEATH, AS THE POLICE ARRIVE
THERE HE IS- AND THE JEWELS! -BUT WHAT IS THAT CARD ON THE TABLE?
BOB KANE

"MEET DOCTOR DEATH- AND HIS DIAMONDS. THEY BELONG TO MRS. JONES SEE THAT SHE GETS THEM-WITH THE COMPLIMENTS OF THE BATMAN-

A NEW ACTION FILLED
BATMAN
STRIP
IN
NEXT MONTH'S
DETECTIVE COMICS

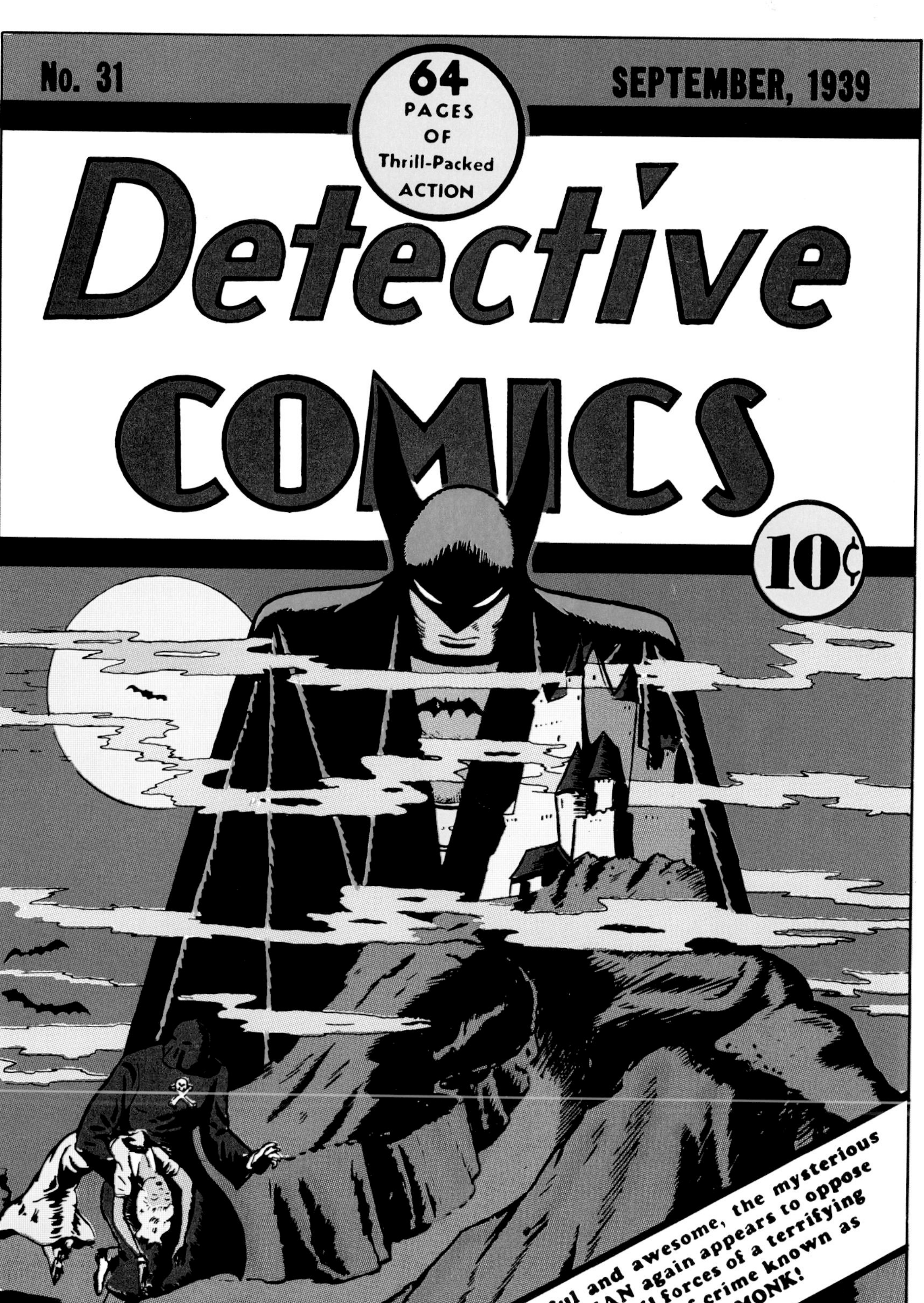
No. 31
64 PAGES OF Thrill-Packed ACTION
SEPTEMBER, 1939
Detective COMICS
10¢
Powerful and awesome, the mysterious BATMAN again appears to oppose the evil forces of a terrifying master of crime known as THE MONK!

BATMAN
THE BATMAN—WEIRD MENACE TO ALL CRIME—AT LAST MEETS AN OPPONENT WORTHY OF HIS METTLE. A STRANGE CREATURE, COWLED LIKE A MONK, BUT POSSESSING THE POWERS OF A SATAN! A MAN WHOSE POWERS ARE UNCANNY, WHOSE BRAIN IS THE PRODUCT OF YEARS OF INTENSE STUDY AND SECLUSION!
BY BOB KANE

THROUGH THE DARK OF A NEW YORK NIGHT...

SOON NOW, AND I SHALL KNOW.

DISTANCE KNOWS NO BOUNDS BY WHICH TO HOLD THE EERIE FIGURE.

HE SIGHTS HIS QUARRY!

I HAVE BEEN SENT TO YOU BY THE MASTER MONK!
I... HELP.. HELP!!

AS IF IN ANSWER TO THE DOOMED MAN...

WHO... WHO ARE YOU?
REMAIN UNTIL I GIVE YOU LEAVE TO GO!!

THE BATMAN RECOGNIZES HIS FIANCEE, JULIE MADISON.
JULIE.. YOU!

WHA-WHAT AM I DOING HERE? WHO ARE YOU?

BUT...IF YOU ARE TAKING ME HOME...HOW DO YOU KNOW WHERE I LIVE? WHY WON'T YOU TALK? YOU WON'T TELL ME A THING!

BUT...WON'T YOU TELL ME WHO YOU ARE?
TELL YOUR FIANCE, BRUCE WAYNE, ALL THAT HAPPENED! G'NIGHT!

THE NEXT MORNING, BRUCE WAYNE IS CALLED TO HIS FIANCEE'S HOME!
BRUCE, THERE IS SOMETHING I MUST TELL YOU. A MAN DRESSED AS AN ENORMOUS BAT FOUND ME LAST NIGHT ON THE STREET ABOUT TO KILL A MAN!
GOOD LORD, JULIE - SUPPOSE YOU HAD! WE'D BETTER SEE DR. TRENT RIGHT AWAY!

AND SCARCELY TWO HOURS LATER.
YOUNG LADY, I'VE SEEN VICTIMS OF AN EXPERT HYPNOTIST EXHIBIT YOUR SYMPTOMS! DON'T YOU RECALL ANYTHING THAT WOULD SUGGEST SOMETHING LIKE THAT? I ADVISE AN OCEAN VOYAGE!

YET, AS DOCTOR TRENT TALKS, BRUCE WAYNE NOTICES HIS STARING EYES AND WONDERS...
YES, YES-AN OCEAN VOYAGE TO PARIS.. AND PERHAPS, LATER, TO HUNGARY-THE LAND OF HISTORY AND WEREWOLVES.

ONE TICKET TO PARIS, PLEASE. PORT CABIN.
LUNAR LINES

I DON'T LIKE THE CRACK THE DOCTOR MADE ABOUT WEREWOLVES, JULIE. AND HE SEEMED HYPNOTIZED HIMSELF, WHEN HE GAVE YOU THAT ADVICE. BUT MAYBE I'M IMAGINING THINGS.
OF COURSE YOU ARE! I'VE WORRIED YOU. BUT I'LL BE GOOD, I PROMISE.

BUT BACK AT THE WAYNE MANSION...
JULIE WOULD BE SURPRISED TO KNOW HER BATMAN IS HER FUTURE HUSBAND.

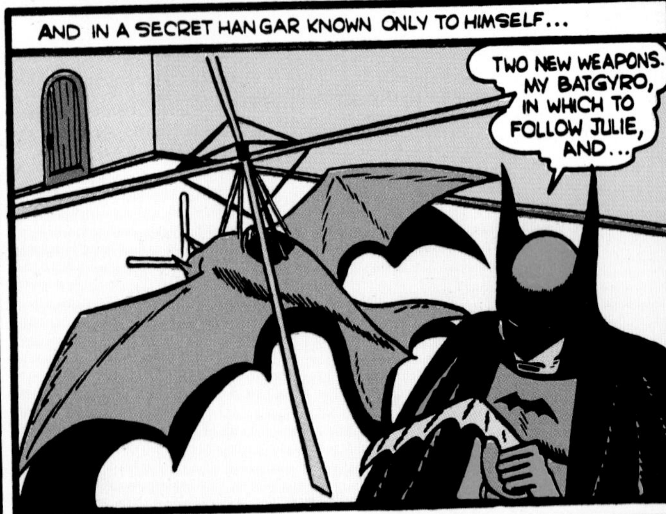
AND IN A SECRET HANGAR KNOWN ONLY TO HIMSELF...
TWO NEW WEAPONS. MY BATGYRO, IN WHICH TO FOLLOW JULIE, AND...

THE FLYING BATERANG. MODELED AFTER THE AUSTRALIAN BUSHMAN'S BOOMERANG!

LOOK!
A BAT!
THE END OF THE WORLD! WE ARE ATTACKED BY MARTIANS!

AND OUT TO SEA...

WHILE ON BOARD THE LUNAR LADY..
A MONSTER BAT! FLYING OVER THE OCEAN.

FIXING HIS AUTOMATIC CONTROLS, THE BATMAN PREPARES FOR A VISIT!

THAT MAN HAS UNCANNY POWERS. I SEEM TO BE HYPNOTIZED. IT IS HARDER AND HARDER TO MOVE.

THE SEARCH BEGINS...

THE TRAIL LEADS EVERYWHERE.

HELP! THE DEVIL HIMSELF.
CAB

THE WEIRD FIGURE IS SEEN ALL OVER PARIS, UNTIL, ONE NIGHT—
JULIE... AT LAST!

BUT A WARM RECEPTION HAS BEEN PREPARED FOR HIM!

THE BATMAN NIMBLY DODGES THE HUGE APE, ONLY TO FLY THROUGH A SLIDING DOOR...

...AND TUMBLES DOWN, DOWN, DOWN, INTO A GIGANTIC NET.

CAUGHT LIKE A RAT IN A TRAP, AS THE NET CLOSES ABOUT HIM . . .

THE BATMAN ONCE AGAIN FACES THE DIABOLICAL MASTER MONK!
RASH MORTAL... TO DARE FACE THE POWER OF THE MONK... LOOK BELOW YOU AT YOUR FATE! WHEN I PULL THIS LEVER-HEH! HEH!!

THE NET BEGINS TO DROP SLOWLY INTO THE DEN OF SNAKES.

IN A FLASH, THE BATMAN FLIPS HIS BATERANG.

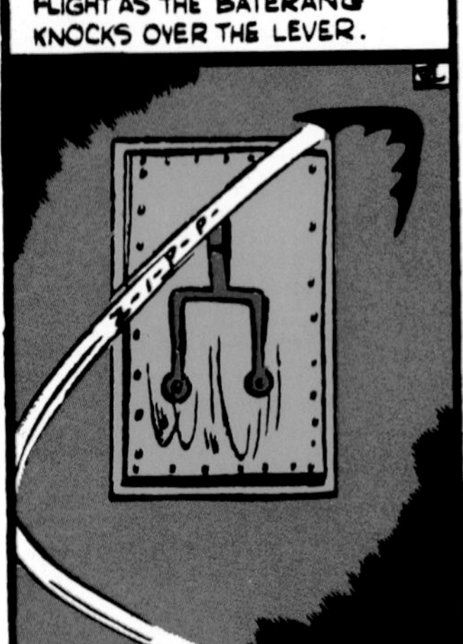
THE NET STOPS IN ITS DOWNWARD FLIGHT AS THE BATERANG KNOCKS OVER THE LEVER.

CONTINUING ON ITS UPWARD SWEEP, IT CRASHES INTO A GLASS CHANDELIER.
ZING

THE BATMAN GRASPS THE BATERANG AND THE BROKEN GLASS!

A HEROIC GESTURE, BUT A FUTILE ONE. THE LEVER WILL REMAIN DOWN THIS TIME!

WORKING AGAINST TIME, THE BATMAN SEVERS STRAND AFTER STRAND.

FREEING HIMSELF NONE TOO SOON..

THE BATMAN, IN FULL PURSUIT OF THE FLEEING MONK...

SUDDENLY, A BARRED DOOR DROPS BETWEEN THE BATMAN AND THE MONK...
DIE HERE, YOU FOOL, WHILE I SEND THE GIRL, JULIE, ON TO MY CASTLE IN HUNGARY, TO FEED MY WEREWOLVES!

THE GIGANTIC GORILLA IS LOWERED, AS THE BATMAN IS CAGED BY BARS ALL ABOUT HIM.

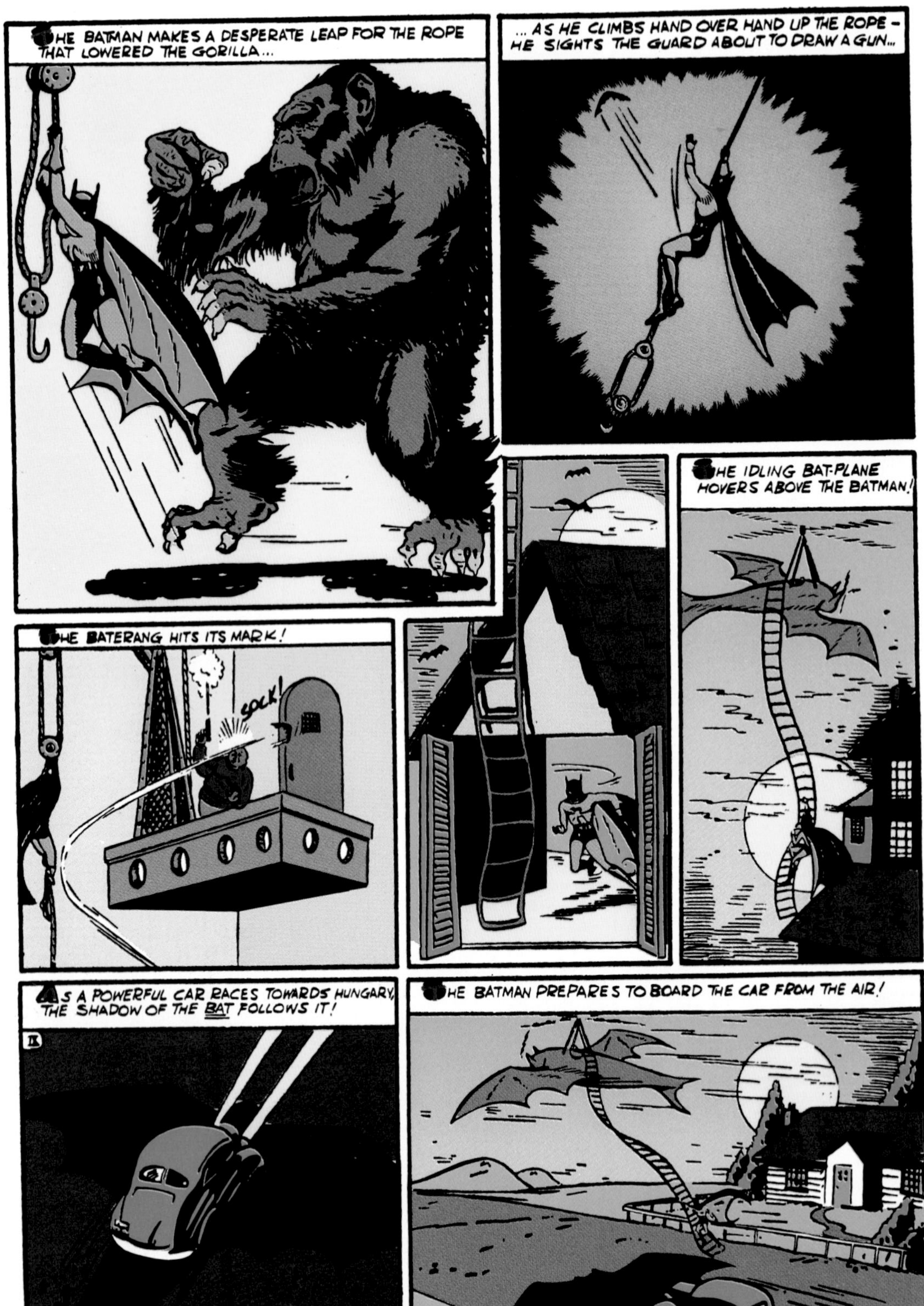
THE BATMAN MAKES A DESPERATE LEAP FOR THE ROPE THAT LOWERED THE GORILLA...
... AS HE CLIMBS HAND OVER HAND UP THE ROPE - HE SIGHTS THE GUARD ABOUT TO DRAW A GUN...
THE BATERANG HITS ITS MARK!
SOCK!
THE IDLING BAT-PLANE HOVERS ABOVE THE BATMAN!
AS A POWERFUL CAR RACES TOWARDS HUNGARY, THE SHADOW OF THE BAT FOLLOWS IT!
IX
THE BATMAN PREPARES TO BOARD THE CAR FROM THE AIR!

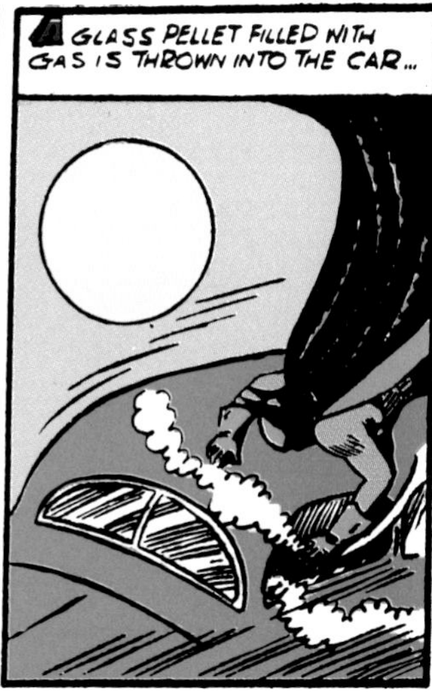
A GLASS PELLET FILLED WITH GAS IS THROWN INTO THE CAR...

THE CAR SWERVES INTO A TREE...
THE MONK KNEW BETTER THAN TO COME -BUT I CAN SAVE JULIE!

THE BATMAN MAKES A VALIANT LEAP FOR THE LADDER OF HIS BAT-PLANE!

WITH JULIE SAFE, THE BATMAN PLANS ON VENGEANCE...
POOR KID!

... AND SETS HIS AUTOMATIC CONTROLS FOR HUNGARY - HOME OF THE VICIOUS MONK AND HIS WEREWOLVES!

Continue THE THRILLING ADVENTURES OF THE BAT-MAN AND HIS COMBAT AGAINST THE MYSTERIOUS MONK! WHAT PLANS HAS THE MONK IN MIND? WHY DOES HE WANT JULIE?
See THE NEXT EPISODE OF THE
BATMAN
BOB KANE

No. 32
OCTOBER, 1939
THE BATMAN
Detective
COMICS
Reg. U.S. Pat. Off.
10¢
ALSO IN THIS ISSUE, AND OTHERS
SLAM BRADLEY, SPEED SAUNDERS,
BUCK MARSHALL, SPY,
LARRY STEELE,
COSMO

BATMAN
BY BOB KANE
LIKE AN ANIMAL OF PREY.. . THE BATMAN WATCHES HIS QUARRY.
—FOLLOWING HIS FIANCEE, THE BATMAN, IN REALITY BRUCE WAYNE, HAS TRAILED A SINISTER FIGURE, COWLED LIKE A MONK, INTO HUNGARY ...
ON THE END OF A SILKEN CORD, THE BATMAN RACES OVERHEAD...
...AND DROPS LIKE A HUGE BAT -
ONTO A SPEEDING CARRIAGE.

HE WHIPS OUT A GLASS PELLET OF CHOKING GAS AND...

THE FUMES OVERCOME THE OCCUPANT OF THE CAB!

INSTEAD OF HIS QUARRY, THE MONK, THE BATMAN FINDS...
WHAT..?

THE EERIE FIGURE RETURNS TO HIS BATPLANE.
I DON'T KNOW WHO SHE IS, BUT I HAVE A FEELING I'LL SOON FIND OUT.

STRANGE FOR ANYONE TO BE TRAVELING ALONE WAY OUT HERE...AND YET THE MONK... I WONDER?

THE BATMAN ARRIVES AT HIS HOTEL, EMBEDDED DEEP IN THE CARLATHAN MOUNTAINS IN HUNGARY...
AH, SHE'S COMING TO! I HOPE JULIE IS SAFE.

WHO... WHO ARE YOU?
MY NAME IS DALA. I SEEM TO HAVE BEEN KIDNAPPED BY YOUR FRIEND HERE.

THAT NIGHT, THE BATMAN SAFEGUARDS HIS FIANCEE AND THE STRANGER.

DURING THE NIGHT, THE BATMAN HEARS SOBBING MOANS!

THROUGH THE OPEN DOOR COMES THE WOMAN, DALA!!

THE BATMAN IS STARTLED TO NOTE BLOOD ON THE WOMAN'S LIPS...

AND FEARS FOR JULIE'S SAFETY.

SUDDENLY, DALA SNAPS OUT OF HER TRANCE, GRABS A STATUETTE AND...

THE BATMAN IS STUNNED MOMENTARILY, ALLOWING THE STRANGE WOMAN TO ESCAPE.

THE BATMAN RETURNS TO JULIE, WHOSE THROAT SHOWS TWO RED SPOTS... MARKS OF THE VAMPIRE!

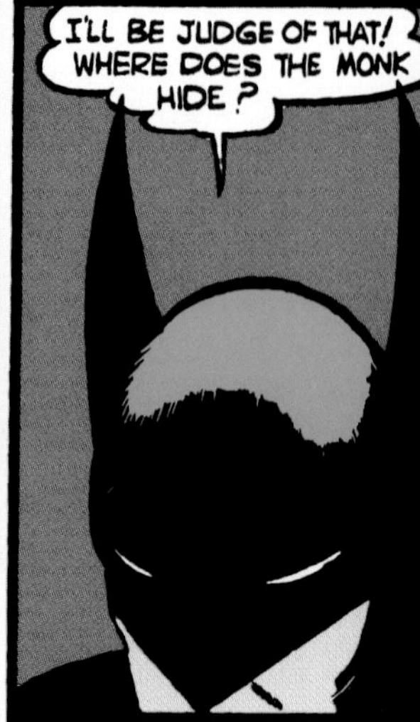

IN THE LOST MOUNTAINS OF CATHALA BY THE TURBULENT RIVER DESS. I SHALL GUIDE YOU.

THIS MONEY WILL SAFE GUARD YOU. I AM GOING. YOU MUST FIGHT AGAINST THE POWER THAT CALLS YOU TO THIS MONK!

OH-I WILL FIGHT. I WILL..., BUT I AM SO AFRAID WITHOUT YOU!!

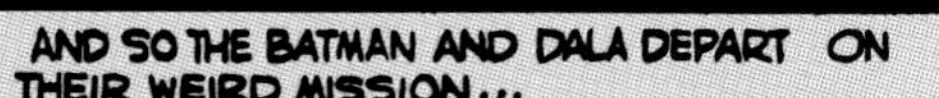
AND SO THE BATMAN AND DALA DEPART ON THEIR WEIRD MISSION...

TOWARD THE STRONGHOLD OF THE 'MONK' WINGS THE EERIE BATPLANE...

SUDDENLY, THE BATMAN SEES...

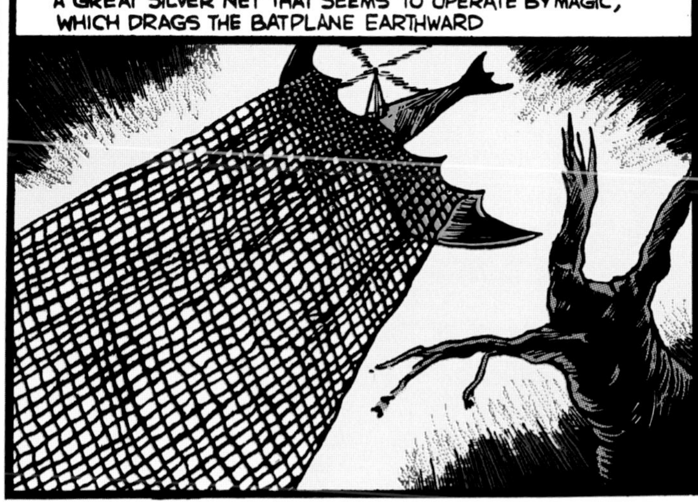
A GREAT SILVER NET THAT SEEMS TO OPERATE BY MAGIC, WHICH DRAGS THE BATPLANE EARTHWARD

YOU FOOL! PITTING YOUR PUNY BODY AGAINST THE MIGHTY MONK.

MY FRIEND, THE BATMAN! SO YOU ARE STILL ALIVE! AH...DALA..WELCOME.

BY HIS MARVELOUS HYPNOTIC POWERS, THE MONK SLOWLY OVERPOWERS THE BATMAN.

YOU MUST GET RID OF THIS BATMAN.
I THINK A TASTE OF THE WERE WOLF DEN WOULD HELP.

WAIT...YOUR VENGEANCE MUST BE PERFECT.

FIRST YOU MUST BRING JULIE HERE! MAKE THE BATMAN SUFFER, KNOWING TO WHAT FATE THE GIRL IS DOOMED!

BY A TREMENDOUS CONCENTRATION OF WILL, THE MONK FORCES HIS POWER THROUGH SPACE.

THE 'MONK'S' MIND FASTENS ON JULIE'S WILL, COMPELLING HER TO COME TO HIM!

THE HELPLESS BATMAN SEES HIS FIANCEE DRAWN INTO THE MONK'S TRAP!
SOON YOUR JULIE WILL BE AS WE ARE - WEREWOLVES TO RAVISH ON ALL LIVING MEN - AND YOU SHALL BE DEAD - HELPLESS TO AVENGE HER!

THE BATMAN IS FORCED TO SUFFER IN SILENCE.
YOU HAVE DONE SOMETHING TO HIM. HIS EYES ARE SUFFERING, BUT HE CANNOT MOVE! OH-YOU FIEND!

INTO THAT DEN OF WOLVES WHICH I SHALL CALL FROM THE FOREST YOU SHALL BE CAST TO DIE BY THEIR THIRSTY FANGS!

BEFORE THE BATMAN'S HORRIFIED EYES, THE MONK BEGINS TO CHANGE...

THE MONK, AS A WOLF, HOWLS THE GATHERING CALL TO THE MOUNTAIN WOLVES...

- AND FROM THE SURROUNDING MOUNTAINS, THE WOLVES GATHER.

YOU SHALL BE THROWN INTO THE ARENA BELOW, TO DIE AT THEIR RENDING FANGS.. AS YOU ARE SCREAMING IN DEATH-REMEMBER THAT JULIE WILL BE A WEREWOLF HERSELF IN TIME! TO RUN WITH THE PACK ON MOONLIGHT NIGHTS!

AS HE IS PUSHED FORWARD, THE BATMAN'S SENSES SUDDENLY RETURN TO THEIR FULL POWER.

HE TWISTS IN MID-AIR AND TRIES A DESPERATE THROW WITH HIS SILKEN ROPE.

— HIS CAST FAILS!

—AND HE FALLS INTO THE WOLF DEN.

THE BATMAN SWIFTLY EXTRACTS A GLASS PELLET FROM HIS BELT!!

THE GAS IN THE EXPLODING PELLET OVERCOMES THE WOLVES..

I CAN HOLD THE WOLVES OFF ONLY AS LONG AS MY GAS PELLETS LAST_ THEN IT'S OVER!

THE LIGHT BUT STRONG ROPE FAILS TO CARRY TO THE PIT'S EDGE.

TOWARD DAWN, THE WOLVES AWAKE..

FLASHING FANGS AGAIN MENACE THE BATMAN!

THE BATMAN'S FINGERS FIND HIS HIDDEN BATERANG!!

ONE STRONG CAST WILL WIN ME FREEDOM.

THE BATERANG SLIPS PAST A STONE POST AND THE ROPE HOLDS.

THE BATMAN CLIMBS TO SAFETY!

AND THEN SEEKS HIS VENGEANCE...

SAFE SO FAR-
NOW FOR THE OTHERS!

A SILVER STATUE! WHILE THE VAMPIRES SLEEP, DURING THE DAYTIME, I SHALL MELT THIS STATUE AND MAKE TWO SILVER BULLETS-ONE FOR DALA AND ONE FOR THE MONK!

ONLY A SILVER BULLET MAY KILL A VAMPIRE!

NOW TO FIND THE OPEN TOMB IN WHICH THESE VAMPIRES SLEEP AND BRING THEM DEATH THAT WILL RELEASE JULIE!

THE BATMAN PAUSES BEFORE THE OPEN TOMBS OF THE VAMPIRES...

NEVER AGAIN WILL YOU HARM ANY MORTAL BEING!

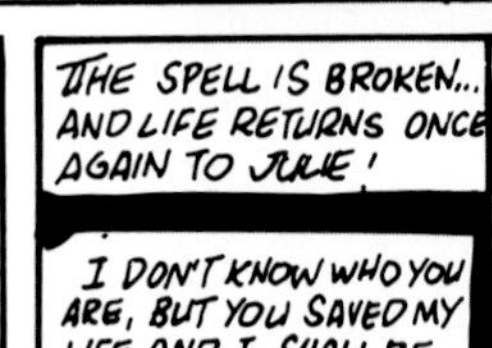
THE SPELL IS BROKEN... AND LIFE RETURNS ONCE AGAIN TO JULIE!

I DON'T KNOW WHO YOU ARE, BUT YOU SAVED MY LIFE AND I SHALL BE FOREVER GRATEFUL!
BOB KANE

FINIS

A NEW INTRIGUING
BATMAN
STORY EVERY MONTH IN
DETECTIVE COMICS

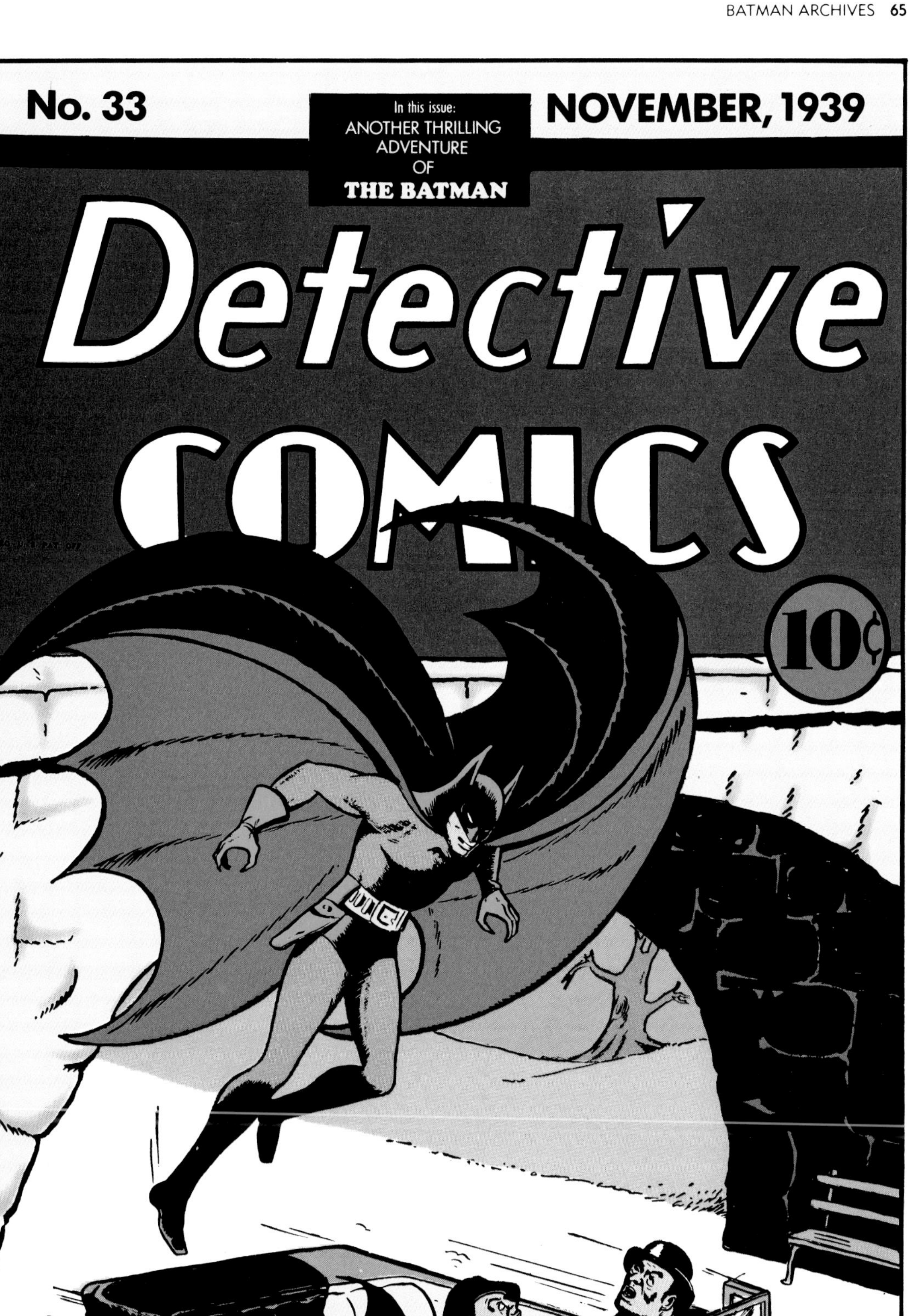
No. 33
In this issue:
ANOTHER THRILLING
ADVENTURE
OF
THE BATMAN
NOVEMBER, 1939
Detective
COMICS
10¢

BATMAN
BY BOB KANE
...EERIE FIGURE OF THE NIGHT - NEMESIS OF CRIME - THIS IS THE BATMAN!
"THE BATMAN WARS AGAINST THE DIRIGIBLE OF DOOM"
LEGEND
THE BATMAN AND HOW HE CAME TO BE !!
SOME FIFTEEN YEARS AGO. THOMAS WAYNE, HIS WIFE, AND SON, WERE WALKING HOME FROM A MOVIE...
W-WHAT IS THIS?
A STICKUP, BUDDY! I'LL TAKE THAT NECKLACE YOU'RE WEARIN' LADY!
LEAVE HER ALONE, YOU. OH..
YOU ASKED FOR IT!
THOMAS! YOU'VE KILLED HIM. HELP! POLICE.. HELP!
THIS'LL SHUT YOU UP!

THE BOY'S EYES ARE WIDE WITH TERROR AND SHOCK AS THE HORRIBLE SCENE IS SPREAD BEFORE HIM.

DAYS LATER, A CURIOUS AND STRANGE SCENE TAKES PLACE.

AND I SWEAR BY THE SPIRITS OF MY PARENTS TO AVENGE THEIR DEATHS BY SPENDING THE REST OF MY LIFE WARRING ON ALL CRIMINALS.

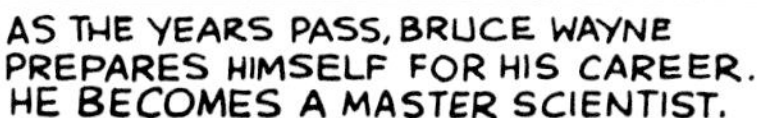

TRAINS HIS BODY TO PHYSICAL PERFECTION UNTIL HE IS ABLE TO PERFORM AMAZING ATHLETIC FEATS.

CRIMINALS ARE A SUPERSTITIOUS COWARDLY LOT. SO MY DISGUISE MUST BE ABLE TO STRIKE TERROR INTO *THEIR HEARTS*. *I MUST BE A CREATURE OF THE NIGHT*, BLACK, *TERRIBLE*.. A. A...

AND THUS IS BORN THIS WEIRD FIGURE OF THE DARK.. THIS AVENGER OF EVIL, 'THE BATMAN'

NIGHTFALL. BRUCE WAYNE WALKS THE CROWDED STREETS OF DOWNTOWN MANHATTAN.

A LITTLE BOY CRIES ALOUD AND POINTS TO THE SKY..
LOOK, MOM! A DIRIGIBLE.
STRANGE-LOOKING SHIP. HMM.. MORE LIKE A ROCKET SHIP.

SUDDENLY RED BEAMS OF LIGHT SHOOT FROM THE SHIP.
RED LIGHTS! WHAT IS IT? HELP! I'M GOING BLIND!

AS THE RAYS STRIKE, THE BUILDINGS EXPLODE. HURLING THEIR WRECKAGE UPON THE CROWDED STREETS BELOW.
HELP!
HELP! THE END OF THE WORLD! HELP!
HELP!

HELP!
HELP! MAMMA, SAVE ME! HELP!!

SUDDENLY FROM THE CRAFT..
WE COME TO RULE THE WORLD. DO NOT RESIST US OR THE RAYS STRIKE AGAIN.. WE, THE 'SCARLET HORDE' WARN YOU..

THE DIRIGIBLE GONE - RESCUE WORK BEGINS. BRUCE WAYNE HELPS.
EASY, OLD MAN.

THE HOME OF BRUCE WAYNE.
-AND THE RESCUE WORK IS STILL GOING ON. THOUSANDS ARE DEAD.. ETC.. ETC..

BRUCE PRESSES A PANEL AND PART OF THE WALL SLIDES AWAY.
I MUST STOP THIS SCARLET HORDE BEFORE THEY BECOME DICTATORS OF THE WORLD.

REVEALING A SECRET LABORATORY..
THOSE RED BEAMS FROM THE DIRIGIBLE. HM. MY FILE MIGHT HELP ME..

BRUCE COMES ACROSS A NEWSPAPER CLIPPING.
PROF CARL KRUGER RELEASED FROM INSANE ASYLUM. SUFFERED FROM NAPOLEON COMPLEX. NOW WORKING ON NEW TYPE DEATH-RAY..

DR. KRUGER MAY BE RESPONSIBLE. THIS LOOKS LIKE A CASE FOR THE BATMAN!

THE BATMAN PREPARES TO VISIT DR. KRUGER

AND NOW MY SILK ROPE AND I'M READY.

THE BATMAN'S HIGH-POWERED CAR SPEEDS TOWARD THE HOME OF DR. CARL KRUGER.

THE CAR WILL BE SAFE HERE. WHERE NO ONE CAN SEE IT.

A WEIRD FIGURE RACES THROUGH THE NIGHT.

A LIGHT! I'LL TRY THAT ROOM!

THINKS HE'S NAPOLEON. HMMM..

- INSIDE THE LIGHTED ROOM!
IT IS WELL THAT YOU THREE JOINED FORCES WITH ME. FOUR GREAT SCIENTISTS, 'THE SCARLET HORDE,' SHALL RULE THE WORLD. TELL ME.. IS OUR ARMY READY?
TWO-THOUSAND STRONG, WAITING FOR YOUR COMMAND

WHEN DO WE STRIKE?
IN TWO DAYS THE DEATH RAY STRIKES AGAIN. DURING THE PANIC OUR MEN WILL LOOT THE BANKS. AND WE WILL HAVE MONEY TO BUILD MORE DIRIGIBLES. YOU TRAVIS, BIXLEY, RYDER, WILL BE MY LIEUTENANTS..

AND I, CARL KRUGER, WILL BE DICTATOR OF THE WORLD!
NAPOLEON

THE THREE MEN LEAVE THE HOUSE OF DR. KRUGER.
MASTER OF THE WORLD. ANOTHER NAPOLEON- AND NO ONE CAN STOP ME!

PERHAPS, I CAN STOP YOU!
THE BATMAN!

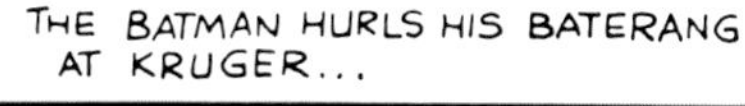
THE BATMAN HURLS HIS BATERANG AT KRUGER...

..WITH THIS!

..WHICH STOPS IN MID-AIR.
FOOL! DO YOU THINK I'D LEAVE MYSELF NO PROTECTION FROM MY ENEMIES! THERE IS A SHEET OF THICK GLASS BETWEEN US.

SUDDENLY THE PAINTING OF NAPOLEON MOVES ASIDE...

HE IS SECURELY BOUND.
MEDDLER! YOU MUST DIE! IN FIVE MINUTES AN INCANDESCERY BOMB WILL GO OFF, SETTING THE HOUSE AFIRE. WHEN YOUR CHARRED BODY IS FOUND, THEY WILL THINK ME DEAD. LEAVING ME TO DO AS I PLEASE HA-HA..

AS KRUGER LEAVES, THE BATMAN ROLLS OVER AND DRAWS FORTH A STEEL BLADE FROM HIS BOOT.

AND HE IS SOON FREE.
GOT TO GET OUT BEFORE THAT BOMB GOES OFF.

AS HE REACHES THE GROUND, A TERRIFIC BLAST BLOWS UP THE HOUSE!
BOOM

THE BATMAN MIRACULOUSLY ESCAPES DEATH..

WHEW! THAT WAS CLOSE. NOW HOME TO REST AND THINK.

THE FOLLOWING NIGHT... THE HOME OF RYDER, ONE OF KRUGER'S LIEUTENANTS.
WHAT IS IT? WHO?

THE BATMAN.
YES.. AND VERY MUCH ALIVE. TELL THAT TO KRUGER. I SHALL BE BACK FOR YOU LATER. GOOD NIGHT.. AND PLEASANT DREAMS.

H..HE'S GONE. BUT HE SAID HE'D BE BACK FOR ME! I'VE GOT TO GET AWAY FROM HERE.

RYDER DRESSES AND SPEEDS AWAY IN HIS CAR. THE BATMAN TRAILS HIM FROM ABOVE IN HIS BATPLANE!

TO THE SECRET HANGAR OF THE DIRIGIBLE.
IT WORKED. HE'S LED ME STRAIGHT TO THE HIDEOUT OF KRUGER.

THE BATMAN BREAKS A GLASS VIAL. A THICK, BLACK, SMOKE POURS FORTH..
THIS WILL PREVENT THE GUARDS FROM SEEING THE PLANE

..WHICH SOON BLANKETS THE WHOLE PLANE!

LIKE A GREAT BLACK CLOUD THE BAT-PLANE FLOATS OVER THE HANGAR.
A BLACK CLOUD..
YEAH. LOOKS LIKE RAIN.

THE BATMAN FIXES HIS AUTOMATIC CONTROLS AND LOWERS HIMSELF ONTO THE HANGAR.

A ROOM INSIDE THE HANGAR.
WHAT ARE OUR INSTRUCTIONS MR. BIXLEY?
THESE SMALL DEATH-RAY MACHINES WILL BE MOUNTED ON TRUCKS. IF THERE IS ANY RESISTANCE BY THE PEOPLE TURN THE MACHINE ON THEM!

SUDDENLY GAS FILLS THE AIR..
I'M CHOKING!
GAS.. OH!!

THAT GAS VIAL DID THE TRICK.

HE ENTERS THE ROOM..
WELL, HERE GOES. I HOPE I DON'T GET BLOWN UP.

THERE IS A BLAST AS A MACHINE GOES OFF, AND BLOWS UP THE OTHERS
BOOM

THOSE RAY MACHINES ARE DESTROYED. NOW FOR THE DIRIGIBLE!

THE BATMAN PICKS UP AN AXE . .

SUDDENLY, A SECRET DOOR OPENS. KRUGER POINTS HIS GUN.. FIRES!!
YOU ARE TOO LATE MY FRIEND_ TOO LATE!

THE BATMAN IS HIT_

HE IS FINISHED! --ANOTHER CONQUEST FOR NAPOLEON! HA-HA-HA!!

I WILL DESTROY HIS BODY WITH A DEATH-RAY MACHINE. GUARD! WATCH THIS BODY. I AM GOING TO GET THE ONE THAT IS LEFT!

KRUGER SOON RETURNS!
IT IS IRONICAL THAT HIS BODY SHALL BE DISPOSED OF WITH THE VERY MACHINE HE TRIED TO DESTROY!

THE DEATH RAY STRIKES THE BATMAN-

THERE IS A BLAST. AND WHERE ONCE HAD BEEN THE BODY OF THE BATMAN_ A HEAP OF ASHES.
MY FUSION OF OZONE GAS AND THE GAMMA RAY HAS AT LAST ELIMINATED THE ONE MAN WHO STOOD IN MY PATH.

SOME TIME LATER. A FIGURE CLIMBS THE ROPE TO THE BATPLANE.

IT IS BRUCE WAYNE, THE BATMAN!

LATER. THE WAYNE MANSION.
IT WAS A GOOD THING MY BULLET-PROOF VEST STOPPED THOSE BULLETS.. JUST A FEW FLESH WOUNDS. LOST SOME BLOOD THOUGH!

-WHEN I OVERPOWERED THAT GUARD AND CHANGED INTO HIS CLOTHING, MY RESCUE WAS COMPLETE... AND NOW TO WORK!

THROUGH THE NIGHT HE WORKS IN HIS SECRET LABORATORY.. MIXING .. PROBING...

A MYSTERIOUS CHEMICAL IS SPRAYED OVER THE BATPLANE.

THE NEXT DAY_
LOOK! THE DIRIGIBLE-
...IT'S BACK!
WE'LL ALL BE KILLED!!

WHEN SUDDENLY.. THE BATPLANE APPEARS.
THOSE RUTHLESS MURDERERS.. TAKING INNOCENT LIVES!

THE BATMAN PLUNGES HIS SHIP FOR THE DIRIGIBLE, WHOSE DEATH-RAYS STRIKE THE PLANE.

BUT IT IS UNSCATHED. THE CHEMICAL SPRAY HAS COUNTERACTED THE DEATH RAY.

A CATAPULT-PLANE IS RELEASED FROM THE AIRSHIP.

SUDDENLY THE BATMAN DIVES..

A TERRIFIC BLAST AND THE DIRIGIBLE AND BAT-PLANE ARE BLOWN TO SMITHEREENS.

– BUT THE BATMAN IS SAFE IN A PARACHUTE.

IN THE CATAPULT-PLANE.. KRUGER!

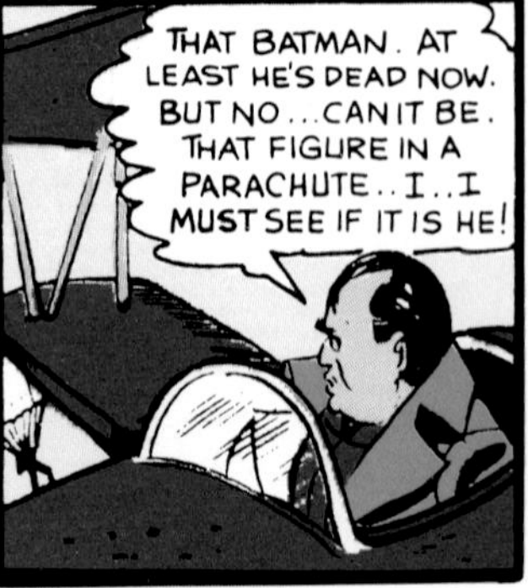

A FEW HOURS LATER _ THE HOME OF BRUCE WAYNE.

. . AND THE BODY OF KRUGER WAS RECOVERED FROM THE WATER. BUT THAT OF THE BATMAN HAS NOT YET BEEN FOUND. LATEST DISPATCHES REPORT THE CAPTURE OF THE ENTIRE SCARLET ARMY. .

THE END

BOB KANE

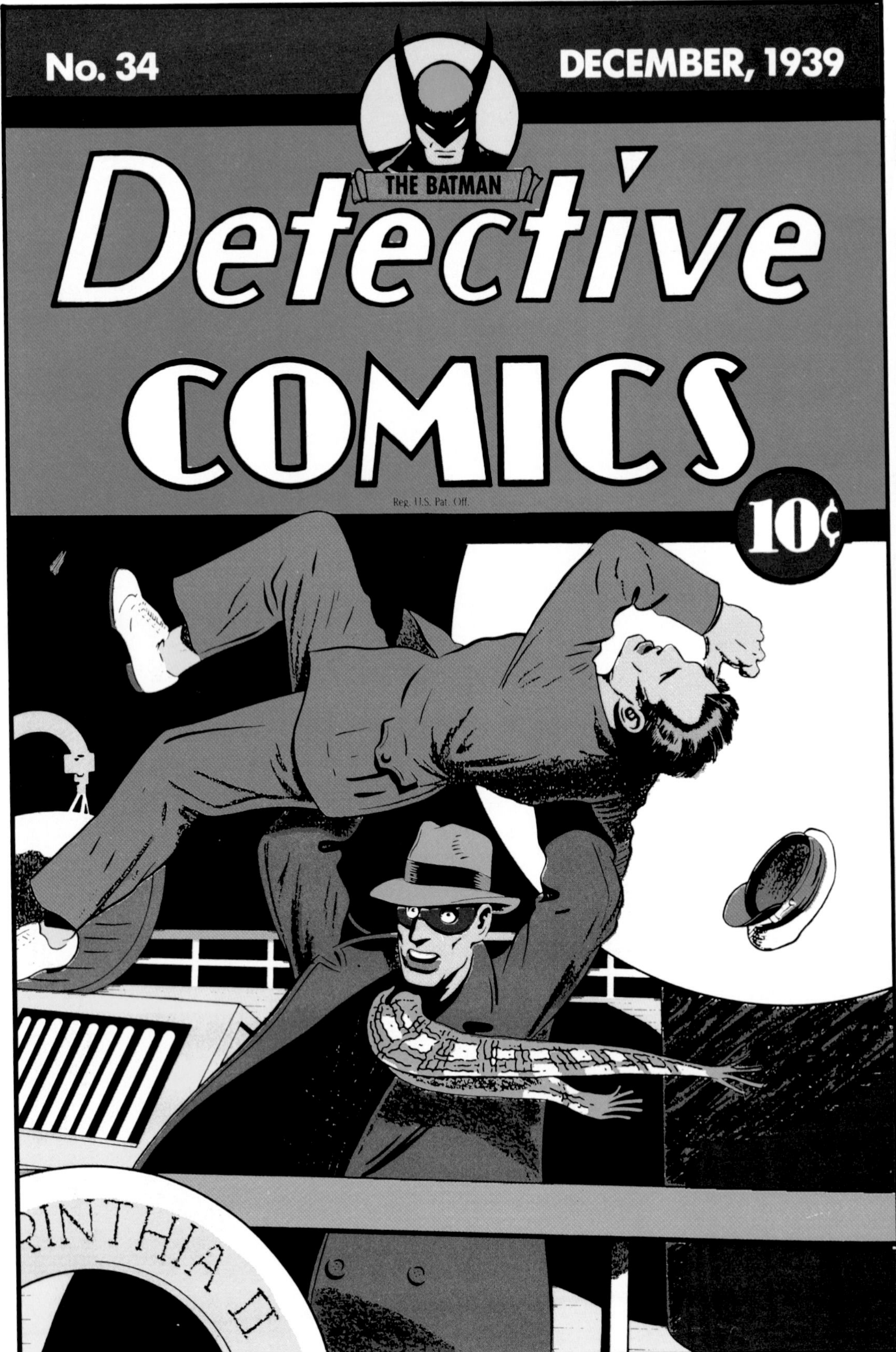
No. 34
DECEMBER, 1939
THE BATMAN
Detective
COMICS
Reg. U.S. Pat. Off.
10¢
RINTHIA II

BATMAN
BY BOB KANE
THE BATMAN, HAVING RESCUED HIS FIANCEE JULIE FROM A SINISTER FIGURE NAMED THE MONK, SEES HER SAFELY ON BOARD A BOAT FOR AMERICA. HE IS TO FOLLOW HER LATER, WHEN HE BECOMES INVOLVED IN A MYSTERY..!
AS BRUCE WAYNE, HE IS LEAVING HIS HOTEL..
THAT LOOKS LIKE OLD JED FARNOL. JED..OH, JED!
JED, I.. OH, I.. LORD!
I DON'T BLAME YOU SIR. I GAVE YOU A SHOCK. NOT HAVING ANY FACE, DIDN'T I. I'M SORRY.
THAT'S MIGHTY QUEER. A MAN WITHOUT A FACE. I'D LIKE TO LOOK INTO THIS, BUT..
IN A MIDTOWN HOTEL.
THE MARK OF DUC D'ORTERRE, MASTER OF THE APACHES! I'M DOOMED TO DIE! WHAT SHALL I DO?
TAXI! TAXI!

AS THE CAR STOPS FOR A TRAFFIC SIGNAL.
THE RUE DE.. OH! I DIDN'T KNOW YOU WERE IN THE CAR.
IT'S ALL RIGHT. MAY I BE OF SERVICE?

WELL. IT SEEMS SOMEONE IS AFTER YOU, YOUNG LADY! WITH DAGGERS AT THAT..
OH! IT'S THE APACHES. THEY SWEAR TO KILL ME.

COME ON! THERE'S NOT A MOMENT TO LOSE. LET'S TAKE ADVANTAGE OF THIS TRAFFIC JAM.

NOW WHAT'S THE MEANING OF ALL THIS MELODRAMA?
IT'S TOO LONG A STORY TO TELL. YOU WOULDN'T BELIEVE ME ANY. OOH!

YOU DID IT. THAT TIME, OLD MAN. SURE SCARED HER SILLY.
SHE IS IN MORTAL FEAR. LET US SEEK PRIVACY.

IN THE MIDTOWN HOTEL.
WON'T YOU TELL ME WHAT THIS MYSTERY IS ALL ABOUT.
I DARE NOT. ASK, CHARLES, HERE. HE WHO OWNS NO FACE. HE CAN TELL YOU. HE IS NOT AFRAID TO DIE.

MY NAME IS CHARLES MAIRE. KAREL HERE IS MY SISTER. WE WERE HAPPY ONCE, BEFORE WE MET THE DUC D'ORTERRE. WE MET AT A BAL MASQUE. HE WAS ENCHANTED OF KAREL. BUT WHEN I INTERFERED.
2

"HE HAD ME CAPTURED AND TAKEN TO HIS UNEARTHLY DEN IN THE PARIS SEWERS."

"ON A HIDDEN ALTAR HE BURNED AWAY MY FACE AND FEATURES WITH A TERRIBLE RAY."

THE DUC D'ORTERRE MUST BE DESTROYED. HE IS AFTER OUR MONEY AND KAREL!
AS MYSELF I CANNOT HELP YOU. BUT IF YOU WILL PARDON ME?

BRUCE WAYNE DISAPPEARS. BUT THE BATMAN ENTERS!
I HAVE HEARD OF YOU! THE BATMAN!
I WILL GIVE YOU INSTRUCTIONS AND MAY THE LORD HELP YOU.

THAT NIGHT AS PARIS SLEEPS..

A DEATH-DEFYING LEAP INTO SPACE..

AND DROPS INTO AN OPEN SEWER.

3

SUDDENLY - FROM A CORRIDOR.
A DRUNK! PROBABLY FROM A BAL MASQUE. GET HIS WALLET..

THE GREAT AGILITY OF THE BATMAN THROWS TERROR INTO THE APACHES!
WHERE IS YOUR LEADER, FOUL ONE!
GLUG! YOU CHOKE. AH HE COMES.

AHA! A VISITOR.

THE BATMAN MAKES A FLYING LEAP TOWARD THE DUC. BUT IS STOPPED BY A BLINDING LIGHT WHICH SHOOTS FORTH FROM THE END OF THE DUC'S CANE.
TOO BAD M'SIEU! YOU ARE TOO IMPETUOUS!

EH, MES AMIS! BRING THIS THING TO MY TEMPLE. I SHALL BE AMUSED FOR A LITTLE WHILE

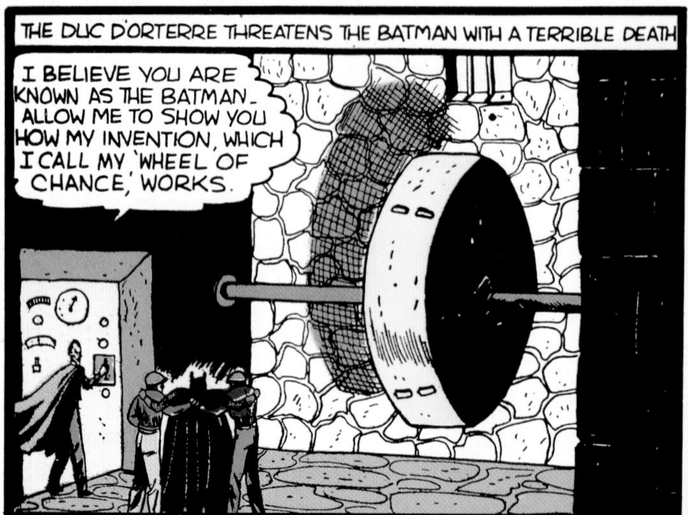
THE DUC D'ORTERRE THREATENS THE BATMAN WITH A TERRIBLE DEATH
I BELIEVE YOU ARE KNOWN AS THE BATMAN. ALLOW ME TO SHOW YOU HOW MY INVENTION, WHICH I CALL MY 'WHEEL OF CHANCE,' WORKS.

OBSERVE THE WHEEL CLOSELY. IT BEGINS TO WHIRL SLOWLY, THEN FASTER AND FASTER. WATCH!

THE WHEEL OF CHANCE BEGINS TO WHIRL.
4

WHEN THE WHEEL REVOLVES ITS FASTEST YOU WILL EITHER BE THROWN AGAINST THE CONCRETE WALLS TO BE CRUSHED..OR BE MADDENED BY THE NEVER-CEASING WHIRLING OF THE GREAT WHEEL. MEANWHILE. I SHALL WATCH FROM BEHIND A GLASS DOOR!

THE BATMAN IS HELPLESS ON THE MIGHTY WHEEL . .

ALL READY? GO!

THE WHEEL BEGINS TO TURN . .

THE WHEEL PICKS UP SPEED.

THE BATMAN TRIES HIS BONDS. BY TENSING HIS STEEL-LIKE MUSCLES, HE BREAKS THE LEATHER THONGS!

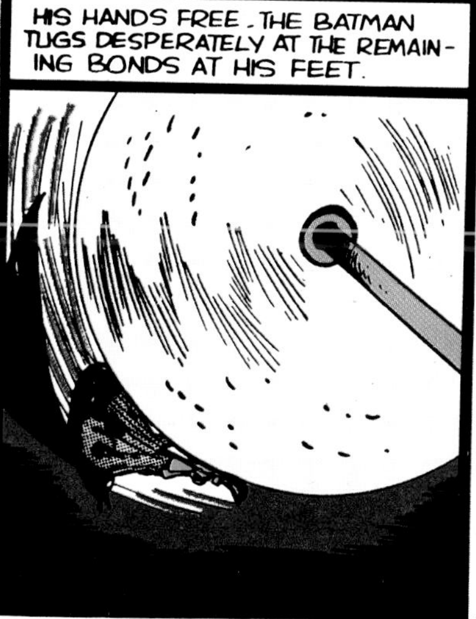
HIS HANDS FREE. THE BATMAN TUGS DESPERATELY AT THE REMAINING BONDS AT HIS FEET.

HE IS WORKING HIMSELF FREE. TURN THE WHEEL FASTER! FASTER.

THE BATMAN IS FREE. BUT THE WHEEL IS SPINNING INCREDIBLY FAST!
I'VE GOT TO CHANCE A JUMP.
5

IN A SWIFT LIMOUSINE THEY ARE SWEPT THROUGH THE UN-SUSPECTING TRAFFIC..

-TO THE DUC D'ORTERRE!
AH, MES AMIS! YOU HAVE COME. I AM SO GLAD.

THIS LITTLE WHEEL WILL TEACH YOUR BROTHER THAT I AM SERIOUS WHEN I SAY I WANT THE MONEY HE HAS HIDDEN AWAY-
YOU FIEND!

MEANWHILE. THE BATMAN SEEMS TO HEAR THE FLOWERS MURMUR.
I SEND MY THOUGHTS TO YOU, STRANGER. YOU MUST RELEASE US! FOLLOW THE HEDGE TO A GLASS DOOR, WHICH LEADS TO THE WHEEL ROOM. THE REST IS UP TO YOU!

A VENGEFUL BATMAN SEEKS RETRIBUTION..

THE WHEEL BEGINS TO MOVE...
HELP! HELP!

-AS THE DUC D'ORTERRE FLEES THROUGH A SECRET DOOR. THE BATMAN MAKES A DESPERATE CAST..

HIS ROPE CATCHES ON TO A BAR ON THE STEEL HUB AND THE WHEEL COMES TO A SUDDEN STOP!
7

WORKING FEVERISHLY, THE BATMAN FREES CHARLES!

THE DUC HAS GONE WITH KAREL TO HIS PALACE IN CHAMPAGNE. YOU MUST OVERTAKE AND KILL HIM! HE IS A FIEND.

FOLLOW HIM! WE WERE LUCKY TO ESCAPE HIS APACHES.. HE WILL TAKE THE HIGHWAY. YOU MUST HURRY. GET A TAXI.

BUT THE BATMAN HAS A BETTER PLAN.

AND SHARP AGAINST THE MOON

SEARCHING, ALWAYS SEARCHING FOR HIS QUARRY.

IN A CAR BELOW...
A PLANE! THE.. THE BATMAN'S PLANE. DRIVER - FASTER!
8

THE BATMAN FIXES HIS AUTOMATIC CONTROLS AND PREPARES TO ATTACK..

AND AN EERIE FIGURE DROPS FROM THE SKY
THE BATMAN GAUGES HIS DISTANCE.
..AND THEN MAKES A VALIANT LEAP ONTO THE SPEEDING CAR!
-AGAIN THE MENACE OF THE RAY CANE..
BUT THIS TIME THE BATMAN IS PREPARED..
SO SORRY TO DISAPPOINT YOU THIS TIME.
AS THE CAR RACES AT A TERRIFIC SPEED - THE BATMAN SWINGS OVER THE SIDE!!
YOU DIE NOW BATMAN!
BUT THE DUC RECKONS WITHOUT HIS CAPTIVE..
UGH!
9

THE BATMAN LEAPS INTO THE TONNEAU OF THE BIG CAR DIRECTLY ONTO THE DUC.

THE FIERCE STRUGGLE UNBALANCES THE CAR..

CAUSING IT TO CAREEN CRAZILY OFF THE NARROW BRIDGE.

SPLIT SECONDS MEANING LIFE OR DEATH. THE BATMAN GRASPS FOR HIS ROPE LADDER..

AND CATCHES IT JUST IN TIME TO ESCAPE SUDDEN DEATH.

LATER.
YOU'VE BEEN WONDERFUL TO US. MERE WORDS CAN'T EXPRESS HOW MUCH WE APPRECIATE IT. BUT WON'T YOU TELL US WHO YOU ARE?
THAT, MY DEAR, MUST BE KEPT A SECRET... AND NOW-- AU REVOIR!

A SMASHING NEW ACTION-FILLED
BATMAN
THRILLER APPEARS IN NEXT MONTH'S DETECTIVE COMICS!

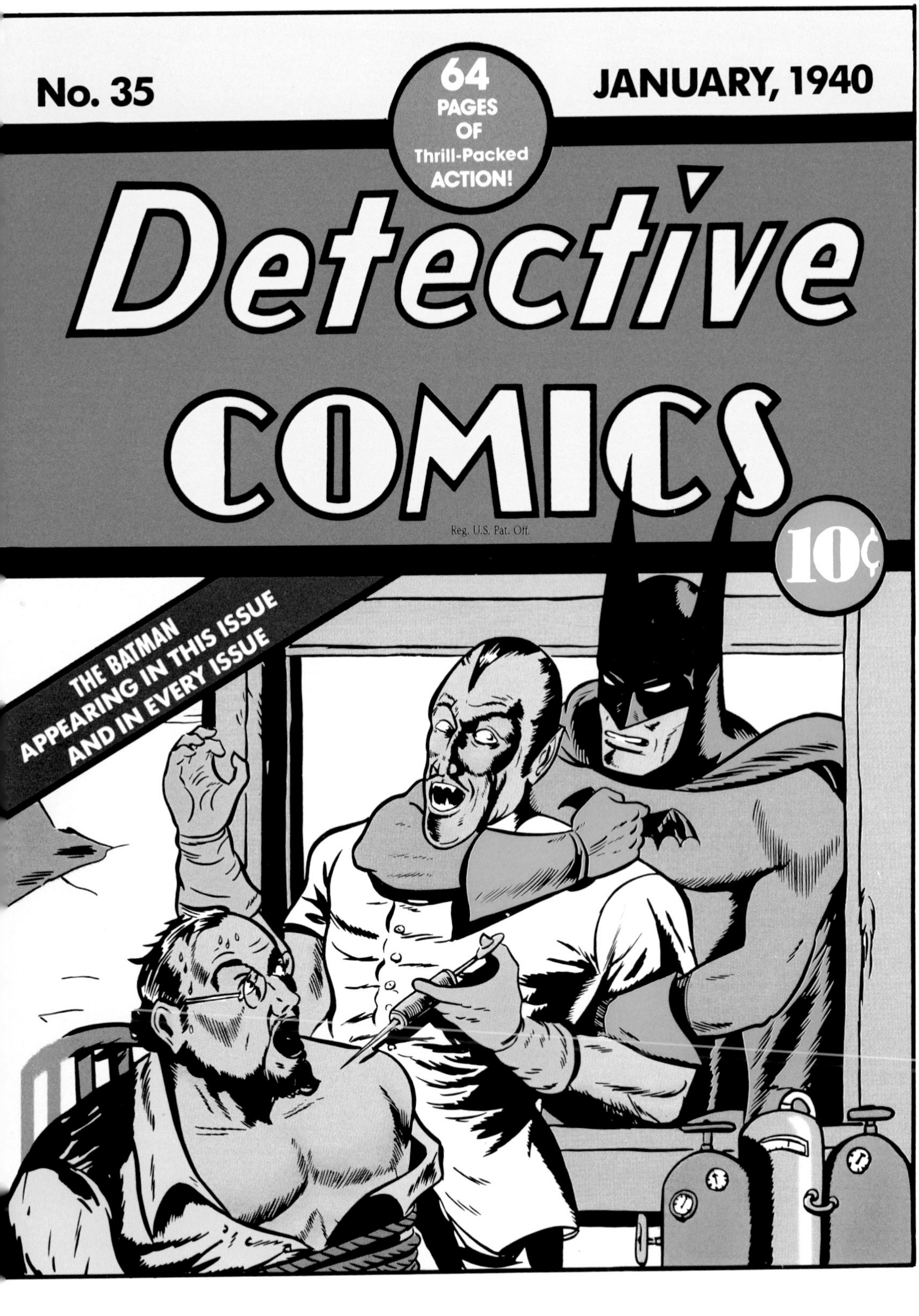

No. 35

64 PAGES OF Thrill-Packed ACTION!

JANUARY, 1940

Detective COMICS

Reg. U.S. Pat. Off.

10¢

THE BATMAN
APPEARING IN THIS ISSUE
AND IN EVERY ISSUE

The BATMAN

THE **BATMAN**, WEIRD FIGURE OF DARKNESS AGAIN PROWLS FORTH TO STRIKE ANOTHER BLOW AGAINST CRIME...

BY BOB KANE

POLICE COMMISSIONER GORDON SITS CHATTING WITH HIS FRIEND 'BRUCE WAYNE', UNAWARE THAT HE IS THE BATMAN.

I TELL YOU, BRUCE, IF I EVER CATCH THE BATMAN!

PARDON ME, SIR, BUT SOMEONE WANTS TO SEE YOU. SAYS IT'S URGENT!

"AS YOU ALREADY MUST KNOW, I AM A SORT OF COLLECTOR OF CURIOS. I EVEN HAVE A SMALL MUSEUM OF MY PIECES.. A FEW NIGHTS AGO, I RECEIVED A VISITOR."

THERE BEFORE ME STOOD THE LARGEST PIECE OF RUBY I HAD EVER SEEN! IT WAS CARVED INTO A LITTLE HIDEOUS STATUE - GLEAMING AS RED AS BLOOD.

WH-WHAT IS IT?
A SOLID CHUNK OF RUBY REPRESENTING THE ANCIENT HINDU-IDOL, KILA.. GOD OF DESTRUCTION.

"OF COURSE I HAD TO HAVE IT! -AND SO I BOUGHT IT FROM LENOX. FIVE DAYS AGO I RECEIVED A THREATENING NOTE!
We the followers of Kila command you to return our God to the Temple from which it was stolen, or else he will bring destruction upon you.

JUST AN HOUR AGO, I RECEIVED ANOTHER NOTE. THIS ONE!

Already destruction visits Lenox the guilty one - You yet may save yourself if you restore Kila to us.

GREAT SCOT, MAN! WE HAVEN'T A MOMENT TO LOSE. LENOX IS IN GREAT DANGER. BRUCE, ARE YOU COMING?
WHY NOT- HINDU IDOL, WORSHIPERS, DEATH-NOTES. ALL SOUNDS VERY MELODRAMATIC- MAYBE I'LL WRITE A STORY ABOUT IT!

SIREN WAILING, THE POLICE CAR SPEEDS THROUGH THE STREETS.

THERE THEY ARE- THEY'VE GOT HIM- AFTER THEM, COMMISSIONER

THE CHASE BEGINS..

THEY'VE HIT A TIRE_ WATCH OUT!

THE TOURING CAR SUDDENLY STOPS ON THE WHARF'S EDGE.
FOR KILA!

THERE IS A SCREAM, A SPLASH, A HINDU'S DEFIANT SHOUT!
KILA IS AVENGED.
THEY'VE KILLED HIM!
YES. AND THROWN HIS BODY INTO THE RIVER. THE RATS!
SPLASH!

THEY GOT AWAY, SIR. I'LL GET THE BOYS TO DRAG THE RIVER FOR THE MAN'S BODY.
FROM NOW ON, WELDON, YOU AND THAT INFERNAL IDOL OF YOURS WILL BE GUARDED BY MY MEN. THEY'LL PROBABLY PAY YOU A VISIT NEXT!!

I'M GOING BACK TO HEADQUARTERS NOW. COMING ALONG BRUCE?
NO COMMISSIONER. I THINK I'LL GO HOME AND WRITE THAT STORY..

THE NEXT DAY
The Tribune
NOTED EXPLORER IS MURDERED BY HINDUS.
POLICE DRAG RIVER FOR BODY OF LENOX BODY NOT YET FOUND
LENOX SOLD MILLIONAIRE WELDON, PRECIOUS STATUE CARVED OF VALUABLE RUBY
SHELDON LENOX

MANY PEOPLE SEEM INTERESTED IN THE NEWS. ESPECIALLY ABOUT THE RUBY IDOL_
YA KNOW, JOE. THAT HUNK OF RUBY MUST BE WORTH AN AWFUL LOT OF DOUGH!
YOU SAID A MOUTHFUL MIKE...

AN ORIENTAL NAMED SIN FANG ALSO SEEMS INTERESTED!
SOON NOW.. SOON.. WHEN THE POLICE ARE TAKEN AWAY!

A FEW WEEKS LATER-
.. AND SO I THINK YOU CAN TAKE YOUR MEN AWAY NOW. THE RUBY IDOL IS IN A BURGLAR-PROOF GLASS AND I'M SURE I'M SAFE ENOUGH!
WELDON, IT'S YOUR RUBY AND IT'S YOUR LIFE. I'LL CALL MY MEN OFF AT ONCE..

.. AND SO THIS GRINNING IDOL OF RUBY IS LEFT UNGUARDED. BEARING ITS CURSE OF DEATH!

SO WELDON HAS TAKEN THE POLICE AWAY. HMM. I'VE GOT A HUNCH SOMETHING'S GOING TO POP TONIGHT AND I WANT TO BE THERE WHEN IT DOES..

WHEN THE POLICE ARE AWAY. THE RATS WILL PLAY. I THINK THE BATMAN WILL TAKE A HAND IN THIS GAME!

THAT NIGHT. THE WELDON ESTATE.

OH-OH! SOME-ONE HERE ALREADY!

C'MON. AIN'T YOU GOT THAT ALARM DIS-CONNECTED YET!

NEED ANY HELP, BOYS?
THE BATMAN!
GET HIM!!

DON'T YOU KNOW IT'S DANGEROUS TO PLAY WITH KNIVES!

THE OTHER GANGSTER RUSHES UP FROM BEHIND AND CATCHES THE BATMAN IN A DEADLY HEADLOCK

OH- YOU BROKE MY ARM- OH!

THE BATMAN TURNS JUST IN TIME TO MEET THE FIRST MAN!
SO. YOU STILL WANT TO PLAY, EH!

SUDDENLY, NEW FIGURES APPEAR ON THE SCENE.. HINDUS.

THIS TIME YOU'LL STAY OUT!

THE CLUB CRASHES DOWN UPON THE BATMAN!

HERE- KILA!! QUICK..

THE HINDU SMASHES THE CASE AS THE ALARM RINGS LOUDLY!
HIST--THE ALARM- QUICK-TAKE THE IDOL!

THE DAZED BATMAN REGAINS CONSCIOUSNESS!

BUT THE ALARM HAS WARNED THE GUARDS..
THERE'S ONE OF THEM-GRAB HIM..
THE CASE IS SMASHED IT'S GONE!

-I HATE TO DO THIS, BUDDY!

THE BATMAN RACES ACROSS THE FLOOR.
SORRY I CAN'T STAY, BOYS.

..LEAPS FOR THE CHANDELIER.
BUT I REALLY...

..AND SWINGS OUT!
..MUST GO!
CRASH!

THE BATMAN CLUTCHES A BRANCH!

– AND DROPS TO SAFETY!

THE BATMAN DASHES TO HIS HIGH-POWERED ROADSTER..
THAT'S THE HINDU'S CAR.. MAYBE I CAN STILL CATCH THEM!

... THEN PURSUES HIS PREY!!

THE BATMAN TRAILS HIS QUARRY INTO CHINATOWN!!
SIN FANG
SIN FANG CHINESE AND ORIENTAL CURIOS.

THE BATMAN, UNNOTICED BY THE HINDUS, WATCHES AT A SAFE DISTANCE..
SIN-FANG! HMMM. I'VE GOT TO FIND OUT ABOUT HIM..
SIN FANG

LATER.. THE HOME OF WONG, UNOFFICIAL MAYOR OF CHINATOWN- A WISE AND HONEST MAN..

OH.. WHAT.. WHO ARE YOU?
-SOME CALL ME THE BATMAN!

I HAVE HEARD OF YOU! YOU ARE A GOOD MAN- YOU FIGHT ALL EVIL.. BUT WHAT CAN THE BATMAN WANT OF WONG?
IN-FORMATION ABOUT ONE CALLED SIN FANG!

THE BATMAN TELLS WONG HIS STORY..
FROM WHAT YOU HAVE TOLD ME I HAVE NO DOUBT THAT THE RUBY IDOL WILL BE CUT INTO SMALL PIECES AND THEN SOLD.. FOR SIN FANG IS REALLY A RECEIVER OF STOLEN GOODS. YOU MUST BE CAREFUL OF SIN FANG

THE BATMAN DECIDES UPON A BOLD RUSE! THAT VERY NIGHT..
SIN FANG
SIN FANG
CHINESE AND ORIENTAL CURIOS

YOU- THE BATMAN!
YES! I'VE COME FOR THE RUBY IDOL..SURELY THE GREAT SIN FANG DOES NOT CARE TO DEAL WITH STOLEN GOODS!

I HAD NOT REALIZED IT WAS STOLEN. IF IT WERE KNOWN THAT SIN FANG DEALT WITH STOLEN GOODS HIS REPUTATION WOULD SUFFER. FOLLOW ME.. AND I WILL RETURN THE IDOL..

YOU'RE A SMOOTH TALKER, SIN FANG- BUT I'M WISE TO YOU..

SUDDENLY, AS SIN FANG OPENS THE DOOR - TWO GIANT MONGOLS WIELDING LARGE, CURVED SWORDS, RUSH FORWARD-

-DUCKING 'NEATH THE FIRST SLASHING BLADE-THE BATMAN CLUTCHES THE MAN'S WRIST AND..

HURLS HIM BACKWARDS..

UPON THE OTHER'S UPRAISED SWORD...
?

THEN SPRINGS FORWARD AND CRASHES HIS FIST AGAINST THE JAW OF THE ASTONISHED MONGOL.!
-AND THAT'S THAT!!

FORGIVE ME! THE GUARDS SEEING YOUR MASKED FACE THOUGHT YOU WERE AN ENEMY. IT WAS PURELY AN ACCIDENT!
I FORGIVE YOU. LEAD ON, MY FRIEND

AS SIN FANG STEPS OUT OF THE ROOM, THE DOOR SUDDENLY SLAMS SHUT UPON THE BATMAN!
SLAM!

GAS! COUGH.. MUSTARD GAS! COUGH....

HE REACHES QUICKLY FOR A PARTICULAR GLASS VIAL IN HIS BELT...

. . AND SLAMS THE PELLET AGAINST THE WALL.
I HOPE I PICKED THE RIGHT VIAL!

THE GAS FROM THE PELLET QUICKLY MIXES WITH THE DEADLY MUSTARD GAS!
THERE. THAT DID IT. THE MUSTARD GAS IS NOW HARMLESS.

I'VE JUST HAD ANOTHER LITTLE ACCIDENT. YOU'VE GOT BAD PLUMBING IN YOUR HOUSE, SIN FANG. THERE IS GAS ESCAPING FROM THE PIPES..
TSK. TSK. I SHALL HAVE IT REMEDIED AT ONCE..

IN THE NEXT ROOM SIN FANG STEPS BEHIND A WALL AND..
JUST A MOMENT AND I'LL GET THE IDOL FOR YOU..

SUDDENLY THE BATMAN DROPS THROUGH A TRAP DOOR.
THIS TIME DIE, BATMAN! IT IS NO ACCIDENT!

DOWN-DOWN-DOWN, FALLS THE BATMAN TO A WATERY GRAVE..

IF I CAN JUST GRAB THAT PIPE . . .

-AND THE BATMAN'S CLUTCH FOR SAFETY IS SUCCESSFUL..
GOT IT!

THAT TRAP DOOR IS SLIGHTLY OPEN. IF I STOOD ON THIS PIPE AND LEAPED I COULD JUST ABOUT REACH IT AND GET OUT OF HERE..

A FEW MINUTES LATER THE BATMAN IS FREE..
WHEW! THAT WAS A TIGHT SQUEEZE. NOW FOR SIN FANG. AND SETTLE A LITTLE SCORE WITH HIM...

THE BATMAN SOON FINDS HIS FOE. HE STEALTHILY OPENS THE DOOR..
WITH THE BATMAN DISPOSE OF NO ONE CAN TAKE YOU FROM ME MY PRECIOUS RUBY.. HA! THE BATMAN. IF HE HAD KNOWN WHO I AM— HA! HA!

SUDDENLY THE ORIENTAL BEGINS PEELING OFF THE SKIN OF HIS HANDS - REVEALING WHITE FLESH UNDERNEATH..
-WITH THESE YELLOW-SKIN GLOVES OFF..

- THIS MAKEUP WASHED OFF AND I REALLY AM...

SHELDON LENOX!
YOU... ALIVE!!

I HAD A FEELING YOU WERE BEHIND ALL THIS. ESPECIALLY WHEN THE POLICE FAILED TO RECOVER YOUR BODY FROM THE RIVER.. YOU NEEDED MONEY AND MADE A DEAL WITH SIN FANG TO CUT UP THE RUBY. YOU MADE USE OF THE DESTRUCTION LEGEND IT WAS SUPPOSED TO HAVE, AND WROTE THOSE NOTES..

YOU HIRED THOSE FAKE HINDUS. STAGED YOUR DEATH AND THEN HAD THE RUBY STOLEN! WHERE IS SIN FANG? HAVE YOU KILLED HIM?
WE HAD A QUARREL.. OVER MONEY! SO I KILLED HIM AND SINCE I SPEAK CHINESE, I MADE UP TO LOOK LIKE HIM AND TOOK HIS PLACE...

-A GUN SUDDENLY APPEARS IN LENOX'S HAND!
-AND NOW, BATMAN. IT IS YOUR TURN TO DIE!

AS A SHOT TEARS THROUGH THE BATMAN'S CAPE. HE REACHES FOR THE RUBY IDOL. KILA...

AND HURLS IT AT LENOX!

LENOX FALLS THROUGH AN OPEN WINDOW

-AND HURTLES TO HIS DEATH
YAAAAAH

WITH BITTER IRONY. ACROSS THE CRUSHED BODY FALLS THE BLOOD-RED IDOL. KILA, GOD OF DESTRUCTION!

NEXT DAY. AT POLICE HEADQUARTERS
THAT BATMAN. HE'S DONE IT AGAIN! HE'S MAKING THE POLICE DEPARTMENT LOOK RIDICULOUS. I WISH I COULD GET MY HANDS ON HIM.
BOB KANE

DON'T MISS THE NEXT EXCITING EPISODE OF THE SENSATIONAL BATMAN...
...AS HE CRASHES THROUGH TO SMASH ANOTHER BLOW AT CRIME!!! NEXT MONTH!

No. 36
FEBRUARY, 1940
THE BATMAN
Detective
COMICS
Reg. U.S. Pat. Off.
10¢

BATMAN

BY BOB KANE

ALREADY AN ALMOST LEGENDARY FIGURE, THE COWLED SHADOW OF THE **BATMAN** PROWLS THROUGH THE NIGHT PREYING UPON THE CRIMINAL PARASITE, LIKE THE WINGED CREATURE WHOSE NAME HE HAD ADOPTED.

WENDING HIS WAY HOMEWARD, THE **BATMAN** SUDDENLY SEES A MAN LEAP FROM A SPEEDING CAR---

HE'S DEAD! PERHAPS THERE IS SOMETHING IN HIS POCKETS THAT MIGHT TELL ME SOMETHING!

HERE'S SOMETHING! A NOTEBOOK WI... POLICE!
THE BATMAN!
HE'S KILLED SOMEONE! SHOOT HIM DOWN!

THE BATMAN RUNS DOWN AN ALLEY---

--- EASILY CLEARS A SIX FOOT FENCE ---
SO YOU WANT TO PLAY COPS 'N' ROBBERS, EH?

--- AND DISAPPEARS INTO THE BLACK NIGHT!
WELL, HE'S GONE, NO USE CHASING HIM ANY FURTHER, WE CAN'T SEE HIM IN THE DARK ANYWAY!
YOU MIGHT AS WELL CHASE A GHOST!
LATER THE "GHOST," ALIAS THE BATMAN, ALIAS BRUCE WAYNE, SITS AT HOME PUZZLING OVER THE WORDS OF THE DEAD MAN ---
THE WORDS OF THAT MAN HAVE GOT ME STUMPED. HE KEPT MUTTERING ABOUT A 'FOG,' A "STRANGE" "FOG" --- MM... 'FOG' --- 'STRANGE' --- 'FOG' ---

'FOG' --- 'STRANGE' --- 'STRANGE' --- OF COURSE! HE DIDN'T MEAN A STRANGE FOG, HE MEANT A "FOG" HAD SOMETHING TO DO WITH A PERSON NAMED 'STRANGE' --- PROFESSOR HUGO 'STRANGE'!

PROFESSOR HUGO STRANGE. THE MOST DANGEROUS MAN IN THE WORLD! SCIENTIST, PHILOSOPHER AND A CRIMINAL GENIUS --- LITTLE IS KNOWN OF HIM, YET THIS MAN IS UNDOUBTEDLY THE GREATEST ORGANIZER OF CRIME IN THE WORLD ---
2
--- MAYBE THAT LITTLE BLACK BOOK I FOUND CAN TELL ME MORE ABOUT HIM AND THE 'FOG'! MMM-- ALL THE PAGES ARE BLANK EXCEPT THIS ONE. WHY, IT'S A LIST OF BANKS AND OTHER PLACES! WHAT'S THIS ON THE BOTTOM --- THE F.B.I. --- THEN THAT MAN WAS A G. MAN!
State Trust Co
Wickler Jewel Co
If this book is found please notify the F.B.I.
John Davis

THE F.B.I. IS NOT GOING TO GET THIS BOOK TILL I CLEAR THE BATMAN'S NAME OF SUSPICION OF THE MURDER OF THE G.MAN, AND SOLVE THE MYSTERY OF THE 'FOG'! I THINK I'LL SIT TIGHT, SEE WHAT HAPPENS... AND THEN I'LL ACT!

NOT FAR AWAY, A MAN SITS IN A DIMLY LIT ROOM AND GAZES INTO THE FIRE....

A MALIGNANT 'SMILE' CROSSES HIS FACE AS HE BROODS OVER THE MANY EVIL SCHEMES THAT SURGE THROUGH HIS BRILLIANT BUT DISTORTED BRAIN....

PROFESSOR STRANGE! THAT G.MAN WE WERE SUPPOSED TO TAKE FOR A RIDE...

THE GUNMAN TELLS HIS STORY....
...AND THEN WHEN I SAW THE BATMAN I PULLED AWAY FAST!
YOU COWARDLY FOOL, YOU SHOULD HAVE SHOT HIM DOWN, TOO! THE BATMAN IS THE ONLY MAN WITH THE IMAGINATION TO SENSE THE EXACT NATURE OF OUR PLANS. HOWEVER, SINCE THE G.MAN IS DEAD, HE CAN GET NO INFORMATION FROM THAT QUARTER!

IN THAT CASE WE WILL PROCEED AS PLANNED. TO-MORROW NIGHT THE 'FOG' WILL STRIKE! AND THEN...HA-HA.. AND THEN..HA.. HA-HA..HA!

THE NEXT NIGHT A QUEER THING HAPPENS. A FOG, A THICK FOG SUCH AS ONE WOULD FIND ONLY IN ENGLAND, BLANKETS THE ENTIRE CITY.
3

SOME FOG, EH, CLANCY? I AIN'T EVER SEEN THE LIKES OF IT BEFORE, AND DID YA NOTICE HOW HOT IT'S GOT SINCE THE FOG HIT US?
AYE, THAT I DID, AND IT STRIKES ME AS AN EVIL SIGN. WHY IF I WAS TO HAVE TO CHASE A CROOK, I WOULDN'T BE ABLE TO SEE HIM AT ALL IN THIS FOG. THIS FOG WILL BE A BAD THING FOR THE POLICE FORCE!
TAXI

CLANCY'S WORDS PROVE PROPHETIC, THE TWO FOLLOWING NIGHTS SEE BANKS ROBBED AS THE BANDITS FLEE AND ARE SWALLOWED UP IN THE FOG

POLICE HEADQUARTERS...
- BUT COMMISSIONER, WE CAN'T HELP IT IF WE LOST THE BANDIT'S CAR. DON'T FORGET WE'RE NOT USED TO ANY FOG!
WELL, GET USED TO IT! IF THIS BLASTED FOG KEEPS UP, THIS CITY IS GOING TO HAVE A CRIME-WAVE SUCH AS IT'S NEVER SEEN BEFORE

THE HOME OF BRUCE WAYNE
-FLASH! THE CASE NATIONAL BANK REPORTS A LOSS OF $250,000, AND THE BOND EXCHANGE BANK $100,000... -FLASH! HENRY JENKINS, THE MISSING ELECTRICAL ENGINEER, HAS NOT YET BEEN HEARD FROM. NO CLUES HAVE...

AN ELECTRICAL ENGINEER DISAPPEARS... AN UNUSUAL 'FOG' COVERS THE CITY... THE FIRST NAMES ON THE LITTLE BOOK'S LIST ARE ROBBED... AND A DYING MAN UTTERS THE SINISTER NAME OF PROFESSOR HUGO STRANGE... HMM....

THAT NIGHT AS THE DENSE FOG AGAIN COVERS THE CITY, A MOVING VAN PULLS UP IN FRONT OF THE STERLING SILVER CO.
OPEN UP IN NAME OF THE LAW! I'M A DETECTIVE
STERLING SILVER COMPANY WAREHOUSE
MOVING VAN
4

THE NIGHT WATCHMAN FALLS FOR THE RUSE AND OPENS THE DOORS...
WHO.. WHAT IS THIS?
THIS IS A STICK-UP! GET BACK INSIDE AND BE QUIET!

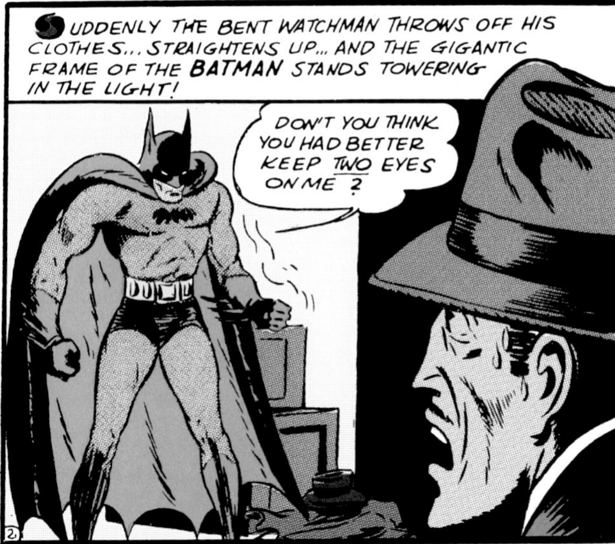

THE BATMAN HURTLES THROUGH THE AIR AND STRIKES THEM LIKE A BOMB-SHELL

THIS, BOYS, IS WHAT THEY CALL A PERFECT STRIKE, ON ANY BOWLING ALLEY!

HANDLE WITH CARE

W-WHAT HIT ME... OHHH! MY HEAD!
SORRY I HAD TO SPOIL YOUR PARTY, BOYS, BUT I GUESS I PLAY TOO ROUGH!
WOT HAPPENED...WUZ WE STRUCK BY DYNAMITE!

THIS OUGHT TO BRING THE POLICE ON IN A HURRY!

AND NOW, PROFESSOR STRANGE, LET'S SEE WHAT YOUR NEXT MOVE WILL BE!!!
I KNEW THOSE SHOTS CAME FROM HERE!
LOOK! A WHOLE GANG OF 'EM! THE PLACE LOOKS LIKE IT WAS HIT BY A CYCLONE!

AGAIN THE ROOM WHERE SITS THE ARCH-CRIMINAL KNOWN AS PROFESSOR STRANGE
THE BATMAN! SIX OF MY MEN IN THE HANDS OF THE POLICE AND ALL BECAUSE OF THE BATMAN!
DAILY GLOBE
...THE THIEVES KEEP SAYING THEY WERE SET UPON BY THE BATMAN WHO

THIS CAN NOT GO ON! I MUST TRAP THE BATMAN!

THE BATMAN KNOWS MY PLANS, POSSIBLY THE G. MAN TALKED BEFORE HE DIED, IF THAT IS SO THEN HE KNOWS THAT THE WOLF BROS. FUR CO. IS NEXT ON THE LIST I THINK I WILL PREPARE A WARM RECEPTION FOR THE BATMAN ON HIS NEXT VISIT... A VERY WARM RECEPTION!

I'LL CRUSH HIM AS READILY AS I CRUSH THIS GLASS!

THE NEXT NIGHT, THE BATMAN AGAIN GOES FORTH ON HIS NOCTURNAL PROWL INTO THE INKY BLACKNESS OF THE NIGHT
6

THE BATMAN APPROACHES THE WAREHOUSE OF THE WOLF BROS. FUR CO.
WOLF BROS. FUR CO.

...CAUTIOUSLY HE STEPS INSIDE...

... SUDDENLY THE LIGHTS BLAZE ON. THE BATMAN IS TRAPPED!

THE BATMAN LEAPS INTO ACTION...
NO SHOTS, MEN! THE PROFESSOR WANTS HIM ALIVE!

THE BATMAN RUNS FOWARD, LEAPS INTO THE AIR... AND GRASPS A DANGLING ROPE!
NOT SO FAST, BOYS!
WHAT TH'?

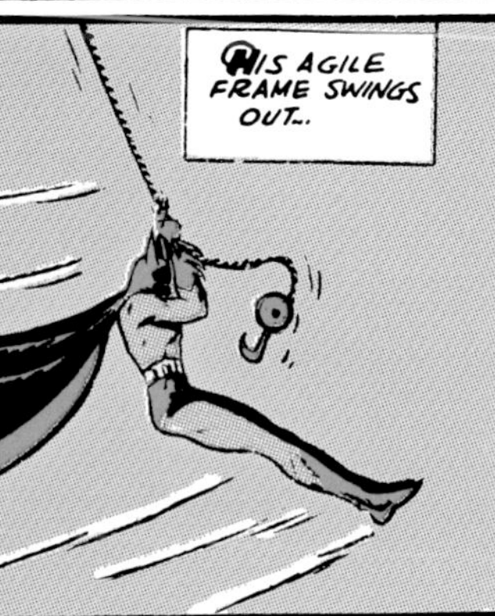
HIS AGILE FRAME SWINGS OUT...

...AND CATAPULTS TO THE BALCONY ACROSS THE ROOM!
AFTER HIM, MEN... UP THE STAIRS!
?

THE BATMAN SPRINGS UP, GRASPS AN OVERHANGING BEAM...
...AND SENDS THE ONCOMING MEN FLYING BACK!
OOFFF!
THEN... A DARING LEAP INTO SPACE...
...AND HE CRASHES ONTO THE MEN BELOW!!!
THE WEIRD FIGURE IS UPON THE OTHERS LIKE A PANTHER, CRUSHING THEM WITH POWER-HOUSE BLOWS!
THIS IS SO YOU WON'T FORGET TO REMEMBER ME!
THE BATMAN KEEPS UP A CEASELESS BARRAGE OF BLOWS UPON THE GUNMEN...
8

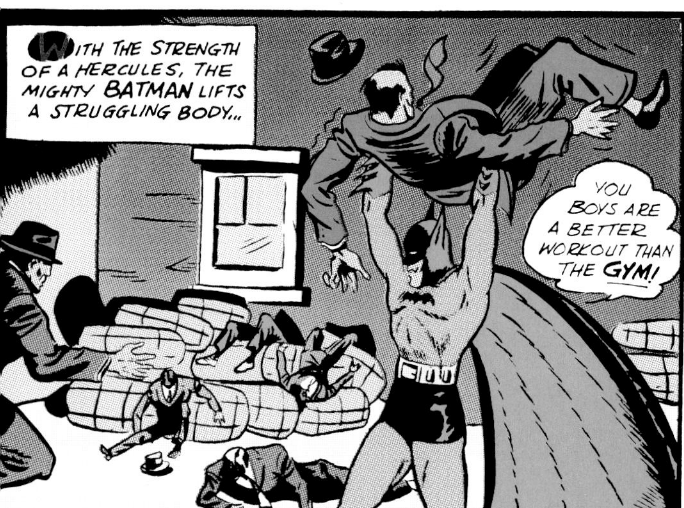
WITH THE STRENGTH OF A HERCULES, THE MIGHTY BATMAN LIFTS A STRUGGLING BODY...
YOU BOYS ARE A BETTER WORKOUT THAN THE GYM!

... AND SENDS HIM FLYING THROUGH SPACE...
YAAAAAA

... UPON THE OTHERS!

SUDDENLY A BLACK-JACK CRASHES DOWN ON THE BATMAN'S HEAD...
THAT OUGHT TO STOP YOU... WHEW! WHAT A GUY!

WELL, HE'S OUT! NOW LET'S GET HIM TO THE PROFESSOR!
YEAH! HE'S OUT! AFTER WRECKING A DOZEN MEN... THAT GUY'S T.N.T- WOW! MY JAW!
8

THE HIDEOUT OF PROFESSOR HUGO STRANGE... A WAREHOUSE NEAR THE RIVER FRONT!

REGAINED CONSCIOUSNESS, BATMAN? GOOD! NOW YOU CAN BE AWAKE TO ENJOY THE ENTERTAINMENT I HAVE PREPARED FOR YOU!

I HAVE BROUGHT YOU HERE ALIVE, SO THAT YOU MAY KNOW WHAT IT MEANS TO INTERFERE WITH PROFESSOR STRANGE!

THE BATMAN IS MADE READY FOR THE LASH!
I'LL TEACH YOU... WITH A TASTE OF THE LASH!

THE WHIP CRACKS DOWN ON THE MASSIVE FIGURE...

WHOSE STEEL MUSCLES SUDDENLY SURGE WITH STRENGTH AND SNAP HIS BONDS!

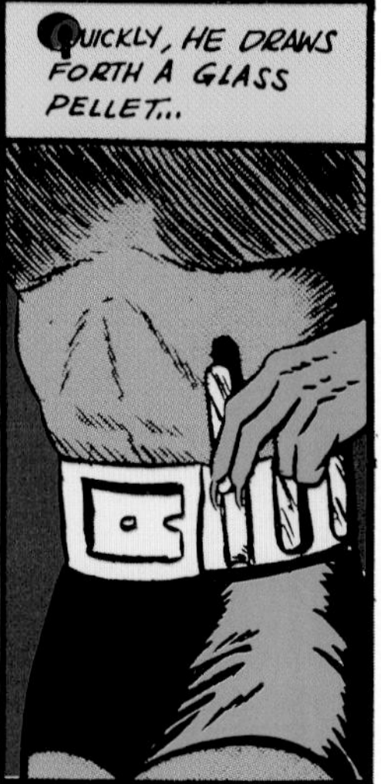
QUICKLY, HE DRAWS FORTH A GLASS PELLET...

...AS HE SLAMS IT TO THE FLOOR, A GAS EMANATES, OVERCOMING THE MEN!
SLEEPING GAS (COUGH) WELL, THAT WON'T GET ME!
GAS!

MAYBE THE GAS WON'T, BUT I WILL!
10

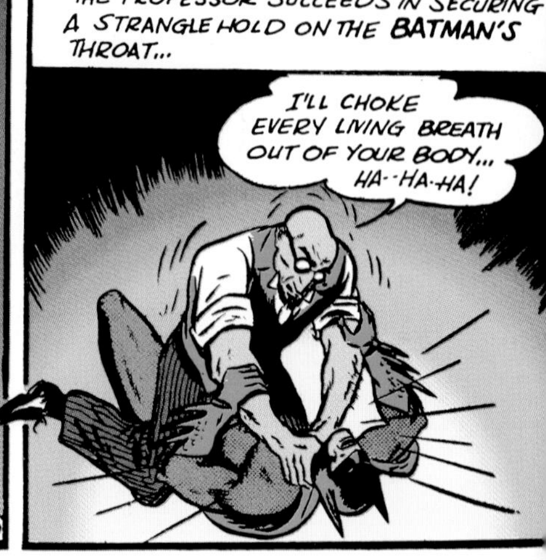
BUT WITH THE POWER OF A MADMAN, THE PROFESSOR SUCCEEDS IN SECURING A STRANGLE HOLD ON THE BATMAN'S THROAT...
I'LL CHOKE EVERY LIVING BREATH OUT OF YOUR BODY... HA-HA-HA!

THE BATMAN DESPERATELY TRIES AN OLD JIU-JITSU TRICK

... AND THIS, PROFESSOR, FOR THE LITTLE WHIPPING INCIDENT!

AS SOON AS I'VE GOT YOU SECURELY TIED, I'M GOING TO SEE HOW YOU WORK THIS "FOG" OF YOURS!

COMING UPON A BARRED ROOM, THE BATMAN STEPS INSIDE AND SEES...

HELP! HELP ME! PLEASE...
WHAT?

DON'T BE FRIGHTENED. I'M THE BATMAN! I'VE COME TO HELP YOU, YOU'RE HENRY JENKINS, THE MISSING ELECTRICAL ENGINEER, AREN'T YOU?
YES! I'VE BEEN HELD PRISONER BY PROFESSOR STRANGE. SOMEHOW HE FOUND OUT ABOUT MY DISCOVERY OF MAKING CONCENTRATED LIGHTNING AND KIDNAPPED ME!

HE FOUND OUT THAT HOT LIGHTNING CAUSED CONDENSED STEAM IN THE AIR, LIKE A SORT OF UN-NATURAL FOG IN THE AIR. HE FORCED ME TO MAKE THIS MACHINE FOR HIM, BUT FOR WHAT PURPOSE I DO NOT KNOW?

HIS PURPOSE WAS OBVIOUS. HE ORGANIZED A CRIME SYNDICATE TO LOOT THE CITY, UNDER THE PROTECTION OF THE FOG, PURSUIT BY THE POLICE WAS ALMOST IMPOSSIBLE. NOW I SUGGEST WE LIFT THIS "FOG" THAT HANGS OVER THIS CITY LIKE A PLAGUE.

THE TWO MEN SPRING TO THE CONTROLS OF THE GIGAN-TIC MACHINE...

...AND SOON...
AH! THE FOG IS LIFTING! 'TIS A FINE THING F'R THE POLICE FORCE!
IT'S NICE TO SEE A CLEAR MOON AGAIN!

RADIO
...AND SO WE CITIZENS OF THIS CITY OWE OUR THANKS TO ONE MAN, THE BATMAN! BECAUSE OF HIM AN ARCH-CRIMINAL IS AT LAST CAPTURED! THERE IS...
WHO IS THE BATMAN, DADDY?
A GREAT MAN, SON, A GREAT MAN!

BACK AT HIS HOME, BRUCE WAYNE, ALIAS THE BATMAN, LISTENS TO THE BROADCAST...
...THERE IS NO DOUBT THAT PROFESSOR HUGO STRANGE IS PUT AWAY FOR A LONG TIME TO COME.
I WONDER... I WONDER...

AT THE STATE PENITENTIARY...
THEY CAN'T KEEP ME HERE, CAGED LIKE SOME WILD BEAST! I'LL ESCAPE... AND WHEN I DO, I SHALL DEVOTE THE REST OF MY LIFE IN REVENGING MYSELF UPON THE BATMAN!
BOB KANE
FINIS

THE Sensational BATMAN!
AMERICA'S MOST EXCITING MYSTERY, ACTION, ADVENTURE STRIP...
Detective COMICS
10¢
APPEARS ONLY IN DETECTIVE COMICS!

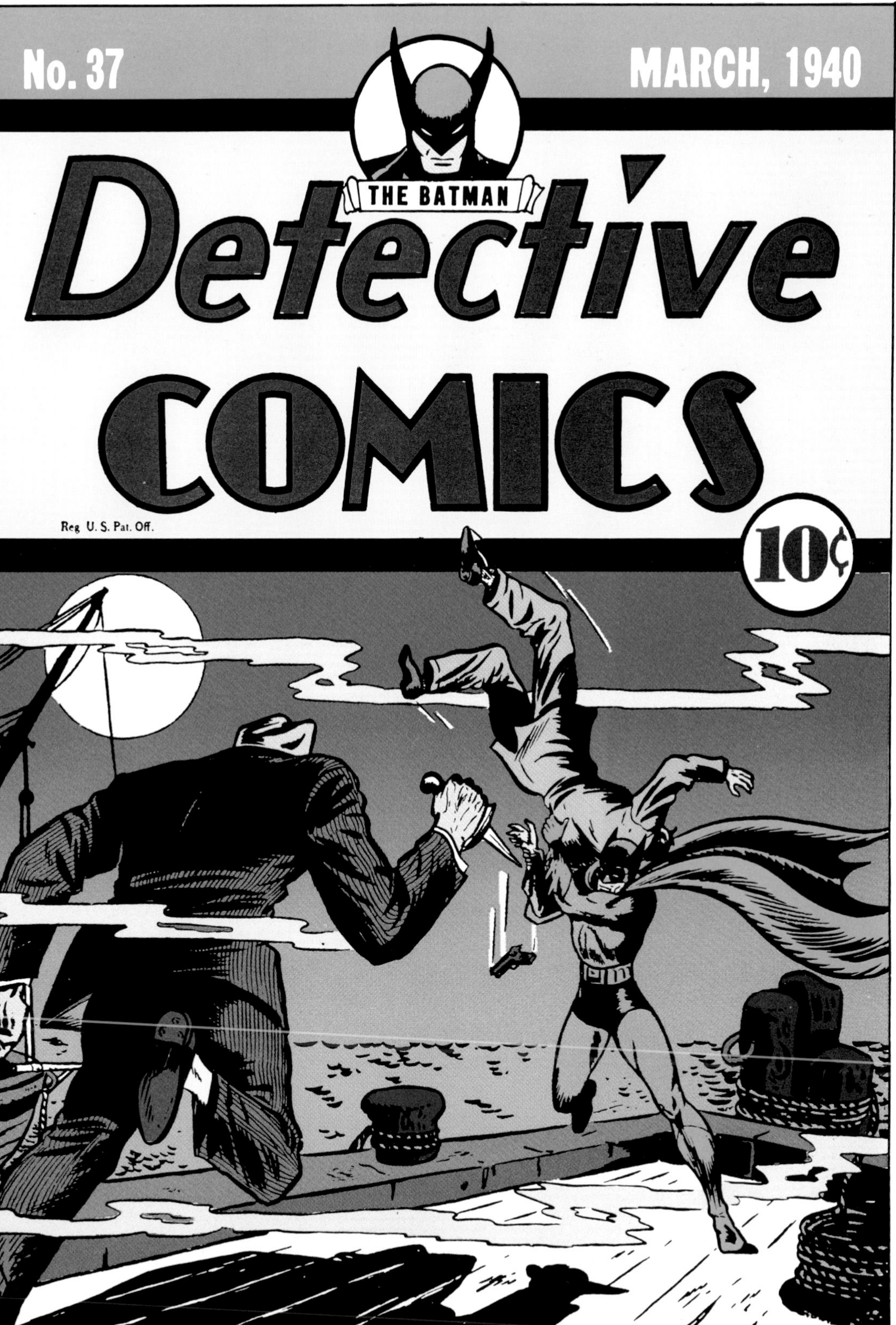
No. 37
MARCH, 1940
THE BATMAN
Detective
COMICS
Reg. U. S. Pat. Off.
10¢

BATMAN

BY BOB KANE

ALREADY AN ALMOST LEGENDARY FIGURE, THE COWLED SHADOW OF THE **BATMAN** PROWLS THROUGH THE NIGHT PREYING UPON THE CRIMINAL PARASITE, LIKE THE WINGED CREATURE WHOSE NAME HE HAS ADOPTED!

THE BATMAN, HAVING LOST HIS WAY ON A LONELY BY-ROAD, STOPS BEFORE A LONE HOUSE TO ASK DIRECTIONS. SUDDENLY, FROM THE HOUSE COMES A SCREAM LIKE THAT OF A WILD BEAST IN PAIN....

OPENING THE DOOR, HE CAUTIOUSLY STEPS INSIDE...

VOICES FROM A LIGHTED ROOM DRAW HIS ATTENTION
SHALL I GIVE IT TO HIM AGAIN?
NO! NO! DON'T! PLEASE DON'T!

DON'T DO IT!
WHEN WE TELL TURG THAT YOU'VE BEEN SELLING INFORMATION, HE'LL DO MUCH WORSE TO YOU!
TELL US WHOM YOU SOLD THE INFORMATION TO OR ELSE!

BETTER TELL ME, JOEY-- OR I'LL...
DON'T YOU THINK THAT FELLOW MIGHT CATCH COLD WITH HIS CHEST EXPOSED LIKE THAT?

WHO ARE YOU?
I KNOW WHO HE IS! THAT'S THE BATMAN! HE'S DYNAMITE!
AM I INTRUDING, GENTLEMEN?

A GUN SUDDENLY COVERS THE BATMAN.
THE BATMAN, EH? WELL, YOU'RE NOT SO SMART AS YOU MIGHT SEEM!

ON THE CONTRARY...
2

I HOPE I DON'T PLAY TOO ROUGH!

AS ONE OF THE GUNMEN RISES, THE BATMAN COMES UP WITH A PARALYZING UPPERCUT.
AND THAT IS THAT!

NOW THAT I'VE TAKEN CARE OF THEM, I'LL TAKE CARE OF YOU! JUST ONE MOMENT AND I'LL HAVE THESE ROPES OFF AND WE CAN USE THEM TO TIE THESE FELLOWS UP!

WHILE THE BATMAN TURNS TO TIE UP THE OTHERS
BY THE WAY, WHAT DID THEY HAVE AGAINST YOU?
WELL, ER... YOU SEE...

THE BATMAN IS STRUCK FROM BEHIND!
SORRY, BUDDY!

IF I WASN'T SO GRATEFUL TO YOU, MR. BATMAN, YOU WOULD BE GETTING WHAT THESE BOYS ARE GOING TO GET!
NO! NO! DON'T, JOEY... PLEASE... H-HAVE YOU GONE CRAZY? DON'T...

THREE SHOTS FROM THE GUN AND THE THREE BOUND MEN ARE DEAD MEN!
NOW TURG WILL NEVER KNOW THAT I'VE BEEN DOUBLE-CROSSING HIM. THE BATMAN DON'T KNOW ANYTHING ABOUT IT, AND THESE GUYS... WELL, DEAD MEN TELL NO TALES!

SOME TIME LATER...
WOW! WHAT HIT ME? IF I'M NOT A PRIZE SAP, LETTING THAT GUY CONK ME WHEN I... SAY, THOSE FELLOWS--! I DIDN'T HIT THEM THAT HARD!

THEY'RE ALL DEAD! THAT FELLOW JOEY MUST HAVE DONE IT! I GUESS I SHOULD BE THANKFUL THAT I'M NOT TOO! BUT WHY SHOULD HE WANT TO KILL THEM? HE MUST HAVE HAD A STRONGER MOTIVE THAN JUST REVENGE...

OF COURSE! THEY KNEW TOO MUCH! THEY SAID THEY WOULD TELL A MAN NAMED TURG THAT HE HAD BEEN SELLING INFORMATION. THEY PROBABLY WORKED FOR TURG AND HE HAD TO KILL THEM SO THAT TURG WOULDN'T KNOW. WONDER WHAT THAT INFORMATION WAS?

LATER... THE HOME OF BRUCE WAYNE... ALIAS, THE BATMAN!
TURG IS NOT A COMMON NAME. THERE SHOULDN'T BE MANY OF THEM--AH! HERE THEY ARE! THERE ARE ONLY THREE TURGS IN THE BOOK!

TOMORROW I WILL CALL UPON THE TURGS. SOMEHOW THIS CASE PROMISES TO BE INTERESTING!

WELL, THE OTHER TURGS ARE QUITE RESPECTABLE! NOW I'LL TRY THIS GROCERY STORE WHICH SEEMS TO BE IN A VERY BAD STREET FOR BUSINESS, SEEING THAT THERE AREN'T MANY HOUSES ABOUT!
ROC

I'D LIKE A POUND OF SUGAR, PLEASE!
JUS' A MINUTE AN' I'LL GET IT FOR YOU!

AT THAT MOMENT, FROM THE BACK OF THE STORE...
I'M GOING OUT FOR A WHILE, AL! TAKE CARE OF THINGS!
ALL RIGHT, MR. TURG.

ERY
SO! JOEY, MY COMPANION OF THE OLD HOUSE, WITH MR. TURG, WHO CERTAINLY DOESN'T LOOK LIKE A GROCERY MAN! WHAT'S THAT OLD SAYING ABOUT BIRDS OF A FEATHER FLOCK TOGETHER? HMMM --
4

THAT NIGHT, A WEIRD MASKED FIGURE OF THE BATMAN PAUSES BEFORE THE GROCERY OF ELIAS TURG.

GREETINGS, AL!
WHAT CAN I DO FOR.... WHAT...?!

I'M NOT BUYING ANYTHING THIS TIME!

THE BATMAN OPENS THE BACK DOOR AND MOUNTS THE STAIRS.

THE MESSAGE THAT I HAVE RECEIVED FROM HEADQUARTERS IS... JOEY! WHAT ARE YOU STARING AT? YOU LOOK AS IF YOU'RE SEEING A GHOST!
I-I AM... AND HE'S GOT A MASK ON!

GOOD EVENING, GENTLEMEN! HOW'S THE GROCERY BUSINESS?
WHAT THE! THAT COSTUME! YOU'RE THE BATMAN!

AS HE SPEAKS, THE BATMAN'S HAND STEALS TOWARD THE LIGHT SWITCH.
HOW IS YOUR CHEST, JOEY?
F..F..FINE!
BATMAN...EH!? SHOOT HIM, MEN!

A CLICK ...THEN DARKNESS AND THE RED FLASHES OF GUNFIRE..
THE LIGHTS ARE OUT! GET THEM ON... WE CAN'T SEE HIM IN THE DARK!
5

THE BATMAN PULLS OVER HIS EYES A QUEER TYPE OF GLASS FROM ITS ALMOST INVISIBLE SUPPORT UPON THE BLACK COWL..

THOUGH HE HIMSELF CANNOT BE SEEN WITH THESE GLASSES OF HIS OWN INVENTION, THE BATMAN CAN NOW SEE IN THE DARK AS WOULD A REAL BAT!...
I CAN'T SEE A BLASTED THING!
HE WAS NEAR THE DOOR THE LAST TIME!
MAYBE I GOT HIM WITH MY SHOTS!

JUST A KISS IN THE DARK!

THIS GUN WON'T DO YOU ANY GOOD!
HELP!... HE'S OVER HERE...

THE MEN TURN TO SHOOT IN THE DIRECTION OF THE BATMAN'S VOICE! THE BATMAN, HOWEVER, DEFTLY SHIFTS TO ANOTHER PART OF THE ROOM!..
HIS VOICE CAME FROM OVER THERE!
NO! HE'S OVER HERE!! UGHHHH...

THE MEN SHUDDER IN TERROR AS THEY REALIZE THE "SUPERNATURAL" POWER OF THE BATMAN!
HE CAN SEE IN THE DARK!
JUST LIKE A REAL BAT!
NO WONDER HE'S CALLED THE BATMAN!
IT'S UNCANNY!

AND NOW, GENTLEMEN, I MUST LEAVE YOU... BUT WE SHALL MEET AGAIN, SOON, I PROMISE YOU!
6

THE BATMAN GONE, THE LIGHTS ARE SWITCHED ON...
HE'S GONE!
FUNNY HOW HE KNEW ABOUT US USING THE STORE AS OUR HEADQUARTERS!
I THINK JOEY KNOWS, DON'T YOU? HE SPOKE TO YOU -- HE KNEW YOUR NAME! YOU TOLD HIM ABOUT US!
NO! NO! I SWEAR!

YOU LIE! YOU TRAITOR! DIE A TRAITOR'S DEATH!

DO YOU THINK HE TOLD THE BATMAN OF OUR PLANS TO BLOW UP THE SHIP TOMORROW NIGHT?
HE MUST HAVE!
WE CANNOT DELAY. WE MUST SINK THE SHIP TONIGHT! COME LET US GO TO THE PIER NOW!

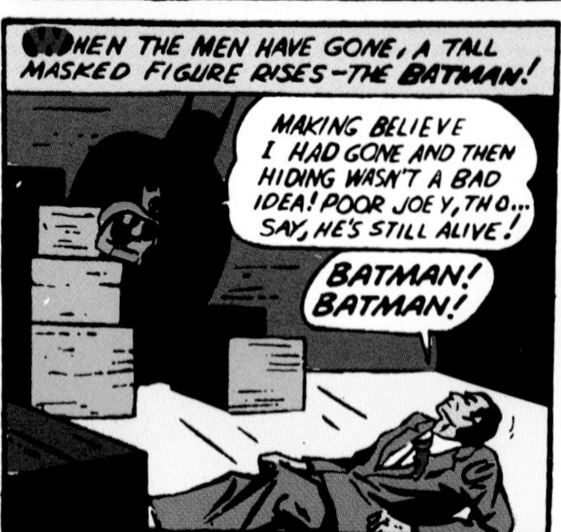
WHEN THE MEN HAVE GONE, A TALL MASKED FIGURE RISES—THE BATMAN!
MAKING BELIEVE I HAD GONE AND THEN HIDING WASN'T A BAD IDEA! POOR JOEY, THO... SAY, HE'S STILL ALIVE!
BATMAN! BATMAN!

JOEY, CAN YOU HEAR ME? WHAT IS THIS ALL ABOUT? WHAT SHIP ARE THEY GOING TO BLOW UP?
THEY'RE SPIES! ...BLOW UP FOREIGN SHIP RONIJ-MAKE IT LOOK LIKE U.S. DID IT... START INTERNATIONAL CRISIS... DON'T KNOW WHO HEAD IS...

STOLE PHONE NUMBER FROM TURG-AL 5743 ...I'M NOT REALLY SPY...NEEDED MONEY...GET THEM FOR GOOD OLE U.S.A.... GET-AHH...
DON'T WORRY, JOEY- I'LL GET THEM!

ON A PIER IN LOWER DOWNTOWN...
WHERE IS TURG? HE HAS NOT YET COME?
HE HAS GONE TO SEE THE HEAD! WE ARE TO GO ON WITH OUR WORK. LISTEN, THE SMALL BOAT BELOW IS LOADED WITH T.N.T. WE LASH THE STEERING WHEEL, HEAD THE BOAT FOR THE RONIJ... AND THEN...
THE EXPLOSION, AND WE ARE FAR AWAY FROM THE SCENE! IT'S PERFECT!

ALMOST A LITTLE TOO PERFECT, I'D SAY!
THE BATMAN!!

BUT ABOVE THE BATMAN...

THE SACK SMASHES DOWN UPON THE BATMAN!

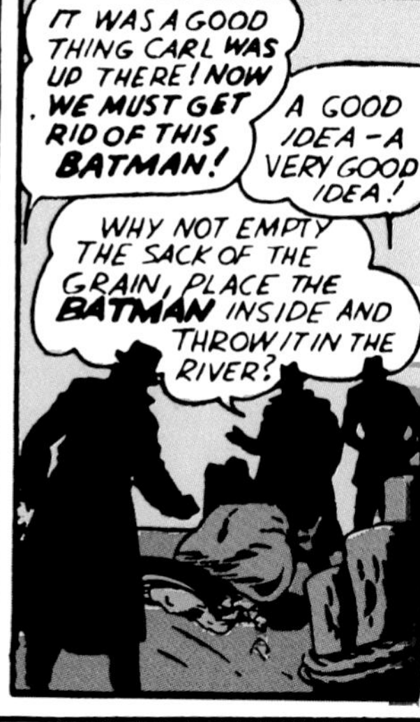
IT WAS A GOOD THING CARL WAS UP THERE! NOW WE MUST GET RID OF THIS BATMAN!
A GOOD IDEA - A VERY GOOD IDEA!
WHY NOT EMPTY THE SACK OF THE GRAIN, PLACE THE BATMAN INSIDE AND THROW IT IN THE RIVER?

THERE YOU ARE, MR. BATMAN! ALL NICE AND READY FOR A WATERY GRAVE! HA! HA!

ONE ... TWO ... THREE ... AND OUT HE GOES!!

THE BATMAN SINKS TO A WATERY GRAVE!

THE SHOCK OF COLD WATER SUDDENLY REVIVES THE BATMAN WHO, QUICKLY REALIZING HIS DANGER, DRAWS A SHARP BLADE..
I'VE GOT TO WORK FAST!

A QUICK SLASH OF THE SHARP STEEL!...
8

THE BATMAN IS FREE!...

WELL, THAT IS THE LAST OF THE BATMAN! NOW MAKE READY THE BOAT TO CARRY THE T.N.T. ON ITS JOURNEY!

THE BATMAN LEAPS FOR THE DANGLING ROPE AND SWINGS ACROSS THE VAST PIER...

HIS FIGURE HURTLES THROUGH THE AIR AND STRIKES THE MEN LIKE A BOMBSHELL...
WHAT IN TH'... THE BATMAN!
SAY, THAT GUY HAS MORE LIVES THAN A CAT!

COME ON, SUCKERS!

HAPPY LANDINGS!
9

SUDDENLY, THE COUGH OF A MOTOR! THE BOAT HAS STARTED WITH ITS LOAD OF DEATH!
TOO LATE! THE BOAT HAS STARTED! MAYBE I CAN STILL MAKE IT!

LIKE A HUMAN BULLET, THE BATMAN STREAKS ACROSS THE PLATFORM..
FEET, RUN LIKE YOU'VE NEVER RUN BEFORE!

A GREAT LEAP INTO SPACE!

THE LEAP IS SUCCESSFUL!

THE ROPES ARE QUICKLY CUT FROM THE STEERING WHEEL.
IT'S A MATTER OF SECONDS NOW!

NEARER.. NEARER.. NEARER- ANOTHER SECOND AND THEN...

THE BATMAN DESPERATELY TAKES THE WHEEL AND TURNS...
IF THIS BOAT DOESN'T TURN IN TIME, I'M A GONER!

THE MOTOR BOAT CARRYING ITS LOAD OF DEATH MISSES THE STEAMSHIP BY INCHES!
10

WHEW! THAT WAS A CLOSE CALL! NOW I'VE GOT SOME MORE WORK TO DO! I'M GOING TO SEE WHO OWNS THAT PHONE-NUMBER THAT POOR JOEY GAVE ME! IF IT'S THE "HEAD"....

THAT PHONE NUMBER BELONGS TO THE SOCIALLY EMINENT COUNT GRUTT! JUST ONE LOOK AT HIM WILL TELL ME IF HE IS THE "HEAD" AND IS ALSO... SOMEONE ELSE!

SOME TIME LATER..
THE COUNT IS BUSY. HE CAN'T SEE ANYBODY!
HE'LL SEE ME!

YOU--
SOMETHING NEW? BUTLERS CARRYING GUNS?

GOING AWAY SOMEPLACE, COUNT GRUTT-- ALIAS THE "HEAD"-- ALIAS ELIAS TURG!
YOU!

YOU DON'T LOOK AT ALL LIKE TURG WITHOUT YOUR GRAY WIG, YOUR PHONEY MUSTACHE AND GLASSES OFF! I HAD A HUNCH YOU WERE THE "HEAD" WHEN YOU DIDN'T SHOW UP TO-NIGHT! SO THE DISTINGUISHED COUNT GRUTT IS REALLY A FOREIGN AGENT!
FOOL!

THE COUNT THROWS THE SWORD DIRECTLY AT THE BATMAN!
YES! BUT YOU'LL NEVER LIVE TO TELL ANYONE ABOUT IT!

IN A FLASH, THE BATMAN PULLS OPEN THE DOOR WHICH IS DIRECTLY IN LINE WITH THE HURTLING STEEL BLADE!

THE POWERFUL THROW SENDS THE SHARP STEEL HISSING THROUGH THE SOFT WOOD.

NOW LET'S SEE HOW YOU CAN FIGHT WITHOUT YOUR SWORDS, RAT!
NO! NO!

THE COUNT TRIES TO ESCAPE BUT THE BATMAN IS QUICKLY UPON HIM AND....

THE COUNT FALLS BACK TOWARD THE STEEL BLADE STICKING THROUGH THE CLOSET DOOR!

A WILD SCREAM-- AND THE FOREIGN AGENT IS IMPALED UPON HIS OWN SWORD!

YA-AA-AA

DEAD! IT IS BETTER THAT HE SHOULD DIE! HE MIGHT HAVE SENT THOUSANDS OF OTHERS TO THEIR DEATH ON A BATTLEFIELD IF HIS PLANS HAD BEEN SUCCESSFUL! THIS HAS BEEN A QUEER CASE... FROM THE OLD HOUSE TO FOREIGN AGENTS... AND TO THE DEATH OF ITS HEAD! YES... A VERY QUEER CASE!
BOB KANE

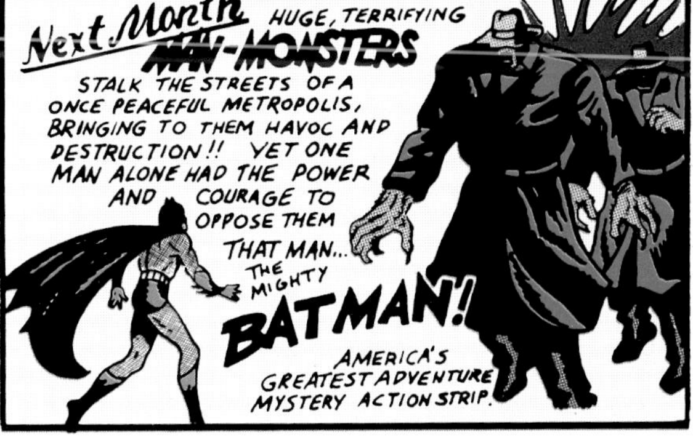
Next Month
HUGE, TERRIFYING MAN-MONSTERS STALK THE STREETS OF A ONCE PEACEFUL METROPOLIS, BRINGING TO THEM HAVOC AND DESTRUCTION!! YET ONE MAN ALONE HAD THE POWER AND COURAGE TO OPPOSE THEM
THAT MAN... THE MIGHTY BATMAN!
AMERICA'S GREATEST ADVENTURE MYSTERY ACTION STRIP.

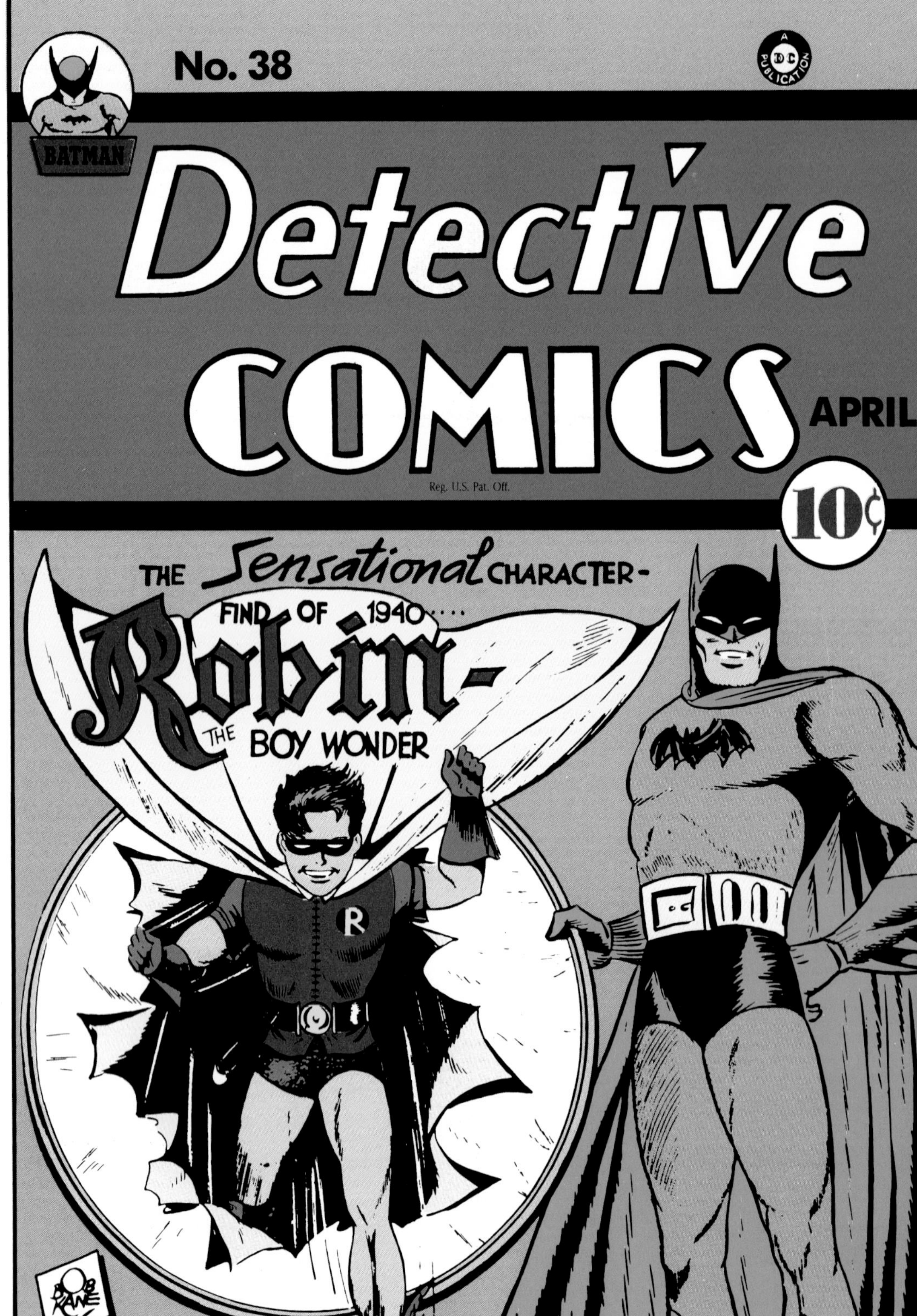
No. 38
BATMAN
A DC PUBLICATION
Detective
COMICS
APRIL
Reg. U.S. Pat. Off.
10¢
THE Sensational CHARACTER-
FIND OF 1940....
Robin-
THE BOY WONDER
R
BOB KANE

The BATMAN
PRESENTS
THE Sensational CHARACTER FIND OF 1940...
Robin-
THE BOY WONDER
BY BOB KANE
THE BATMAN. THAT AMAZING, WEIRD FIGURE OF NIGHT, AT LAST TAKES UNDER HIS PROTECTING MANTLE AN ALLY IN HIS RELENTLESS FIGHT AGAINST CRIME... INTRODUCING IN THIS ISSUE ...AN EXCITING NEW FIGURE WHOSE INCREDIBLE GYMNASTIC AND ATHLETIC FEATS WILL ASTOUND YOU... A LAUGHING, FIGHTING, YOUNG DARE-DEVIL WHO SCOFFS AT DANGER LIKE THE LEGENDARY ROBIN HOOD WHOSE NAME AND SPIRIT HE HAS ADOPTED... ROBIN THE BOY WONDER
LEGEND
ROBIN, THE BOY WONDER AND HOW HE BECAME THE ALLY OF THE BATMAN
OUR SCENE... A RISING YOUNG TOWN OUTSIDE THE BIG CITY WHERE THE HALY CIRCUS PLAYS AN ENGAGEMENT... INSIDE THE BIG TENT THE FLYING GRAYSONS, FATHER, MOTHER AND YOUNG SON, DICK SWING ON THE FLYING TRAPEZE.

LATER··HIS PART OF THE ACT OVER, THE BOY, DICK, IS GOING PAST MR. HALY'S ROOM WHEN HE HEARS VOICES··
··AND IF YOU PAY US WE PROTECT YOU, GET IT, HALY?
YES! I GET IT. YOU'RE GANGSTERS! IT'S A PROTECTION RACKET! I'LL CALL THE POLICE!
OFFICE

YOU DON'T WANT TO DIE, DO YOU? BE SENSIBLE. PAY US AND PROTECT THE SHOW FROM "ACCIDENTS."
GET OUT! GET OUT!
OKAY, BUDDY! IT'S YOUR FUNERAL REMEMBER··· "ACCIDENTS" WILL HAPPEN!

THE NEXT NIGHT···IN THE AUDIENCE···BRUCE WAYNE, THE BATMAN, ENJOYS THE SHOW.
···AND NOW THAT YOUNG DICK GRAYSON IS SAFE BELOW. THE FLYING GRAYSONS WILL PERFORM THEIR DEATH-DEFYING ACT··· THE TRIPLE SPIN!

THE DRUMS ROLL··GRAYSON FLIES OUT··TURNS OVER THREE TIMES··AND STRAIGHTENS OUT
NICELY DONE, JOHN!

SUDDENLY··THE ROPES PART!!
JOHN!
MARY!

MOTHER! FATHER!
T··THEY'LL BE KILLED!
EEE-EE-EE

ARE···ARE TH··THEY OH N-NO THEY...
I'M AFRAID SO, SON.

LATER
TOO BAD ABOUT THAT "ACCIDENT," HALY.
YEAH! BUT THERE WOULDN'T BE ANY "ACCIDENTS" IF YOU PAID US TO PROTECT YOU!
YOU MURDERERS. ALL RIGHT, I'LL PAY-BUT ONLY SO THAT NO ONE ELSE WILL BE KILLED.

BUT OUTSIDE THE DOOR DICK LISTENS··WHEN··
THEY KILLED MY MOTHER AND FATHER! I'M GOING TO THE POLICE!
NO SON, NOT YET!

I'M THE BATMAN! I WANT TO HELP YOU GET THOSE MURDERERS! THEY PUT ACID ON THE TRAPEZE ROPES! BUT YOU CAN'T GO TO THE POLICE--COME WITH ME! AND I'LL TELL YOU WHY.
WHA... WHO?...

WHY CAN'T I TELL THE POLICE?
BECAUSE THIS WHOLE TOWN IS RUN BY BOSS ZUCCO. IF YOU TOLD WHAT YOU KNEW YOU'D BE DEAD IN AN HOUR. I'M GOING TO HIDE YOU IN MY HOME FOR A WHILE.

THE BATMAN THINKS BACK TO THE TIME WHEN HIS PARENTS, TOO, WERE INNOCENT VICTIMS OF A CRIMINAL.
MY PARENTS TOO WERE KILLED BY A CRIMINAL. THAT'S WHY I'VE DEVOTED MY LIFE TO EXTERMINATE THEM.
THEN I WANT TO ALSO! TAKE ME WITH YOU...PLEASE!

THE BATMAN IS RELUCTANT BUT THE TROUBLED FACE OF THE BOY MOVES HIM DEEPLY.
WELL, I GUESS YOU AND I WERE BOTH VICTIMS OF A SIMILAR TROUBLE. ALL RIGHT. I'LL MAKE YOU MY AID. BUT I WARN YOU, I LEAD A PERILOUS LIFE!
I'M NOT AFRAID.

THAT NIGHT TWO GRIM FIGURES TAKE AN UNDYING OATH!
-AND SWEAR THAT WE TWO WILL FIGHT TOGETHER AGAINST CRIME AND CORRUPTION AND NEVER TO SWERVE FROM THE PATH OF RIGHTEOUSNESS!
I SWEAR IT!

THE TRAINING BEGINS...
I'VE BEEN DOING THIS SINCE I WAS FOUR YEARS OLD!
AS FAR AS SWINGING ROPES GO, YOU COULD PROBABLY TEACH ME A TRICK OR TWO!

BOXING
AND, THEN YOU SORT OF SNAP YOUR PUNCH AND PUT YOUR SHOULDER BEHIND IT! DO IT RIGHT AND YOU CAN HIT AS HARD AS ANY FEATHERWEIGHT CHAMP!
LIKE THIS?

JIU JITSU
THAT'S IT... NOW I'LL TEACH YOU ANOTHER TRICK!

AND THUS DICK GRAYSON, BY THE HAND OF FATE, IS TRANSFORMED INTO THAT ASTONISHING PHENOMENON THAT YOUNG ROBIN HOOD OF TODAY-ROBIN THE BOY WONDER!

MANY MONTHS LATER... AFTER STRENUOUS WORK AND STUDY....
WELL, NOW THAT I'M READY, WHATS OUR NEXT MOVE?
NOW, DICK, WE'RE GOING TO GO BACK TO THE SMALL TOWN AND GO TO WORK! YOU'RE GOING TO GET A JOB AS A NEWSBOY AND...

INSIDE THE MYSTERIOUS HOUSE....
WELL, BOSS, THERE IT IS. THE TAKE OF THE WEEK!
IT ISN'T ENOUGH! SEE! YOU'VE GOT TO GET MORE MONEY OUT OF OUR CUSTOMERS. SEE! I WANT YOU TO GO TO THE BUTCHERS, THE TAILORS, LAUNDRYS AND THE REST AND MILK 'EM DRY. SEE!

ALL OF THEM GET IT, SEE! EVEN THE NEWSBOYS AND THE REST OF THE SMALL STUFF! AND IF THEY DON'T PLAY BALL, YOU KNOW WHAT TO DO. SEE!! START TOMORROW NIGHT!

TOMORROW NIGHT! WOW! I BETTER TELL THE BATMAN RIGHT AWAY!

NEXT NIGHT · A TAILOR STORE
BUT I CAN'T PAY YOU ANY MORE! I HAVEN'T GOT IT!
GET IT!
··AND IF YOU DON'T··

SUDDENLY FROM BEHIND...
DON'T TALK SO MUCH!!

HOLLOW... JUST AS I THOUGHT!

IF YOU SEE BOSS ZUCCO, TELL HIM THE BATMAN WAS HERE.
GOOD DAY GENTLEMEN!

IN A BUTCHER SHOP...
PAY UP OR ELSE YOU'LL..WHA...?

...OR ELSE YOU'LL GET A SOCK ON THE JAW!

TELL ZUCCO I JUST DROPPED IN TO SAY "HELLO"! AU REVOIR!

IN A GAMBLING HOUSE OWNED BY BOSS ZUCCO.

PARDON THE INTRUSION, GENTLEMEN!
IT'S THE BATMAN!
GET HIM!

SO YOU WANT TO PLAY, EH?..WELL.....

...HERE'S A ROULETTE TABLE TO PLAY WITH!

THE BATMAN SWEEPS THROUGH THE ROOM LIKE A CYCLONE, OVERTHROWING THE GAMBLING TABLES!
HE'S THROWING ALL THE MONEY ON THE FLOOR!
GET IT!
THE MONEY!

WITH NO ONE TO STOP THEM BECAUSE OF THE FIGHT, THE GAMBLING CROWD RUNS AMUCK GRABBING ALL THE MONEY!
A HUNDRED DOLLAR BILL! WHOOPIE!! HERE'S MY CHANCE TO GET BACK WHAT I LOST!
THEY'RE TAKIN' ALL THE DOUGH!
THEY'RE WRECKING THE PLACE! WAIT TILL ZUCCO HEARS ABOUT THIS!

ADIEU, GENTLEMEN... I HOPE I HAVEN'T CAUSED ANY DISTURBANCE...

OUTSIDE A LAUNDRY STORE
AND TELL ZUCCO HE NEEDS A LITTLE CLEANING HIMSELF!
LAUND
19
DRY

IN THE STORES HOLDING ZUCCO'S SLOT MACHINES....
BUT WHAT'LL I TELL ZUCCO'S MEN?
JUST SAY... THE BATMAN!

AN HOUR LATER
AND THEN THE BATMAN!
THE BATMAN! SHUT UP ABOUT THE BATMAN! SEE! THAT GUY WALKS IN AND OUT OF MY PLACES AND NOBODY STOPS HIM! I'M BOSS OF THIS TOWN. SEE! NO ONE CAN DO THAT TO ME, SEE!

SAY, BOSS. THIS PACKAGE JUST CAME BY EXPRESS FOR YA.
WELL, BLADE, OPEN IT UP! OPEN IT UP!

WELL I'LL BE... A BAT!!
IT MUST BE FROM THE BATMAN!
LOOK! THERE'S A NOTE INSIDE THE BOX!

Get out of town, Zucco.
I know you are also
trying to get protection
money from the company
that is putting up the
Canin Building. Stay away
I'm protecting that building
from your protection mob.

OH YEAH! I'M BOSS OF THIS TOWN, SEE! NO ONE CAN TALK TO ME LIKE THAT AND GET AWAY WITH IT! C'MON, BOYS, WE'RE GOING TO THE CANIN BUILDING. I'M STILL BOSS ZUCCO, SEE!
I GOTCHA, BOSS!

AS THE CAR LEAVES, THERE RIDING ON THE TIRE RACK...ROBIN, THE BOY WONDER!
THE BATMAN'S PLAN WORKED! ZUCCO IS SO MAD HE'S GOING TO DO THE JOB PERSONALLY!

the CANIN BUILDING

OKAY! I TIED UP THE WATCHMAN!
GOOD! YOU STAY DOWN HERE AS GUARD. NOW I'M GOING TO CONVINCE CANIN HE SHOULD PAY UP! BRING THE DYNAMITE BOYS!

AS ZUCCO AND HIS MEN GO UP, SUDDENLY FROM THE SHADOWS THE STREAKING FIGURE OF ROBIN. THE BOY WONDER
HEY...

SORRY, BOY, BUT I'M GOING UP!

NOW WE'LL JUST BLOW UP THE TOP OF THE BUILDING TO SCARE CANIN INTO PAYING. AND IF HE DON'T, THE NEXT TIME....
BOSS, LOOK! OVER THERE... SOMEONE ON THE GIRDER...

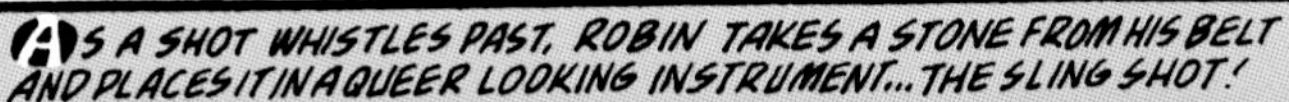
AS A SHOT WHISTLES PAST, ROBIN TAKES A STONE FROM HIS BELT AND PLACES IT IN A QUEER LOOKING INSTRUMENT... THE SLING SHOT!

SHOOT HIM!

LIKE DAVID FIGHTING GOLIATH ROBIN FIGHTS THE GANGSTERS!

A BULLS-EYE!
Z-I-N-G

AN AMAZING LEAP...

A SWEEPING SWING...

...AND THE YOUNG DARE-DEVIL LANDS AMONG THE MURDEROUS GUNMEN!
W-WHY, IT'S ONLY A KID!

USING HIS KNOWLEDGE OF JIU JITSU TAUGHT BY THE BATMAN, THE PLUCKY BOY PUTS UP A STIFF FIGHT AGAINST OVERWHELMING ODDS!

BUT AS THE GANGSTER STEPS ON ROBIN'S FINGERS THE WONDER BOY TWISTS HIS BODY UP AND AROUND THE GIRDER.

BUT SWINGING THROUGH THE AIR...THE BATMAN..
MIND IF I JOIN THE PARTY, ZUCCO? SO SORRY TO DROP IN SO UNEXPECTEDLY THIS WAY...
1

WHAT PLEASURE THIS GIVES ME, YOU'LL NEVER KNOW!
2

THE BATMAN! I'M GETTING OUTA HERE!
3

A ROPE SUDDENLY LOOPS ABOUT BLADE AND JERKS HIM OFF THE GIRDER!
4

AS THE GANGSTER DANGLES, THE BATMAN PRODUCES A SMALL VIAL.
DO YOU KNOW WHAT'S IN THIS VIAL, BLADE? IT'S ACID...THE SAME ACID THAT YOU PUT ON THE TRAPEZE OF THE FLYING GRAYSONS...AND IT'S GOING TO EAT AWAY THE ROPE UNLESS YOU SIGN A CONFESSION NAMING NAMES!
I'LL CONFESS! PULL ME UP! PULL ME UP!
5

BLADE SIGNS A FULL CONFESSION...
IT WAS ZUCCO THAT PUT ME UP TO IT! I SWEAR IT!
YOU DIRTY SQUEELER!
6

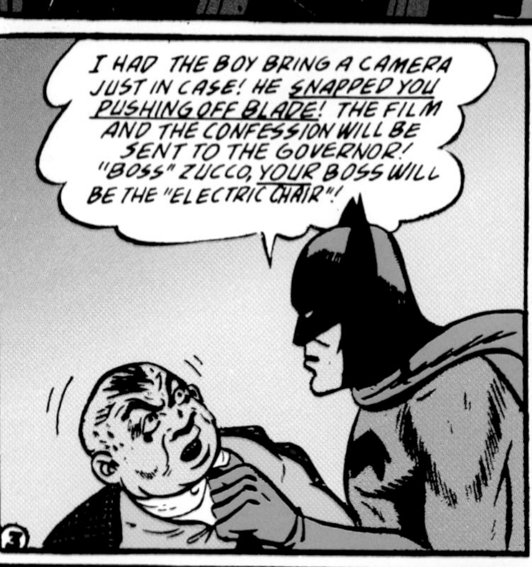

EXTRA!
ZUCCO GUILTY OF MURDER! GOVERNOR TO CLEAN UP CITY POLITICS! EXTRA!
ZUCCO GUILTY

THRILLS
THRILLS AND MORE THRILLS...
IS WHAT THAT AMAZING CHARACTER
the BATMAN
AND
THE Sensational FIND OF 1940
Robin
BOY WONDER OF THE COMIC STRIPS... GIVE YOU IN EVERY ISSUE... WITH THEIR ASTOUNDING EXPLOITS
WATCH FOR NEXT MONTH'S THRILLING EPISODE

No. 39

A DC PUBLICATION

The BATMAN

Detective COMICS

MAY

10¢

THE Sensational ADVENTURES OF The
BATMAN
WITH
Robin
THE BOY WONDER
BOB KANE
AGAIN THE INTREPID BLACK-CLAD FIGURE OF THE BATMAN AND HIS AIDE, ROBIN, THE LAUGHING YOUNG DARE-DEVIL, COMBINE FORCES TO BATTLE AGAINST THOSE WHO WOULD MENACE A PEOPLE·· TWO FIGURES, A MAN AND A BOY·· TWO FIGURES ALWAYS OUTNUMBERED BUT NEVER OUTFOUGHT·· TWO FIGURES TO FIGHT·· THE HORDE OF THE GREEN DRAGON!

IT IS NIGHT AND THE MILLIONAIRE HENRY CRANDALL STEPS TO HIS CAR..

SUDDENLY

NOT FAR AWAY, ANOTHER MILLIONAIRE, JOHN COBB, WALKS TO A WAITING CAR..

SUDDENLY-THREE SILHOUETTED FIGURES SPRING FROM THE SHADOWS..

HEY! WHAT'S GOING ON HERE?

SUDDENLY THERE IS A HISS.. AND A SICKENING THUD!
YA-A-A-A..

SPLITTING THE HEAD OF THE CHAUFFEUR ... A HATCHET!!

NEXT DAY NEWSPAPERS SHRIEK THEIR HEADLINES..
HERALDE
EXTRA
TWO MILLIONAIRES KIDNAPPED
CHAUFFEUR OF JOHN COBB MURDERED WITH HATCHET
WIVES RECEIVE NOTES DEMANDING $100,00

THE HOME OF BRUCE WAYNE - THE BATMAN!
AND THEY DEMAND $100,000 RANSOM! WHEW! WHAT A STORY!
THE CHAUFFEUR WAS KILLED WITH A HATCHET..HMMM

A HATCHET! THERE'S ONLY ONE KIND OF PEOPLE THAT KILL WITH A HATCHET·· THE ·· WHA?··
LOOK! THERE'S AN AD IN THE PAPER ADDRESSED TO THE BATMAN!

NOTICES
BATMAN A FRIEND NEEDS YOUR HELP. COME AT ONCE!
Arrived Yesterd

THE TYPE WAS SET IN CHINESE STYLE. THE SENDER DID IT PURPOSELY!
YES, TO LET ME KNOW HE WAS CHINESE! A FRIEND-- OF COURSE, WONG OF CHINATOWN! HE HELPED ME IN THE CASE OF THE "RUBY IDOL"

A FEW MINUTES LATER
DICK! YOU STAY HOME AND GUARD THE FORT. THE BATMAN IS GOING TO VISIT A FRIEND!

CHINATOWN·· A CITY WITHIN A CITY·· WHERE THE MYSTERY OF THE EAST COMES TO THE STREETS OF THE WEST

WONG-UNOFFICIAL MAYOR OF CHINATOWN--A WISE, HONORABLE M
GOOD EVENING, WONG!
AH, BATMAN! YOU HAVE COME! YOU UNDERSTOOD MESSAG

I HAVE COME TO HELP A FRIEND! WHAT IS YOUR TROUBLE?
OPIUM! A NEW TONG HAS ARISEN CALLED THE GREEN DRAGON! THEY ARE EVIL MEN, AND WORK MANY WICKED ENTER-PRISES. WORST OF ALL, THEY ARE SELLING OPIUM TO MY PEOPLE. THOUGH IT IS DANGEROUS TO DO SO, I HAVE GATHERED MUCH INFORMATION.

AS THE MEN SPEAK THEY DO NOT NOTICE THAT A PICTURE HAS MOVED ASIDE AND AN EVIL EYE WATCHES

BY TOMORROW NIGHT AT EIGHT O'CLOCK I WILL HAVE SOME INFORMATION ABOUT THE DWELLING PLACE OF THE GREEN DRAGON AND THEIR LEADER, BUT I WILL NEED YOUR HELP IN HIS CAPTURE!
YOU CAN COUN ON ME, WONG. I'LL BE HERE AT EIGHT!

..AND SO WILL WE— O BATMAN!

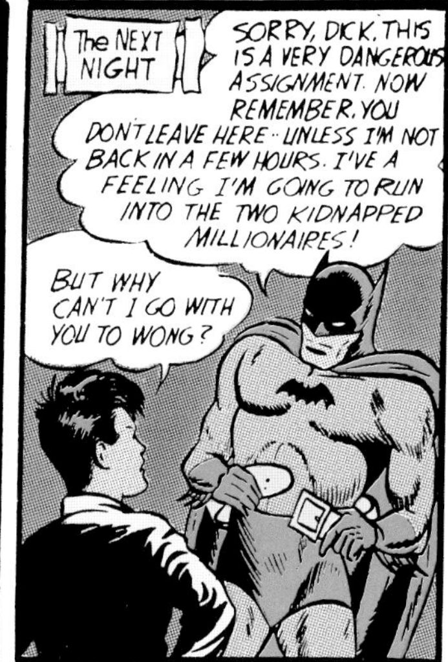
The NEXT NIGHT
SORRY, DICK, THIS IS A VERY DANGEROUS ASSIGNMENT. NOW REMEMBER, YOU DON'T LEAVE HERE.. UNLESS I'M NOT BACK IN A FEW HOURS. I'VE A FEELING I'M GOING TO RUN INTO THE TWO KIDNAPPED MILLIONAIRES!
BUT WHY CAN'T I GO WITH YOU TO WONG?

SOMETIME LATER.. AN EERIE FIGURE PAUSES OUTSIDE A WINDOW OF THE HOUSE OF WONG.
WELL, WONG, HERE I AM!

WONG, I'M HERE! THAT STARE!...... IT'S THE BATMAN!

WONG! WHAT'S THE MATTER, WONG?

WONG SUDDENLY SLUMPS FORWARD, AND THERE, BURIED DEEP IN THE BACK OF HIS HEAD.. A HATCHET!

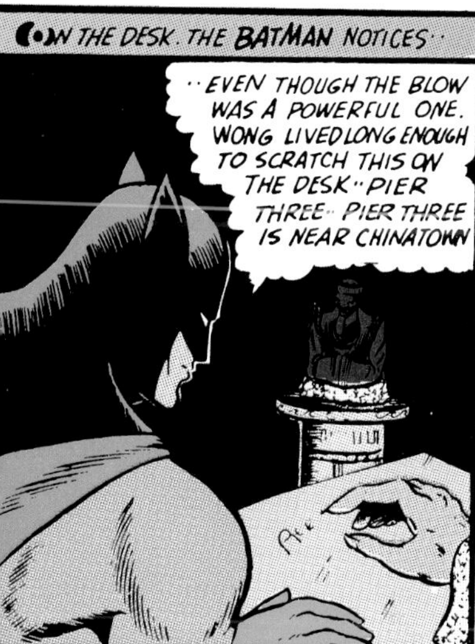
ON THE DESK, THE BATMAN NOTICES..
..EVEN THOUGH THE BLOW WAS A POWERFUL ONE, WONG LIVED LONG ENOUGH TO SCRATCH THIS ON THE DESK.. PIER THREE.. PIER THREE IS NEAR CHINATOWN

SUDDENLY THE BATMAN SEES ON THE FLOOR.. A SHADOW!

A QUICK DROP TO THE FLOOR, A HISS.. AND THEN A THUD!

FROM BEHIND THE SCREEN... THE DREADED CHINESE HATCHET MEN!
ENTER THE VILLAINS!

A QUICK JERK ON THE CARPET AND...
SLIPPERY, ISN'T IT?

THE BATMAN LEAPS TO THE ATTACK!

AS THE BATMAN STRUGGLES, THE HATCHET MAN REGAINS HIS GRISLY WEAPON AND STEALTHILY CREEPS FROM BEHIND...

THE BATMAN SENSES HIS DANGER AND SWIFTLY MOVES...

YOU SHOULD WEAR GLASSES, FELLA!

THE TRICKY CHINAMAN MAKES ANOTHER TRY FOR HIS INTENDED VICTIM.....

SUDDENLY THE CHINESE JERKS HIS HAND LOOSE AND CHOPS DOWN AT THE BATMAN . . .

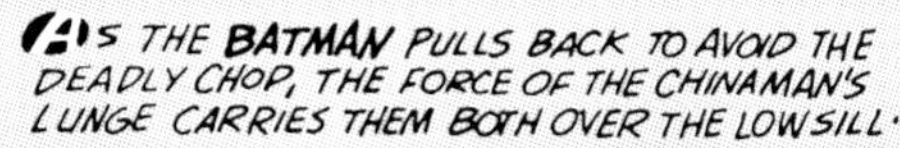
AS THE BATMAN PULLS BACK TO AVOID THE DEADLY CHOP, THE FORCE OF THE CHINAMAN'S LUNGE CARRIES THEM BOTH OVER THE LOW SILL..

THE MEN FALL TO THE PORCH ROOF AND ROLL DOWN THE SLANT.

FOR A MOMENT THEY HOVER ON THE ROOF EDGE, AND THEN PLUNGE TO THE GROUND!

BUT THE CHINAMAN IS UNDERNEATH, AND AS THEY HIT THE GROUND, HIS BODY ACTS AS A SHOCK-ABSORBER!

THE BATMAN, HOWEVER, RECEIVES A GLANCING BLOW ON THE HEAD AND ROLLS OVER UNCONSCIOUS!

A LITTLE LATER . . . INSIDE WONG'S HOUSE, ANOTHER ENTERS THE MURDER ROOM.. ROBIN THE BOY WONDER!!

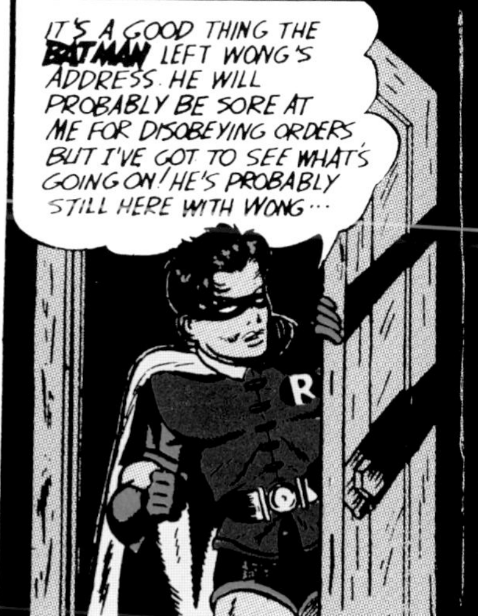
IT'S A GOOD THING THE BATMAN LEFT WONG'S ADDRESS. HE WILL PROBABLY BE SORE AT ME FOR DISOBEYING ORDERS BUT I'VE GOT TO SEE WHAT'S GOING ON! HE'S PROBABLY STILL HERE WITH WONG...

KILLED.. WITH A HATCHET LIKE THE MURDERED CHAUFFEUR! THEN THE BATMAN WAS RIGHT.. THIS CASE DOES TIE IN WITH THE KIDNAPPED MEN!

AN ADDRESS SCRATCHED BY WONG WHEN HE WAS KILLED! - PIER THREE...

SOMETHING MYSTERIOUS IS GOING ON AND I'M PRETTY SURE THE ANSWER IS OVER AT PIER THREE.. AND THAT'S WHERE I'M GOING, RIGHT NOW!

AS ROBIN LEAVES.. THE FIRST HATCHET MAN UNSTEADILY RISES TO HIS FEET..
DARK BATMAN FIGHTS LIKE PANTHER! HUH! NO ONE HERE? PERHAPS BATMAN CAPTURED AND IS NOW AT GREEN DRAGON.. MUST GO THERE AT ONCE!

THE WATERFRONT CLOAKED IN THE INK OF MIDNIGHT... PIER 3!!

THE ONLY THING THAT LOOKS LIKE IT MIGHT BE A HIDE-OUT IS THAT SCHOONER OVER THERE. I'M GOING TO TAKE A LOOK AT IT!

BUT ROBIN IS SEEN! A SKULKING FIGURE FOLLOWS... THE HATCHET MAN!
SOMEONE IS VERY INQUISITIVE ABOUT OUR SHIP. HE ALSO WEARS A CLOAKED COSTUME LIKE THE DARK BATMAN.. IT WOULD BE BETTER IF HE IS CAPTURED...

A MOMENT LATER.. THE FLAT OF A HATCHET CRASHES DOWN ON THE BOY!

THE UNCONSCIOUS BOY IS CARRIED ACROSS THE SHADOWY PIER TO THE SHIP OF MYSTERY.. TO THE LAIR OF THE GREEN DRAGON!
1

WHEN ROBIN AWAKENS, HE IS AWARE OF TWO CHAINED FIGURES. CRANDALL AND COBB.. THE KIDNAPPED MILLIONAIRES.. AND THERE UPON HIS THRONE.. THE MASTER OF THE TONG OF THE GREEN DRAGON!
AWAKE, EH? HMM.. PECULIAR COSTUME YOU WEAR.. VERY DIFFERENT.. BUT VERY SIMILAR TO THAT OF.. A.. ER.. THE.. BATMAN! AH! YES! HEE! HEE!
2

I SHOULD LIKE TO KNOW WHERE THE BATMAN RESIDES. WILL YOU TELL ME OR MUST I USE.. ER.. PERSUASION? EH?
NEVER! YOU CAN TORTURE ME ALL YOU LIKE BUT I WON'T TELL YOU ANYTHING ABOUT THE BATMAN!
3

YOU ARE STUBBORN, EH? YOU KNOW, I LIKE TO SEE THINGS WRIGGLE. YOU SHALL WRIGGLE BEFORE ME.. WITH PAIN! HEE! HEE! HEE!
4

FIRST WE SHALL SEE HOW ADEPT YOU ARE AT DUELING! I WARN YOU MY MAN IS QUITE EXPERT.. HE SLICED MANY AN OPPONENT!
5

BUT IT WILL BE UNFAIR, MY SWORD IS MADE OF.. WOOD!
UNFAIR PERHAPS.. BUT SO INTERESTING.. HEE! HEE! HEE! HEE!
6

AS ROBIN SKILLFULLY PARRIES THE MONGOL'S THRUST.. THE STEEL BLADE SLICES OFF PART OF THE WOODEN ONE!
7

AGAIN THE THRUST, AGAIN THE PARRY · AND MORE OF THE WOODEN SWORD IS LOPPED OFF!
ONE MORE PARRY AND I'LL HAVE NO MORE SWORD!

ANOTHER THRUST·· AND THE STEEL BLADE SLASHES THROUGH AT THE HILT!
THAT'S IT!

HEE! HEE! WELL, BOY, WHAT WILL YOU DO NOW? CAN YOU PULL A TRICK OUT OF YOUR SLEEVE? HEE! HEE!

AS ROBIN SIDE-STEPS ANOTHER WICKED SLASH OF THE BLADE·· HE REACHES INSIDE HIS JACKET··
I WON'T PULL A TRICK OUT OF MY SLEEVE·· BUT MY COAT!

the SLING!
··AND A STEEL PELLET··

ARMED WITH JUST THE PUNY SLING, ROBIN FACES THE ATTACKING MONGOL!

THAT'S ONE TRICK YOU DIDN'T COUNT ON!
--Z--I--N--G--

DON'T BE SO HASTY! HAVE YOU FORGOTTEN ALL ABOUT ME?
FOOLS! WHY DID YOU NOT SEARCH HIM? CAPTURE HIM OR ... WHA?

BATMAN!
GOOD EVENING, FRIEND, BUT THEN AGAIN, IS IT?

A MIGHTY LEAP...

A GIANT SWING...

..AND BATMAN LANDS ON THE PLATFORM.
CAPTURE HIM! YOU ARE MANY, HE IS ONLY ONE! DO NOT BE AFRAID!

AS THE ATTACKING CHINESE DASH ACROSS THE FLOOR, THE DYNAMIC BATMAN LEAPS TOWARD THE GREEN DRAGON... GRIMLY BRACES HIMSELF..AND WITH A SUPREME EFFORT..

..MANAGES TO TOPPLE THE ENORMOUS IDOL OFF BALANCE!

MORE FUN THAN A PUNCHING BAG!

BUT ROBIN..
BOY! WHAT A PARTY THIS TURNED OUT TO BE!

WELL, DOGGONE! ALL I CAN SAY IS, HE CERTAINLY IS AN APT PUPIL!

THE BATMAN FILES AWAY THE CHAINS AND THE KIDNAPPED MEN ARE FREED!
WHY, THEY CHLOROFORMED US AND BROUGHT US HERE. WHEN I TOLD THE CHINAMAN THAT THE POLICE WOULD GET HIM HE ONLY LAUGHED!
AND THEN WHAT HAPPENED?
YES, HE SAID THE POLICE WOULD PROBABLY HUNT FOR WHITE GANGSTERS AND NEVER SUSPECT A CHINESE OF KIDNAPPING, VERY SMART.

YES, HE WAS.. ONLY ONE OF HIS MEN SPOILED THE PLAN BY KILLING THE CHAUFFEUR WITH A HATCHET! ONLY THE CHINESE HATCHET MAN WOULD USE THAT TYPE OF WEAPON! ONCE I KNEW THAT, IT WAS A MATTER OF FINDING THE HIDEOUT. HERE IT WAS THAT HE INDULGED IN THE SMUGGLING OF OPIUM AND CHINESE!

THE NEXT DAY BRUCE WAYNE, THE BATMAN, IS OUT STROLLING WITH HIS FIANCEE.
BATMAN FREES MILLIONAIRES. BREAKS UP OPIUM RING! EXTRA! EXTRA!
WHAT AN EXCITING CHARACTER, THAT BATMAN ...WHY CAN'T YOU BE THAT SORT OF MAN?!

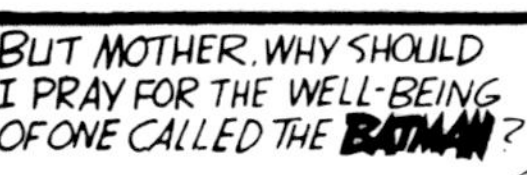
BUT MOTHER, WHY SHOULD I PRAY FOR THE WELL-BEING OF ONE CALLED THE BATMAN?

BECAUSE, LITTLE ONE, HE HAS SAVED THE SOULS OF MANY OF OUR PEOPLE. BUT FOR HIM THE DREAD OPIUM WOULD HAVE ENSLAVED THEM AS IT DID THE GENERATIONS IN THE PAST!

THE WAYNE HOME...
IT'S A PITY THAT WONG HAD TO DIE BECAUSE HE KNEW TOO MUCH!
BOB KANE
HIS SACRIFICE WAS NOT IN VAIN! HIS PEOPLE ARE FREE. IT IS THE END OF THE TONG OF THE GREEN DRAGON.

BEWARE OF CLAYFACE
A BLACK-CLOAKED, HIDEOUS FIGURE THAT MENACES THE LIVES OF THE BATMAN AND HIS AIDE, ROBIN THE BOY WONDER...
AS HE LEAVES BEHIND A TRAIL OF DEATH....
COMING NEXT MONTH

No. 40
A DC PUBLICATION
The BATMAN
Detective COMICS
JUNE
10¢
BOB KANE

BATMAN

WITH Robin -THE BOY WONDER-

AGAIN THE MIGHTY BATMAN AND THAT YOUNG, LAUGHING ROBIN HOOD OF TODAY, ROBIN THE BOY WONDER, PLUNGE DEEP INTO BAFFLING MYSTERY. AGAIN THEY FIGHT A MASTER OF CRIME, A MASTER OF MURDER! A BLACK CLOAKED, HIDEOUS FIGURE THAT MENACES THEIR VERY LIVES AS HE LEAVES BEHIND A TRAIL OF CORPSES!

BY BOB KANE

BRUCE WAYNE SPEAKS TO YOUNG DICK GRAYSON, WHO IS THE ONLY LIVING PERSON TO KNOW HIM AS BATMAN!

YEP, JULIE IS NOW A MOTION PICTURE ACTRESS. I'M GOING OVER TO THE STUDIO TO MEET HER

SO YOUR FIANCÉE IS ACTING IN THAT NEW HORROR PICTURE THEY'RE MAKING OVER AT ARGUS?

THE STUDIO OF THE ARGUS MOTION PICTURE COMPANY.

AND THIS, BRUCE, IS MR. BENTLEY, HEAD OF ARGUS PICTURES

HOW DO YOU DO?

MR. WAYNE, IF JULIE KEEPS UP HER FINE WORK SHE'LL BE A STAR IN NO TIME...

MR. KENNETH TODD IS THE NEW STAR OF THE PICTURE, "DREAD CASTLE." HE PLAYS "THE TERROR." YEARS AGO, IN THE OLD VERSION, THIS ROLE WAS PLAYED BY THE GREATEST CHARACTER AND MAKEUP ARTIST, BASIL KARLO!

DID SOMEONE SPEAK MY NAME? HELLO, BENTLEY.
BASIL KARLO!

JUST DROPPED IN TO WISH SUCCESSOR TO MY ROLE GO LUCK, TODD. I ONLY HOPE YO ARE AS SMART AS I WAS FOOL LOTS OF LUCK TO YOU!
THANK YOU, KARL I GUESS I'LL NEVER AS GOOD A CHARAC ACTOR AS YOU WER

WHEN KARLO LEAVES..
WHAT DID KARLO MEAN BY THAT "SMART" AND "FOOLISH" CRACK?
OH, YOU REMEMBER HOW AFTER HE BECAME A BIG STAR HE GOT INTO SCRAPES AND DID A LOT OF CRAZY THINGS. HE GOT A LOT OF BAD PUBLICITY BECAUSE OF IT. AFTER THE PAPERS GOT THROUGH WITH HIM, THE PEOPLE WOULDN'T GO TO SEE HIS PICTURES EVEN IF THEY GAVE AWAY PRIZES!

AT THAT MOMENT.
LOOK HERE, BENTLEY, WHAT'S THE IDEA OF STOPPING MY DIRECTING ON "DREAD CASTLE"?
NED NORTON.. SO YOU FINALLY SHOWED UP?

YOU GO OUT AND DISAPPEAR FOR DAYS AND YOU WANT TO K WHY! FIRST PROVE YOU CAN BE RELIED ON AND THEN PERHAPS I'LL GIVE YOU WOR
SO I'M FIRED, EH?

I WON'T FORGET THIS, BENTLEY. I WON'T FORGET THIS! REMEMBER, YOU'LL NEVER FINISH THIS PICTURE WITHOUT ME!

BENTLEY SHOWS BRUCE ABOUT THE STUDIO.
AND THERE IN THE BACK IS THE SET OF "DREAD CASTLE." FOR THIS PICTURE I HAD A REAL CASTLE BUILT —WITH A MOAT AROUND IT! NO EXPENSE WAS SPARED!
2

SUDDENLY THE SOUND O ANGRY VOICES REACHES TH
WE'RE THROUGH, FRE WALKER, THROUGH! AN THAT'S FINAL!
YOU CAN' WALK OUT ME NOW! WHAT ABO OUR LOVE
OH, OH! A TIFF!

HAT'S LORNA DANE, MY STAR! SHE'S GETTING RID OF HER SWEETHEART, FRED WALKER, JUST LIKE SHE'S RID HERSELF OF ALL HER OTHER SWEETHEARTS, THE GOLD DIGGER!
AND NONE TOO GENTLY, EITHER!

OUR LOVE? HA! HA! DON'T MAKE ME LAUGH! LISTEN, FRED, YOU HAVEN'T HAD A ROLE IN MONTHS. I CAN'T AFFORD TO LET MYSELF BE TIED TO AN ACTOR THAT'S SLIPPING!
YOU VIXEN, I OUGHT TO KILL YOU! YOU DON'T DESERVE TO LIVE!

LAUGH AT ME, WILL YOU! WHEN I GET THROUGH WITH YOU, YOU WON'T LAUGH AGAIN ... EVER!

LATER...
WELL, MR. BENTLEY, IT'S BEEN VERY ENJOYABLE, BUT IT'S GROWING LATE.
ALL RIGHT. TAKE JULIE HOME, BUT BE CAREFUL,... SHE IS VALUABLE PROPERTY-NOT ONLY TO ME BUT TO YOU, EH? HA! HA!

AS THEY LEAVE, A SATURNINE-LOOKING MAN APPROACHES BENTLEY...
HYA, BENTLEY. DECIDED TO ACCEPT MY OFFER YET?
ROXY BRENNER!

OFF! YOU GANGSTER! OFF THE LOT! I REFUSE TO PAY YOU "PROTECTION" MONEY! NOW GET OFF BEFORE I CALL THE POLICE!
OKAY, BENTLEY, IT'S YOUR FUNERAL! BUT DON'T BLAME ME IF ANYTHING HAPPENS TO ANY OF YOUR STARS!

NOBODY TALKS TO ROXY BRENNER LIKE THIS! WHEN I GET THROUGH WITH YOU, YOU'LL LEARN TO KEEP YOUR MOUTH SHUT! SEE YOU SOON, BENTLEY!

LATER.. THE WAYNE HOME...
SOMETHING IS GOING TO HAPPEN OUT AT THE STUDIO! THERE SEEMS TO BE AN AURA OF HATE PERVADING THE VERY ATMOSPHERE OF THE PLACE! YESSIR! SOMETHING IS GOING TO HAPPEN-AND SOON!
3

BUT FROM THE DARKENED CORNER OF THE SET, A HIDEOUS FACE WATCHES WITH BALEFUL EYES...

THOUGH POLICE INVESTIGATE, AT THE END OF A WEEK, THEY ARE FORCED TO REPORT... LORNA DANE MURDERED BY PERSON OR PERSONS UNKNOWN!"

A MOMENT LATER... BATMAN, THE DARK KNIGHT, AND ROBIN, THE BOY WONDER

ALL SET?

LET'S GO!

THE GATES OF ARGUS PICTURES!

IT SAYS "NO ADMITTANCE"... BUT THAT DOESN'T MEAN US, ROBIN!

INSIDE THE STUDIO..

YOU SAID SOMETHING WOULD HAPPEN TO MY STARS..YOU.. YOU GANGSTER! DID YOU KILL LORNA DANE?

BETTER PAY UP, BENTLEY!

MAYBE, BETTER PAY UP THE "PROTECTION" MONEY OR ELSE YOU WON'T HAVE ANY DOUBTS!

CHINESE GARDEN SET

SUDDENLY HURTLING THROUGH THE AIR... BATMAN AND ROBIN, THE BOY WONDER!!

I THINK YOU'RE THE ONE WHO IS LOOKING FOR TROUBLE!

WHA...? I'M ATTACKED BY AN ELF!

IF YOU'RE LOOKING FOR TROUBLE, BENTLEY, WHY...SAY...!!

?

THE COURAGEOUS PAIR QUICKLY ROUT THE GANGSTERS

BATMAN QUESTIONS BENTLEY:
I'M GOING TO CLEAN UP YOUR MYSTERY FOR YOU. NOW THAT ROXY BRENNER IS OUT, WHO ELSE WOULD WANT TO KILL LORNA DANE?
FRED WALKER, HER OLD SWEETHEART.. OR PERHAPS NED NORTON DID IT SO HE COULD GET EVEN WITH ME AND STOP THE PICTURE.

ROBIN, YOU STAY HERE AND KEEP YOUR EYES OPEN.. I'M GOING TO PAY A VISIT TO FRED WALKER, LORNA DANE'S JILTED SWEETHEART!
RIGHT!
LATER BATMAN CLEARS THE FENCE SURROUNDING WALKER'S HOME!

A PASS KEY IS USED AND THE DOOR SLOWLY OPENS..
HMM NOBODY HOME?

THE BATMAN SEARCHES FRUITLESSLY THROUGH THE HOUSE. THEN IN A FINAL CLOSET...
GOOD HEAVENS! WHAT'S THIS?

DANGING FROM A HOOK IN THE CLOSET IS FRED WALKER!
H..HELP.. HELP ME!
WALKER! WHAT IS IT? WHAT'S HAPPENED?

WALKER! CAN YOU HEAR ME? WHO DID THIS TO YOU?
CLAYFACE!.. CLAYFACE.. HE..A..AAAAAH!

DEAD! CLAYFACE.. HE SAID! WHO IS CLAYFACE? NOT ROXY BRENNER. CERTAINLY NOT THIS DEAD MAN...CAN IT BE NED NORTON, THE DIRECTOR... OR PERHAPS KEN TODD???

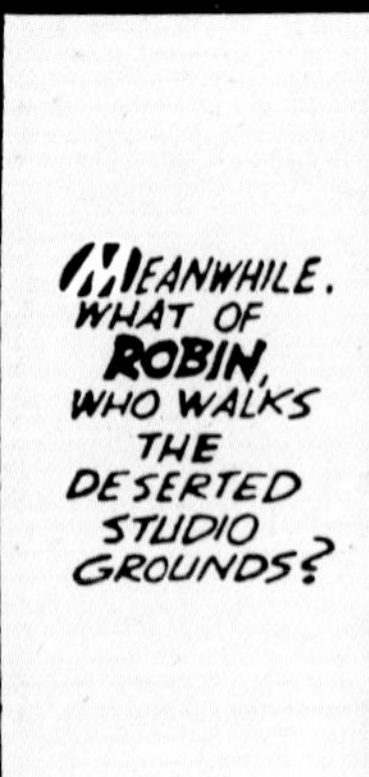
MEANWHILE. WHAT OF ROBIN, WHO WALKS THE DESERTED STUDIO GROUNDS?

SUDDENLY HE SPIES... LIGHT ON DREAD CASTLE!
LIGHT! IT SEEMS I'M NOT THE ONLY ONE OUT TONIGHT!

...THINK I'LL INVESTIGATE!

BUT FROM HIGH ABOVE. THE BOY IS SPIED.. THE MYSTERIOUS CLAYFACE!
HMM. SOMEONE IS INQUISITIVE.. BUT NOT FOR LONG.. AHAA!

ROBIN ENTERS THE GLOOMY CASTLE.
GOSH! WHAT A SPOT FOR A MURDER!

UNAWARE OF THE LURKING TERR
AT THE TOP ROBIN ASCENDS THE LO
WINDING STAIRCASE TO THE LAST TOWE
LOOKS LIKE MY GUEST IS WALKING HIS LAST MILE!

CLAYFACE LEAPS..
HEY!

BUT THE AGILE ROBIN DUCKS AND THE MURDEROUS CLAYFACE GOES HURTLING OVER HIS SHOULDER!
8

I NEED NO KNIFE... I CAN KILL YOU WITH MY BARE HANDS!
WOW! I'M IN A SPOT!

AS ROBIN STEPS BACK TO AVOID A CLUTCHING HAND, HE TRIPS ON THE FALLEN LAMP!
CRACK!

I'LL DRAG THIS FOOL BOY TO THE PARAPET AND THROW HIS BODY INTO THE WATERS OF THE MOAT BELOW!

HA! THAT IS THE END OF YOU, MY PRYING YOUNG FRIEND!

BUT AT THAT MOMENT THE BATMAN, WHO HAS RETURNED, SEES THE FALLING BODY.
THAT LOOKS... THAT IS... ROBIN!

THE BATMAN CLEAVES THE WATER JUST AS THE BODY SINKS! ....

A FEW MOMENTS LATER...
ARE YOU ALL RIGHT, KID?
I G-GUESS SO -- WOW! WHAT HIT ME? OH, NOW I REMEMBER - THE MONSTER UP IN THE TOWER!
9

ONCE MORE IN THE TOWER··BUT CLAYFACE··GONE!
HE'S GONE! I WONDER WHAT HE WAS DOING UP HERE ANYWAY?
PROBABLY SURVEYING THE SCENE FOR HIS NEXT MURDER!··CLAYFACE ···I WONDER IF···

NEXT MORNING··IN A DIMLY-LIT ROOM, A MAN APPLIES A GROTESQUE MAKEUP··CLAYFACE!
ONCE MORE I DON THE GARMENTS OF DEATH!

THIS MORNING MISS JULIE BEGINS HER "MURDER" SCE
IN "DREAD CASTLE"··PERH
IT SHALL PROVE PROPHET
HA! PROPHETIC!

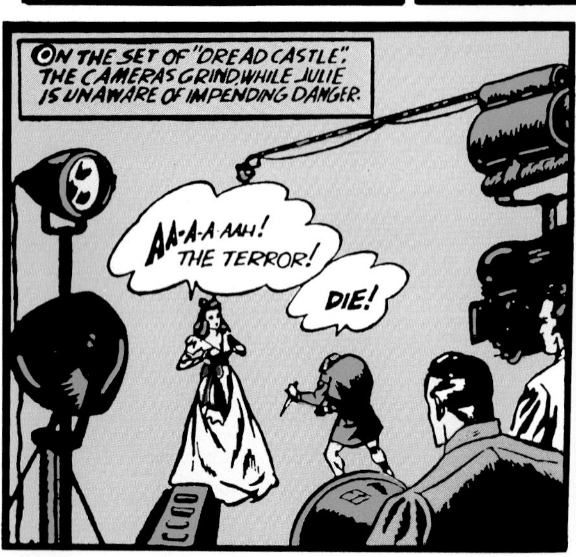
ON THE SET OF "DREAD CASTLE", THE CAMERAS GRIND, WHILE JULIE IS UNAWARE OF IMPENDING DANGER.
AA-A-A-AAH! THE TERROR!
DIE!

BUT UP ON THE DARKENED CATWALK A GHASTLY FIGURE RAISES HIS KNIFE FOR THE THROW··· CLAYFACE!
DIE - JULIE!

BUT SUDDENLY A ROPE ENCIRCLES THE MURDERER'S WRIST···
?

MAY I CUT IN ?
···THEN WITH THE SPEED OF THOUGHT A MIGHTY TACKLE·· BATMAN!

FOCUS THE CAMERAS! THE SHOTS WILL BE KNOCKOUTS!
LOOK! ON THE CATWALK! THE BATMAN!

CLAYFACE, FIGHTING WITH THE STRENGTH OF A MADMAN, SUDDENLY UNLEASHES A TERRIFIC BLOW!!!
FOOL, NO ONE SHALL TAKE ME ALIVE!

THE MANIAC LEAPS FOR A DANGLING ROPE...
THAT ROPE!

BUT CLAYFACE HAS RECKONED WITHOUT ROBIN, THE BOY WONDER!
HERE'S WHERE I GET EVEN WITH THAT GUY!

I'LL BET YOU'RE SURPRISED!

HERE'S SOMETHING I OWE YOU!

A ROPE SUDDENLY HISSES THROUGH THE AIR AND JERKS CLAYFACE OFF HIS FEET....

THE BATMAN HAS WON THE LAST TRICK!
CLAYFACE, FROM NOW ON YOUR NAME IS MUD!

A FEW MOMENTS LATER...
NOW I'M GOING TO SHOW YOU THE MURDERER OF LORNA DANE AND FRED WALKER
THAT MAKEUP! I ONCE SAW IT IN ONE OF MY PICTU ..CLAYFACE..IT W PLAYED BY..

THE BATMAN PROCEEDS TO REMOVE THE GHASTLY MAKEUP FROM THE HORRIBLE CLAYFACE..WHOSE REAL FACE BELONGS TO

IT'S... BASIL KARLO !!
RIGHT! YOU SEE, HE HATED YOU FOR USING TODD IN A REMAKE OF ONE OF HIS OLD STARRING PICTURES! HE WANTED TO STOP THE PICTURE!
BUT WHY DID HE KILL LORNA DANE AND THEN TRY FOR ME? WHY DIDN'T HE KILL TODD FIRST?

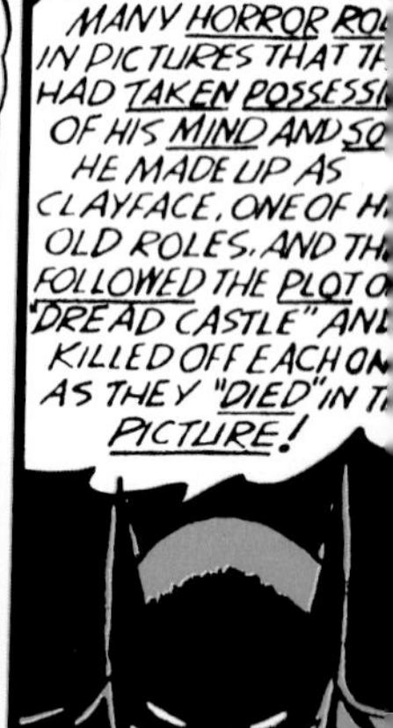
HE HAD PLAYED SO MANY HORROR RO IN PICTURES THAT T HAD TAKEN POSSESSI OF HIS MIND AND SO HE MADE UP AS CLAYFACE, ONE OF H OLD ROLES, AND TH FOLLOWED THE PLOT O "DREAD CASTLE" AN KILLED OFF EACH ON AS THEY "DIED" IN T PICTURE!

IN THE LAST REEL, TODD, AS "THE TERROR," WAS SUPPOSED TO "DIE"..THAT'S WHEN HE INTENDED TO KILL HIM! IN THIS WAY BASIL KARLO WOULD AGAIN BE THE REAL TERROR! ONCE MORE HE WOULD STAR! FANTASTIC, WASN'T IT?
BUT WHY DID HE KILL WALKER?
HE RECOGNIZED ME IN MY CLAYFACE DISGUISE WHEN I GOT LORNA. HE WANTED TO BLACKMAIL ME, SO I KILLED HIM..AS FOR YOU, BATMAN, I'LL GET YOU YET!
BOB KANE

SENSATIONAL! YOU TWO ARE SENSATIONAL! I GOT YOU BOTH IN FIGHT PICTURES! STAY WITH ME AND YOU HAVE A CAREER IN THE MOVIES!
SORRY! OUR CAREER IS OUR CONSTANT BATTLE AGAINST CRIME AND EVIL!
THEY'RE WHAT I CALL A PAIR OF REAL HEROES AND I DON'T MEAN REEL! HO! HUM! IF ONLY BRUCE WAS SO DASHING!

ONE O
America
MOST OUTSTANDI ADVENTUR STRIPS!
THE AMAZING BATMA
WITH HIS SENSATIO AIDE
Robin
WILL AGAIN THRILL YOU NEXT MONTH IN DETECTIVE COMICS WITH THEIR DARING EXPLO
DON'T MISS THEM!!

No. 41
The BATMAN
Detective
Comics
JULY
10¢
HERE COMES
THE BATMAN
AGAIN!
BOB KANE

BATMAN
WITH Robin
- THE BOY WONDER -
FEATURED IN THIS SPECIAL ISSUE
ONCE AGAIN THE MIGHTY BATMAN AND ROBIN, THE BOY WONDER, GLIDE THROUGH THE PERILOUS MAZES OF GRIPPING MYSTERY AS A DREADED MASKED FIGURE THREATENS THEIR VERY LIVES! TO ROBIN, THE BOY WONDER FALLS THE TASK OF BRINGING ABOUT THE FALL, OF A MASTER CRIMINAL .... A MASTER MURDERER!
BY BOB KANE
BLAKES SCHOOL FOR BOYS
ON A CERTAIN EVENTFUL NIGHT.... IMPORTANT INCIDENTS TAKE PLACE THAT ARE TO INVOLVE MANY PEOPLE, INCLUDING BATMAN AND ROBIN, THE BOY WONDER !!!
A HOMICIDAL MANIAC MAKES GOOD HIS ESCAPE FROM AN INSANE ASYLUM...
HEE! HEE! HOLD ME, WILL THEY? HEE HEE! CALL ME CRAZY, EH? HEE HEE! I'M SMART ENOUGH TO ESCAPE!
LATER, ON THE GROUNDS OF THE FASHIONABLE PRIVATE SCHOOL FOR BOYS NEARBY, THE SUPERINTENDENT IS FOUND MURDERED.. STRANGLED....

2 NEW YORK WORLD MONDA

YOUNG BOY DISAPPEARS FROM BLAKES BOYS SCHOOL

ATTENDANT FOUND MURDERED ON GROUNDS MANIAC ESCAPED FROM A NEARBY ASYLUM IS SUSPECTED

POLICE ARE MYSTIFIED BY THE MURDER OF AN ATTENDANT OF THE WEALTHY AND FASHION-ABLE BLAKE SCHOOL AND THE DISAPPEARANCE OF ONE OF ITS PUPILS

IT LOOKS AS IF GREER HAS IT IN FOR YOU!

POPPYCOCK! HE'S HARMLESS! COME NOW, I'LL INTRODUCE YOU TO THE REST OF THE STAFF! THEIR SLEEPING QUARTERS ARE IN THE HOUSE, YOU KNOW!

LATER
AND NOW I WANT YOU TO MEET MR. GRAVES, THE ART INSTRUCTOR.
AH! ANOTHER PUPIL TO ABSORB THE FINE POINTS OF ART! I SHALL MAKE A MASTER CRAFTSMAN OF YOU, MY BOY... A MASTER!
HOW DO YOU DO!
HOW DO, YOU DO!

IT SEEMS YOU ARE A MASTER. MR. GRAVES. I NOTICE THESE FINE ENGRAVINGS HAVE YOUR NAME ON THEM!
THOSE ARE NOTHING! I WOULD LIKE TO SHOW YOU SOME REALLY FINE WORK I HAVE DONE THEY ARE MASTERPIECES!
MODEST GUY!

ANOTHER MAN ENTERS..
THIS IS MR. HODGES, THE HISTORY INSTRUCTOR!
HOW DO YOU DO, MR. HODGES!
WELCOME TO BLAKE SCHOOL! AND NOW IF YOU'LL EXCUSE ME.. GOOD DAY!

BRRR! DID WE GET THE COLD SHOULDER!
HODGES MAY BE A BIT RESERVED, BUT HE'S A FINE TEACHER!
HE KEEPS TO HIMSELF. NEVER TALKS TO ANOTHER! NO-ONE HERE LIKES HIM! I DON'T TRUST HIM!

HURRIED INSTRUCTIONS ARE GIVEN TO DICK BY BRUCE WAYNE..
POLICEMEN ALL OVER THE PLACE LOOKING FOR THE ESCAPED MANIAC AND THAT MISSING BOY!..LOOKS LIKE THERE WON'T BE MUCH PRIVACY FOR THE BATMAN TO WORK ABOUT HERE!
GUESS I'LL HAVE TO WORK ALON EH?

YES, BUT KEEP IN TOUCH WITH ME.. YOU KNOW HOW! SEND ME DETAILS ON WHATEVER DEVELOPS! GOOD LUCK, AND WATCH YOURSELF!
RIGHT!

DICK IMMEDIATELY GETS TO WORK ON ONE OF HIS NEW FELLOW PUPILS

AND YOU SAY THAT THE POLICE SEARCHED TED SPENCER'S ROOM FOR A DIARY?
YES, THEY FIGURED HE MIGHT HAVE WRITTEN DOWN SOMETHING THAT HAD TO DO WITH HIS DISAPPEARANCE, BUT COULDN'T FIND IT!

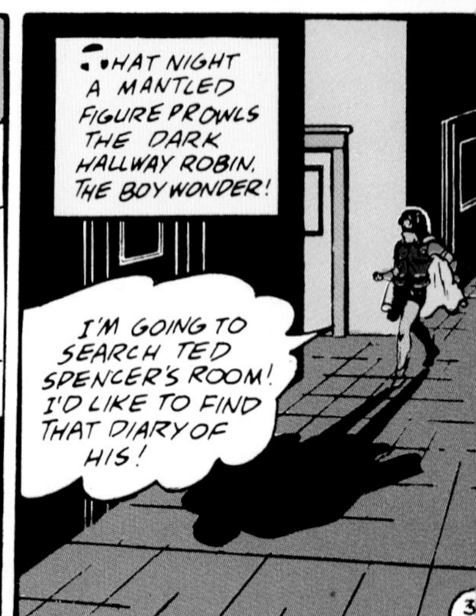
THAT NIGHT A MANTLED FIGURE PROWLS THE DARK HALLWAY ROBIN, THE BOY WONDER!
I'M GOING TO SEARCH TED SPENCER'S ROOM! I'D LIKE TO FIND THAT DIARY OF HIS!

ON THE BOY'S ROOM .. HE SEARCHES UNTIL...
THE DIARY! NO WONDER THE POLICE MISSED IT...IT WAS COVERED LIKE HIS OTHER SCHOOL BOOKS! AND LYING AMONGST THEM!

WOW! JUST WHAT I'VE BEEN LOOKING FOR THE LAST ENTRY!

THE LAST ENTRY MADE BY THE MISSING BOY!
"LAST NIGHT I SAW A MASKED MAN WALKING DOWN THE CORRIDOR! I WONDER WHO THE MASKED MAN IS? I AM GOING TO TELL MR. BLAKE, THE PRINCIPAL, ABOUT IT!

ABRUPTLY...
I'LL TAKE THAT!
THE MASKED MAN!
I DON'T KNOW WHO YOU ARE, BUT KEEP YOUR DISTANCE! I MEAN TO HAVE THIS BOOK!

YOU'RE NOT THE ONLY ONE WHO WANTS THAT DIARY!

A SMALL BUT COMPACT FIST SHOOTS OUT?
TAG! YOU'RE IT!
4

BUT AS ROBIN LAUNCHES FORWARD ONCE MORE...
FOOL OF A BOY!

A CHAIR CRASHES DOWN ON THE UNPROTECTED HEAD OF ROBIN ... THE WONDER BOY!

I WARNED YOU!

WOW! MAYBE I SHOULD HAVE HEEDED THAT GUY'S WARNING AFTER ALL! HE MEANT IT!

BY THE TIME ROBIN REACHES THE DOORWAY...
GONE! AND THE DIARY WITH HIM! I WISH I COULD HAVE READ THE REST OF THAT LAST ENTRY!

IT'S TIME I LET THE BATMAN KNOW WHAT HAPPENED! BETTER GET STARTED ON MY SENDING SET!

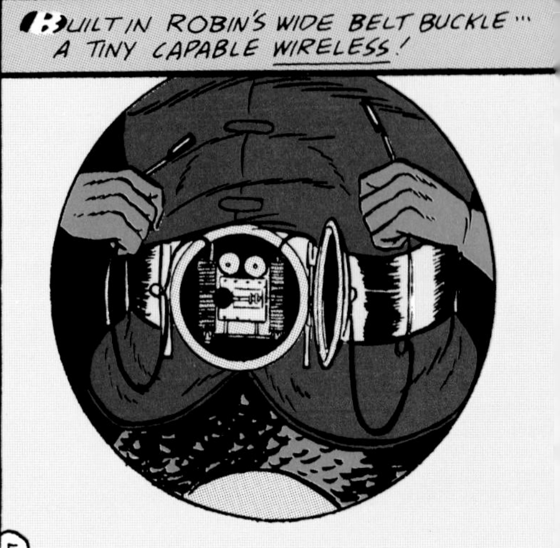
BUILT IN ROBIN'S WIDE BELT BUCKLE ... A TINY CAPABLE WIRELESS!
5

OUTSIDE THE SCHOOL WALL, THE BATMAN IS CONTACTED!
THE PORTABLE PHONE...ROBIN HAS SOME NEWS FOR ME!

THE BATMAN IS INFORMED OF ALL THAT HAS TRANSPIRED!
AND THEN HE DISAPPEARED WITH THE DIARY!... WHAT SHALL I DO NOW?
THE MISSING BOY'S DIARY MENTIONED THE PRINCIPAL, MR. BLAKE WHY NOT SEARCH HIS ROOMS.. MAYBE HE KNOWS SOMETHING!

IN A LARGE GLOOMY ROOM A MAN STANDS READING BEFORE A ROARING FIRE. THE SINISTER MASKED MENACE!
HMM!.. GOOD THING I SECURED THIS DIARY.. MIGHT HAVE GIVEN THE POLICE A CLUE TO MY ACTIVITES HERE!

BETTER IF I RID MYSELF OF IT! NOTHING LIKE THE ALL-CONSUMING FLAME TO DEVOUR EVIDENCE.. NOW I'M FREE TO CONTINUE MY WORK!

THE NEXT NIGHT, ROBIN IS ONCE MORE ON THE PROWL!
THAT'S BLAKE'S ROOM UP THERE! BEST I CLIMB THAT VINE AND ENTER THE OUTSIDE WINDOW INSTEAD OF THE DOOR!

AN AGONIZING SCREAM SUDDENLY SPLITS THE NIGHT AIR!
WHA.. SOMEONE IN TROUBLE!
AAGH! HELP! HELP!
IT CAME FROM AROUND THIS CORNER!
6

ROUNDING THE BUILDING, ROBIN STANDS TRANSFIXED WHEN HE SEES...
TRY TO TELL ME YOU'RE A JANITOR, EH! I KNOW YOU'RE A KEEPER LIKE THE OTHER ONE I KILLED!

SUDDENLY THE MADMAN SEES ROBIN··AND LEAPS!
ANOTHER ONE! ALL TRYING TO TAKE ME BACK! I ESCAPED, BUT YOU WON'T HEE! HEE! YOU WON'T!

A SWIFT MOVE AND THE DEADLY SLASHING BLADE HISSES PAST!
YOU'RE NOT GOING TO CUT ME WITH THAT OVERGROWN PENKNIFE!

A LIGHTNING GRASP OF THE WRIST··
AND NOW I GRAB YOUR HAND··THUSLY!

A QUICK TWIST AND
OVER YOU GO THUSLY!

LIKE A JUNGLE CAT HE POUNCES UPON THE MADMAN!
OKAY, FELLA, IT LOOKS LIKE YOUR KNIFE-STICKING DAYS ARE OVER!
7

I HEARD IT COME FROM OVER THIS WAY.
LOOK! SOMEONE OVER THERE CAN'T SEE WHO IT IS!
TIME FOR MY EXIT!
R

NEXT MORNING THE SCHOOL BUZZES WITH EXCITEMENT OVER SENSATIONAL NEWS ···

THEY SAY THE MANIAC THOUGHT THE UNIFORMED JANITORS WERE KEEPERS TRYING TO TAKE HIM BACK TO THE INSANE ASYLUM!
THEN I IMAGINE THE POLICE WILL BE CALLED OFF THE GROUNDS NOW?
SO IT WAS THE MANIAC WHO KILLED THE FIRST JANITOR AND THEN TRIED TO KILL ANOTHER LAST NIGHT!
OH, YES. THE CASE IS FINISHED NOW!

THAT'S WHAT YOU THINK!... WHAT ABOUT THE MISSING BOY AND HIS DIARY!.. AND THE MASKED MAN! YESSIR, THIS CASE IS JUST BEGINNING!

ANOTHER HAS HIS OPINION··· HODGES!!
SO THE CASE IS FINISHED IS IT, MR. BLAKE?.. YOU HAVE FORGOTTEN ABOUT THE MISSING TED SPENCER! YOU HAVE LESS BRAINS THAN I THOUGHT YOU HAD.. OR HAVE YOU?

THAT NIGHT THE BOY WONDER IS AGAIN ON THE MOVE!
LAST NIGHT I DIDN'T GET A CHANCE TO LOOK IN THE PRINCIPAL'S ROOM, BUT NOTHING IS GOING TO STOP ME NOW!

SWIFTLY THE AGILE FIGURE SCALES THE HIGH WALL···

WRAITHLIKE, HIS FIGURE GHOSTS INTO THE ROOM!
WELL, I'M IN, AND··· GOOD HEAVENS, WHAT'S THAT ON THE FLOOR?
8

BLAKE..... MURDERED!

ON THE MORNING THE BODY IS DISCOVERED.. POLICE INVESTIGATE.. GREER IS ARRESTED ON SUSPICION OF MURDER!
YOU KILLED BLAKE, DIDN'T YOU!
YOU HATED HIM BECAUSE HE DISCHARGED YOU FROM SCHOOL!
NO.. NO.. I DIDN'T.. I TELL YOU I DIDN'T!
YOU THREATENED TO FIX HIM!

WHAT DID YOU DO WITH TED SPENCER, THE MISSING BOY?
YOU HATED HIM! YOU WANTED REVENGE! YOU KIDNAPPED HIM!
WE FOUND OUT THAT SPENCER WAS THE PUPIL WHO FAILED THAT TEST! IT WAS BECAUSE OF HIM THAT YOU WERE DISCHARGED!
NO.. NO.. NO.. !!

YOU HATED BLAKE AND THE BOY!
YOU SATISFIED YOUR REVENGE. DIDN'T YOU? DIDN'T YOU?
YOU KILLED BLAKE AND PERHAPS HAVE ALREADY KILLED THE BOY!
NO.. NO.. I'M INNOCENT!

WHO DO YOU THINK IS THE MYSTERY MURDERER? WHO DO YOU THINK IS THE MASKED MENACE? CHECK WHICH PERSON YOU THINK IS GUILTY!
GREER ... THE SUSPECTED ONE ?
BLAKE ... THE PRINCIPAL .. WAS HE THE MASKED MAN?
GRAVES .. ... THE ECCENTRIC ART TEACHER?
.. THE ESCAPED MANIAC ... WAS HE THE MASKED MAN?
HODGES. THE MYSTERIOUS HISTORY TEACHER?

ONCE MORE THE PANEL SLIDES OPEN.. THIS TIME TO ADMIT THE WONDER BOY!
YOU DON'T KNOW IT. MR. MASKED MAN, BUT YOU'VE GOT COMPANY!

INTO DARKENED DEPTHS STEPS THE FEARLESS BOY!
THIS MUST BE AN OLD DESERTED TUNNEL ABANDONED WHEN THE SCHOOL WAS BUILT!

OUT OF THE OLD TUNNEL THE MASKED MENACE STEPS INTO THE OPEN AIR!

AND ENTERS AN OLD DWELLING NEARBY!

INSIDE THE OLD HOUSE THE MISSING BOY·TED SPENCER!
DIDJA GET IT, BOSS?
SURE, I KNEW WHERE BLAKE KEPT IT 'THIS IS REAL. MONEY. NOT THE COUNTERFEIT STUFF WE'VE BEEN MAKING!
BLAKE SURE COINED A LOTTA DOUGH BY STICKING WITH US··UNTIL HE GOT PANICKY AND WANTED TO QUIT·BUT YOU FIXED HIM, EH, BOSS?

YEAH· AND NOW SO THAT THIS KID DON'T TALK· I'LL FIX HIM!
SURE. GET RID OF HIM · HE'S TOO RISKY TO KEEP AROUND!

ABRUBTLY THE DOOR BURSTS OPEN A HUMAN AVALANCHE STRIKES!
OUTA MY WAY..! THE EXPRESS IS COMIN' THRU!
10

A LONE BOY FIGHTS AGAINST OVERWHELMING ODDS!
YOU'RE IN FINE FORM, ROBIN, BUT I THINK YOU COULD USE SOME HELP!
THAT KID AGAIN.. GET HIM!
WE'LL KNOCK HIM SILLY!
PERHAPS IT WILL BE JUST THE OPPOSITE!
HUH?
ANOTHER FIGURE DECIDES TO JOIN THE PARTY... THE MIGHTY BATMAN!
THE BATMAN!
I SAW YOU EMERGE TO FOLLOW OUR MASKED FRIEND HERE, SO I DECIDED TO SEE WHAT WAS UP!!
LEMME OUTA HERE.. THAT GUY'S DYNAMITE!
BATMAN... HOW DID YOU GET HERE?
I DON'T LIKE THESE BOYS, ROBIN.. WHAT DO YOU SAY TO ROUGHING THEM UP A BIT!?
C'MON! LET'S TAKE 'EM!
THE NEXT MOMENT SEES A TANGLE OF ARMS AND LEGS... SWINGING FISTS... JAWS ARE CRACKED.. GRUNTS EXPLODED.. MEN GO FLYING.. THE BATMAN AND ROBIN ARE HAVING FUN!
ARE YOU ALL RIGHT, ROBIN?
HELP! THE JOINT'S BEEN HIT BY A TORNADO!
DON'T WORRY ABOUT ME.. I'M HAVING A SWELL TIME!
ROBIN!.. GET THAT GUY.. HE'S GETTING AWAY!
HE WON'T GET FAR!
11
FROM WITHIN HIS VEST THE BOY WONDER PRODUCES AN ANCIENT BUT FORMIDABLE WEAPON... THE SLING!
YOU'RE PRETTY FAST ON YOUR FEET, MR MASKED MAN.. BUT I HAVE SOMETHING THAT'S EVEN FASTER!

GRAVES AND THE PRINCIPAL WERE PARTNERS! GRAVES USED TO SNEAK OUT OF HIS ROOM AND USE THE TUNNEL TO GET HERE! ONE NIGHT HE WAS SPOTTED.. BY THE BOY TED SPENCER!

I SEE, AND WHEN SPENCER TOLD BLAKE THAT HE SAW A MASKED MAN IN THE SCHOOL, BLAKE TOLD GRAVES, WHO KIDNAPPED HIM SO THAT HE WOULDN'T TELL ANYONE ELSE!

ROBIN, the ORIGINAL BOY WONDER, WILL BE BACK NEXT MONTH IN DETECTIVE COMICS TO THRILL YOU AGAIN IN ANOTHER EXCITING AND FAST-MOVING ADVENTURE WITH THE BATMAN!

No. 42
A DC PUBLICATION
The BATMAN
Detective Comics
AUG.
10¢
BOB KANE

BATMAN

WITH

Robin
-THE BOY WONDER-

BY BOB KANE

WHEN BRUCE WAYNE, THE BATMAN, WENT TO MR. WYLIE'S FASHIONABLE PARTY AND MET ANTAL THE ARTIST, LITTLE DID HE REALIZE THAT HE WAS SOON TO PLUNGE INTO THE DEPTHS OF A FANTASTIC MYSTERY! WHEN ANTAL PAINTED, SOMEONE DIED.... HOW.. ... WHY? THIS WAS THE PUZZLE OF "THE CASE OF THE PROPHETIC PICTURES!"

THE HOME OF BRUCE WAYNE, THE BATMAN, AND DICK GRAYSON, WHOM ALL CALL ROBIN THE BOY WONDER!

BOY, YOU SURE ARE PUTTING ON THE DOG TONIGHT! WHERE ARE YOU GOING?

TO A PARTY THAT THE SOCIALLY EMINENT MR. WYLIE IS THROWING FOR AN ARTIST HE DISCOVERED WHILE TRAVELLING IN EUROPE!

AN ARTIST, EH?

YES, WYLIE IS QUITE INSANE ABOUT PAINTINGS. HE'S BEEN THE PATRON OF MANY A STARVING GENIUS! WELL, I GUESS I'M ALL SET NOW!

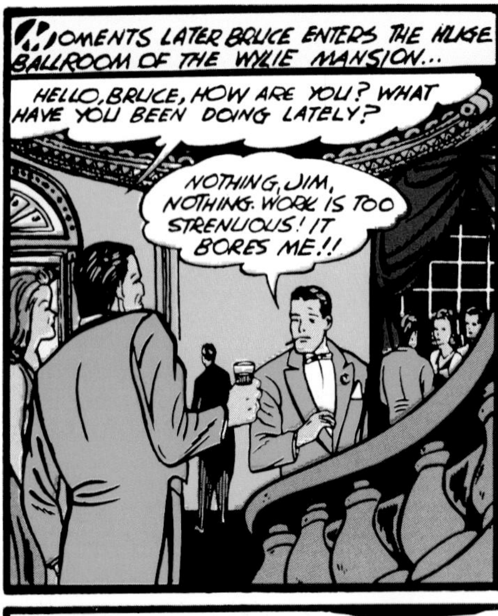
MOMENTS LATER BRUCE ENTERS THE HUGE BALLROOM OF THE WYLIE MANSION...
HELLO, BRUCE, HOW ARE YOU? WHAT HAVE YOU BEEN DOING LATELY?
NOTHING, JIM, NOTHING. WORK IS TOO STRENUOUS! IT BORES ME!!

BORED! EVERYTHING BORES THAT FELLOW! IF HE EVER GOT EXCITED ABOUT ANYTHING I THINK THEY WOULD DECLARE A NATIONAL HOLIDAY!
THEY SAY HE IS PROBABLY THE LAZIEST, MOST USELESS CHAP IN OUR SET!

AH, MY HOST, MR. WYLIE!

WAYNE, MEET ANTAL, WHO WILL PROBABLY BE THE BEST KNOWN PAINTER IN AMERICA BY THE TIME I'M THROUGH WITH HIM!
MR WAYNE.
HOW DO YOU DO!

THIS IS MY AGENT AND MANAGER, MR. BLEEK!
MR. WYLIE INTENDS TO MAKE ANTAL THE MOST FASHIONABLE SOCIETY PORTRAIT PAINTER. HE WILL PAINT ALL OF SOCIETY, EH MR. WYLIE?

ABRUPTLY..
ANTAL! YOU WRETCH! SO YOU ARE HERE IN AMERICA!
MIKOFF! YOU!

I SHOULD KILL YOU AS YOU KILLED MY DEAR SISTER! YOU- YOU - KEEP OUT OF MY WAY. I WARN YOU.... ELSE NEXT TIME I THROTTLE YOU!

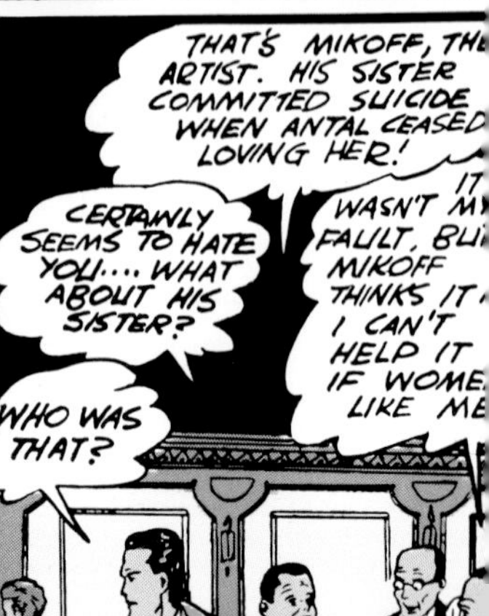
CERTAINLY SEEMS TO HATE YOU.... WHAT ABOUT HIS SISTER?
WHO WAS THAT?

OMETIME LATER, AS BRUCE TROLLS ON THE TERRACE, HE EARS ANGRY VOICES....
BUT, MR. RYDER, YOU ARE MISTAKEN! YOU....
YOU HEARD ME! STAY AWAY FROM MY WIFE! THIS IS THE LAST TIME I'LL TELL YOU!
HM! ANTAL SEEMS TO BE QUITE THE CASANOVA!

LOOKS LIKE ANTAL HAS MADE AN ENEMY IN THE SOCIALLY EMINENT MR. DRAKE! THAT MAN HAS A QUICK TEMPER!

LATER THAT EVENING-
OH, IT'S YOU, BRUCE! HAVE A GOOD TIME? DID ANYTHING HAPPEN?
NOT TONIGHT BUT FROM WHAT I'VE SEEN, IT LOOKS LIKE SOMETHING WILL...SOON!

IN THE ENSUING WEEKS, ANTAL'S FAME GROWS WITH EACH FINISHED PORTRAIT....
...AND THEY SAY THIS NTAL PERSON S MARVELOUS!
HEARD HE'S A VERY FINE PAINTER!
VANGILD HAD ONE DONE OF HIMSELF LATELY!

BUT AT THAT MOMENT IN THE VANGILD HOME...
.... I TELL YOU, SIR, THAT IS THE WAY I FOUND THE PICTURE AS I PASSED IT BEFORE! .... A KNIFE STICKING INTO IT!
IT'S INSANE! WHY SHOULD ANYONE PLUNGE A KNIFE INTO MY PORTRAIT? I DON'T UNDERSTAND! WHY?

THE NEXT DAY VANGILD LEARNS ONLY TOO LATE... THE CRYPTIC MEANING IS- DEATH!

IN THE HOME OF CARMEN LARGO THE OPERA STAR....
DEAR, LOOK, YOUR NEW PORTRAIT PAINTED BY ANTAL... IT HAS A DART DRIVEN INTO IT!
...A DART- IN MY THROAT!

NEXT NIGHT AT THE OPERA... AS THE STRONG, VIBRANT VOICE RINGS OUT--- SUDDENLY....
AHHHHH

THEN... AS THE AUDIENCE SITS SPELLBOUND, SHE COLLAPSES TO THE STAGE.
DEAD!... A DART IN HER NECK.... JUST LIKE ON HER PICTURE!
CARMEN, MY CARMEN!

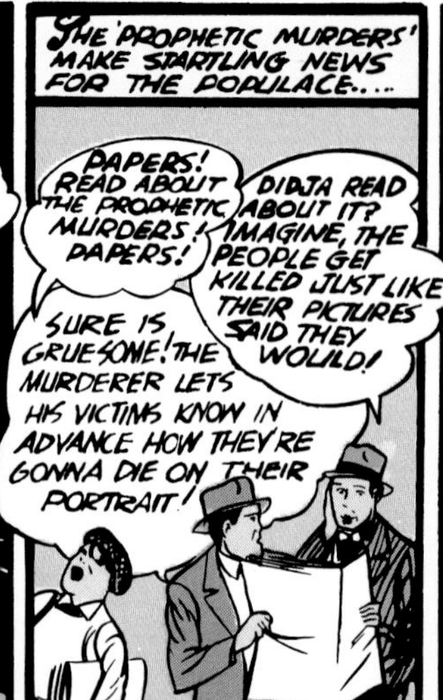
THE 'PROPHETIC MURDERS' MAKE STARTLING NEWS FOR THE POPULACE....
PAPERS! READ ABOUT THE PROPHETIC MURDERS! PAPERS!
DIDJA READ ABOUT IT? IMAGINE, THE PEOPLE GET KILLED JUST LIKE THEIR PICTURES SAID THEY WOULD!
SURE IS GRUESOME! THE MURDERER LETS HIS VICTIMS KNOW IN ADVANCE HOW THEY'RE GONNA DIE ON THEIR PORTRAIT!

NEXT DAY ANOTHER PATRON OF ANTAL'S MAKES A HORRIFYING DISCOVERY.
MY PICTURE.... THAT ROPE.. I'M GOING TO DIE LIKE THE OTHERS! I'M GOING TO BE HANGED!

A FRANTIC APPEAL IS MADE....
YOU'VE GOT TO PROTECT ME! I'M A DOOMED MAN! LOOK AT MY PICTURE!
DON'T WORRY, MR. WARREN, I'LL HAVE MEN STATIONED OUTSIDE YOUR ROOMS! NO ONE WILL BE ABLE TO GET IN HERE WHILE I'M AROUND!

THE HOME OF BRUCE WAYNE....
BET I KNOW WHERE YOU'RE GOING.... TO WARREN'S PLACE!
RIGHT! I'M KIND OF CURIOUS TO FIND OUT WHY PEOPLE WHO HAVE HAD THEI PORTRAITS PAINTED BY ANTAL SUDDENLY DIE!

THE SITE OF WARREN'S DUPLEX PENTHOUSE APARTMENT...
TOO MANY POLICE WATCHING THE ENTRANCES! I'LL HAVE TO TRY THE BACK OF THE BUILDING!

NOTHING BUT MY SUCTION PADS WILL GET ME TO THE TOP OF THIS BUILDING!

NOW.. FOR MY HUMAN FLY ACT!
THE CLINGING SUCTION PADS PUT ON, THE BATMAN BEGINS HIS PERILOUS ASCENT!

LIKE A HUGE BAT, THE BATMAN MOVES UP THE SHEER FACE OF THE BUILDING...
A FEW MOMENTS LATER, ATOP THE PENTHOUSE...
A HOARSE CRY ESCAPES THE BATMAN'S LIPS AS HE SEES...
GOOD LORD! WARREN! I'M TOO LATE!
SUDDENLY--AS THE DOOR OPENS...
I THINK WE'LL TAKE A LOOK AND SEE HOW WARREN IS!
WELL, NOBODY GOT PAST US, AND IT'S A CINCH THAT NO ONE COULD GET IN HERE BY THE WINDOWS, WHAT WITH A BLANK WALL OUTSIDE!
LOOK! WARREN! HANGING!
BATMAN! SO YOU'RE THE GUY THAT'S BEHIND THESE MURDERS! WELL, YOU SLIPPED THIS TIME!
SURELY YOU DON'T BELIEVE I HAD ANYTHING TO DO WITH THIS! MY METHODS MAY BE-ER, DIFFERENT, BUT I'VE ALWAYS WORKED ON THE SIDE OF THE LAW!
HE'S RIGHT! I DON'T BELIEVE HE DID IT!
A SUDDEN LEAP....
A LONG, SWEEPING SWING!
THE BATMAN LANDS ATOP THE STAIRS OF THE DUPLEX APARTMENT!
TOO BAD ROBIN ISN'T HERE! HE'D ENJOY THIS!

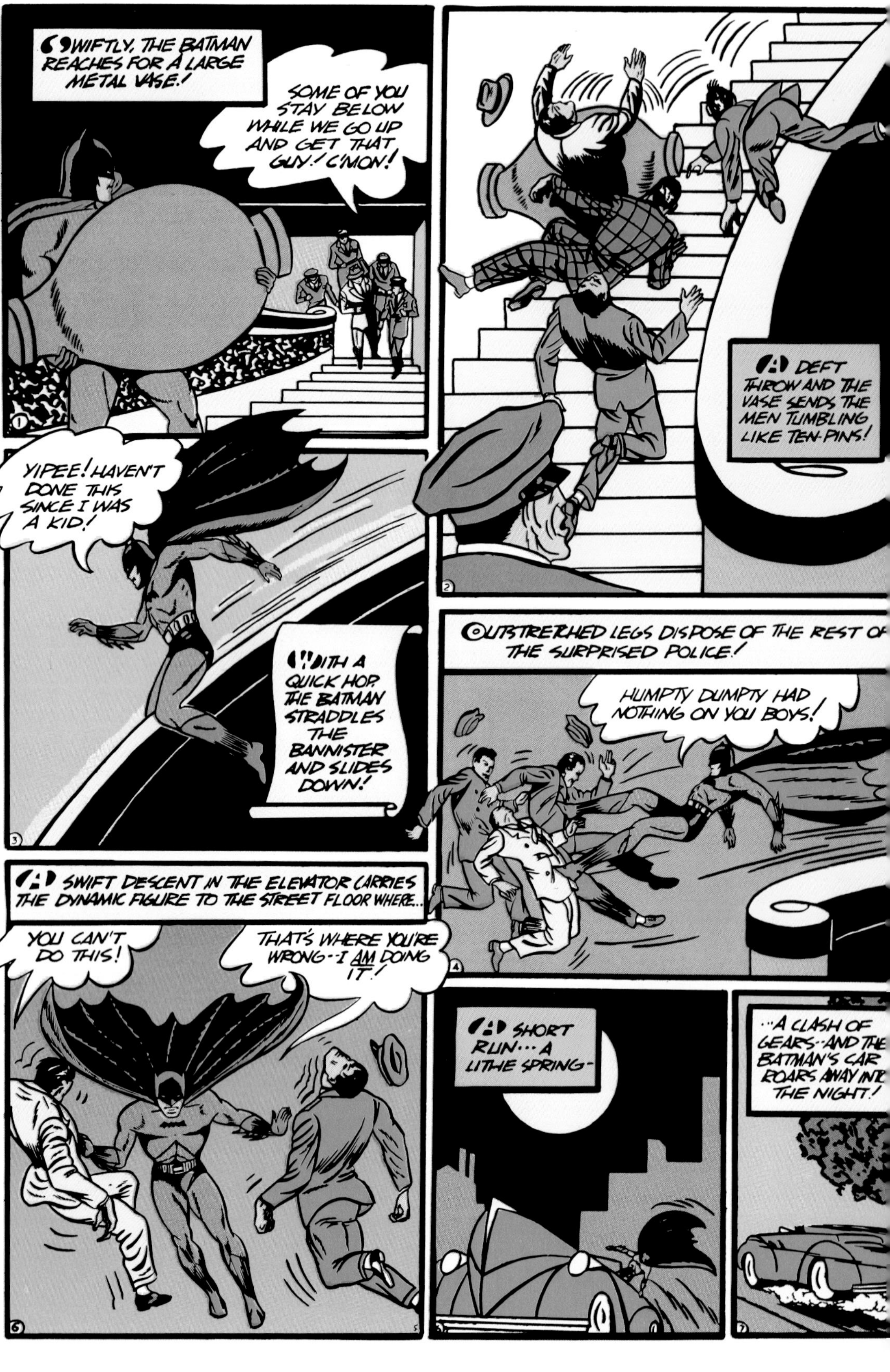

SWIFTLY, THE BATMAN REACHES FOR A LARGE METAL VASE!
SOME OF YOU STAY BELOW WHILE WE GO UP AND GET THAT GUY! C'MON!
A DEFT THROW AND THE VASE SENDS THE MEN TUMBLING LIKE TEN-PINS!
YIPEE! HAVEN'T DONE THIS SINCE I WAS A KID!
WITH A QUICK HOP, THE BATMAN STRADDLES THE BANNISTER AND SLIDES DOWN!
OUTSTRETCHED LEGS DISPOSE OF THE REST OF THE SURPRISED POLICE!
HUMPTY DUMPTY HAD NOTHING ON YOU BOYS!
A SWIFT DESCENT IN THE ELEVATOR CARRIES THE DYNAMIC FIGURE TO THE STREET FLOOR WHERE...
YOU CAN'T DO THIS!
THAT'S WHERE YOU'RE WRONG--I AM DOING IT!
A SHORT RUN... A LITHE SPRING-
...A CLASH OF GEARS--AND THE BATMAN'S CAR ROARS AWAY INT THE NIGHT!

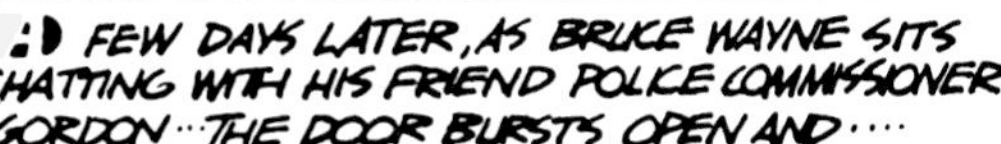
A FEW DAYS LATER, AS BRUCE WAYNE SITS CHATTING WITH HIS FRIEND POLICE COMMISSIONER GORDON···THE DOOR BURSTS OPEN AND····

COMMISSIONER, YOU'VE GOT TO DO SOME-THING! PEOPLE ARE CANCELLING ORDERS! THEY'RE SAYING EVERY TIME I PAINT SOME-ONE, HE DIES!

SOMEONE IS TRYING TO RUIN YOU, THAT'S EVIDENT! GOT ANY ENEMIES, ANTAL?
MIKOFF, THE ARTIST, BECAUSE HIS SISTER COMMITTED SUICIDE OVER ME!···OR, PERHAPS IT IS DRAKE! HE IS A JEALOUS MAN! HIS WIFE, YOU KNOW!

THEN AGAIN, MY AGENT, BLEEK··· I FIRED HIM! PERHAPS HE···
PERHAPS! BUT WOULD THESE PEOPLE KILL OTHER INNOCENT HUMANS JUST TO SETTLE AN OLD SCORE WITH YOU? THAT'S THE QUESTION!

ABRUPTLY--A WILD, DISHEVELED MAN ENTERS····
WYLIE! WHAT'S HAPPENED TO YOU?
PLENTY! WHEN I SAW MY PORTRAIT YESTERDAY, IT HAD BULLET HOLES IN IT! I FOOLISHLY KEPT IT TO MYSELF! LAST NIGHT I HAD A VISIT FROM THE MURDERER!

WE HAD QUITE A TUSSLE! HE NICKED ME IN THE ARM! I'M AFRAID HE'LL COME BACK AND TRY TO FINISH THE JOB!
LISTEN, WYLIE, I WANT YOU TO GO HOME AND STAY THERE! I'LL POST MEN OUTSIDE YOUR ROOM... YOU WON'T BE ABLE TO GET OUT AND THE MURDERER WON'T GET IN!!

COMMISSIONER GORDON HAS YET ANOTHER VISITOR···
WHAT SORT OF POLICE FORCE DO WE HAVE HERE, ANYWAY? LOOK WHAT I FOUND PIERCING MY PORTRAIT TODAY!··· AN ARROW!
WHAT!··ANOTHER ONE!
LOOKS LIKE THIS OFFICE IS THE MAIN HIGHWAY!
WHY, IT'S MR. TRAVERS! HIS WAS THE LAST PICTURE I MADE!

MR. TRAVERS, YOUR LIFE IS IN GREAT DANGER! I'LL ASSIGN SOME MEN TO·····
BAH! IF MY LIFE IS IN DANGER I'LL SAVE MYSELF! I'LL TAKE A CRUISE ON MY FRIEND RODGERS' YACHT! I WON'T BE AROUND WHEN THE MURDERER APPEARS! HAH!

THAT VERY NIGHT...
THEN I'M TO GO TO THE RODGERS YACHT ALONE, EH?
RIGHT! I'VE GOT TO DO A LITTLE INVESTIGATING OF SOME BANK STATEMENTS! REMEMBER, ROBIN, A MAN'S LIFE IS IN YOUR HANDS!

LATER, A SLEEK BOAT CLEAVES THE FOG-LADEN WATERS..
THE RODGERS YACHT!

THE NEXT MOMENT, ROBIN DRAWS ALONG-SIDE OF THE YACHT AND STEALTHILY CREEPS ABOARD..

ROBIN'S KEEN EYES SUDDENLY GAZE UPON A GHASTLY SCENE...
THE MURDERER-- ABOUT TO SHOOT AN ARROW AT TRAVERS!

SWIFTLY, THE BOY WONDER DRAWS FROM HIS BELT THE SLING AND
THIS HAD BETTER WORK! IF IT DOESN'T...

EVEN AS THE ARROW BOLTS FROM THE TAUT STRING, SO DOES THE STEEL PELLET STREAK FORWARD, STRIKING IT IN MID-AIR!
Z-I-N-G
8

THE BOY WONDER LEAPS AT THE GHASTLY MURDERER!
AN INTRUDER, EH?.. I'LL TAKE CARE OF YOU!

AS ROBIN STAGGERS, THE MENACING FIGURE PLACES AN RROW IN THE BOW...DRAWS THE STRING TAUT AND LETS FLY!
CURIOUS, EH?...WELL, CURIOSITY KILLED THE CAT...AND WILL YOU, TOO!
51

INSTINCTIVELY ROBIN SWERVES...AND THE WINGED MESSENGER OF DEATH HISSES PAST... PINNING HIS CAPE TO THE WALL!
WHEW!... CLOSE!...
R

EVEN AS THE BOY WONDER TEARS LOOSE, THE HOST-LIKE FIGURE RACES FORWARD AND LEAPS TO HIS WAITING BOAT!

BEST ESCAPE NOW BEFORE ALL THE CREW AWAKENS!

AS THE BOAT PLOWS FORWARD, ROBIN LEAPS AFTER IT....

BUT THE SPEED BOAT IS TOO FAST FOR EVEN THE ONDER BOY AND HE PLUNGES INTO THE SEA!...

MISSED! HECK!

HE'S ESCAPED, BUT AT LEAST I'VE SAVED A MAN'S LIFE! THAT'S SOMETHING!
9

LATER THAT EVENING..
HELLO! GOSH, YOU LOOK EXCITED! YOU MUST HAVE FOUND OUT SOMETHING TONIGHT!
I HAVE! I KNOW WHO OUR MURDERER IS--BUT I CAN'T PROVE IT! HATE IS NOT HIS MOTIVE--BUT THE ROOT OF ALL EVIL--MONEY!

NEXT DAY--
SAY, WHERE ARE YOU GOING? I THOUGHT YOU WERE WORKING ON OUR MURDER CASE!
I HAVE NO TIME FOR THAT NOW! I'M GOING TO HAVE MY PORTRAIT PAINTED BY ANTAL!

AT ANTAL'S STUDIO.
YOU--YOU WA YOUR PORTRA PAINTED--BY ME? DO YOU KNOW WHAT H HAPPENED TO THE OTHERS WHOSE PORTRAI I HAVE DONE?
UTTER FANTASTIC R STOP YOUR WILD BABBLING AND GET T WORK!

WORK ON THE PAINTING PROGRESSES RAPIDLY.
YOU ARE A BRAVE MAN, MR. WAYNE! WHAT COULD HAVE POSSESSED YOU TO HAVE YOUR PORTRAIT MADE?
VANITY--SHEER VANITY! I LIKE TO LOOK AT MYSELF! ALWAYS ENJOY LOOKING IN THE MIRROR!

DAYS LATER--
AT LAST--FINISHED! NEVER REALIZED HOW HANDSOME I AM! I SHALL HAVE TO HANG IT IN A PROMINENT PLACE!
EITHER H IS A MAN WITHOUT FEAR, OR THE MOST CONCEITED F I HAVE EVER SEE

RATHER GOOD LIKENESS, DON'T YOU THINK?
YEAH!.. SURE!..
WHAT'S GOT INTO HIM? WONDER IF HE'S GOT SOMETHING UP HIS SLEEVE?
10

THE FOLLOWING MORNING!...
SEEMS WE'VE HAD A VISITOR DURING THE NIGHT--MUST HAVE USED A SILENCER ON HIS GUN!
BULLET HOLES! THE MURDERER IS TELLING YOU THAT YOU'RE GOING TO BE SHOT IN THE HEAD! WHAT ARE YOU GOING TO DO?

DO?... WHY, NOTHING! I'M GOING TO SIT IN THIS CHAIR AND WAIT FOR THE MURDERER!
HUH?

THAT NIGHT, A SHADOWY FIGURE SILENTLY ENTERS THE WAYNE LIBRARY...

STEALTHILY, WITH SILENCER POISED, HE MAKES HIS WAY TO THE UNSUSPECTING MAN...

THEN, LEVELING HIS REVOLVER AT BRUCE'S HEAD...FIRES POINT-BLANK!

SUDDENLY, A VOICE... THE BATMAN!
THAT'LL BE ENOUGH OF THAT!
WHA... WHO... ARE YOU?

MY CARD, SIR!

THE BATMAN. AT YOUR SERVICE!
11

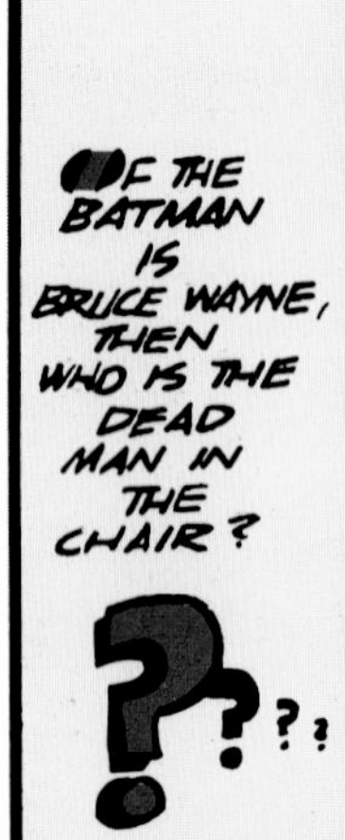

OKAY, DICK, IT'S ALL OVER! WELL, WHAT DO YOU THINK OF MY IDEA OF HAVING A DUMMY PUT OVER YOU?

IT WORKED SWELL! WHEN I WORKED MY HANDS IN THE SLEEVES, IT REALLY LOOKED ALIVE! AND SINCE I'M TOO SMALL TO REACH THE OF THE DUMMY, THE WENT OVER MY HEA INTO THE DUMMY'S HEAD.

THE MASK OFF, A FAMILIAR FACE IS REVEALED IN THE LIGHT - MR. WYLIE!

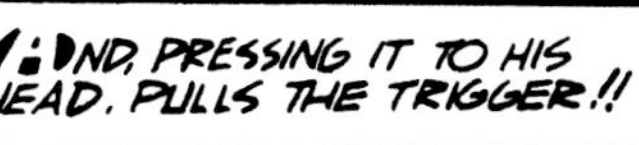

No. 43
The BATMAN
Detective
SEPT.
COMICS
10¢
BOB KANE

BATMAN
WITH
Robin
-THE BOY WONDER-
BY BOB KANE
"CRIME WAS KING WHEN A CZAR OF EVIL TOOK OVER A QUIET CITY AND CHANGED IT INTO THE BATTLEGROUND OF THE UNDERWORLD- THEN IT WAS THAT THE BATMAN AND HIS LAUGHING YOUNG AIDE, ROBIN, THE BOY WONDER, DECIDED TO BURROW INTO THIS DEN OF CRIME AND BRING AN END TO... "THE CASE OF THE CITY OF TERROR"
DECIDING TO TAKE A VACATION FROM CRIME-HUNTING, BRUCE WAYNE, IN REALITY THE BATMAN, AND YOUNG DICK GRAYSON, WHO IS ROBIN THE BOY WONDER, ARE ON A CROSS-COUNTRY TOUR..
CITY AHEAD! WE CAN PUT UP AT ONE OF THE LOCAL HOTELS FOR THE NIGHT!
THIS IS THE LIFE! NO WORRIES ABOUT GANGSTERS AND NUTTY SCIENTISTS WHO WANT TO RULE THE WORLD!
YOU SAID A MOUTHFUL! FOR AWHILE, AT LEAST, WE'RE GOING TO LEAD A QUIET, PEACEFUL LIFE OF EASE!
5 MILES

QUIET? PEACEFUL? BRUCE SPEAKS TOO SOON. FOR ALREADY THEY ARE ENTERING UPON ONE OF THE MOST EXCITING CASES THEY HAVE EVER TACKLED.
OKAY, KID... THIS IS OUR PLACE FOR THE NIGHT!
AFTER LOOKING AT IT, I CAN BELIEVE, "THERE'S NO PLACE LIKE HOME!"
HOT
SUDDENLY THE SOUND OF ANGRY VOICES REACHES THEIR EARS, AND THEY TURN TO SEE...
SO YOU DON'T LIKE THE WAY THE MAYOR'S RUNNIN' THINGS, EH, RYDER?
MAKIN' SOAP-BOX SPEECHES AIN'T YA?
I'VE GOT A RIGHT TO SAY WHAT I WANT! FREE SPEECH IS....
FREE SPEECH, EH?- YOU AIN'T GONNA BE SO FREE WITH IT FROM NOW ON!
OOH!
WE'LL FIX YOU FER GOOD!
AS THE CROWD LOOKS ON..... SUDDENLY THE TWO POLICEMEN BEAT THEIR VICTIM MERCILESSLY AND-
-AND THAT'S WHAT HAPPENS TO ANYBODY ELSE THAT TALKS AGAINST THE MAYOR!
TAKE A TIP AND KEEP YOUR LIPS BUTTONED UP-TIGHT!
THE DIRTY RATS!
I'D LIKE TO...
SHUT UP, YOU FOOL! MAYOR GREER MAY HAVE HIS MEN PLANTED AMONG US!
BRUCE QUESTIONS ONE OF THE MEN....
PARDON ME, BUT COULD YOU TELL ME WHY YOU PEOPLE ALLOW THIS SORT OF THING!? WHY DON'T YOU REPORT THOSE POLICEMEN?
UH- PARDON ME, I GOT WORK TO DO!
BRUCE QUESTIONS MORE PEOPLE, BUT WITH THE SAME RESULT- ALL LOOK AT HIM WITH FRIGHTENED EYES AND HURRIEDLY DEPART!
QUEER! ALL EVADE MY QUESTIONS! AND THEIR EYES-THERE WAS FEAR THERE-AND TERROR, TOO!
BRUCE, I HAVE A FEELING WE'RE NOT GOING TO HAVE MUCH OF A VACATION, AFTER ALL!
YOU'RE RIGHT! IT ENDS RIGHT NOW. TO-NIGHT WE'RE GOING TO WORK... AND FIND OUT WHY THESE PEOPLE ARE AFRAID!

LATER THAT NIGHT..... BRUCE WAYNE DONS A FANTASTIC GARB...
WHERE ARE YOU GOING?
I'M GOING TO PAY A VISIT TO A MR. CARTER, THE MOST RESPECTED MAN IN TOWN! HE'S RICH AND HAS A LOT OF INFLUENCE!

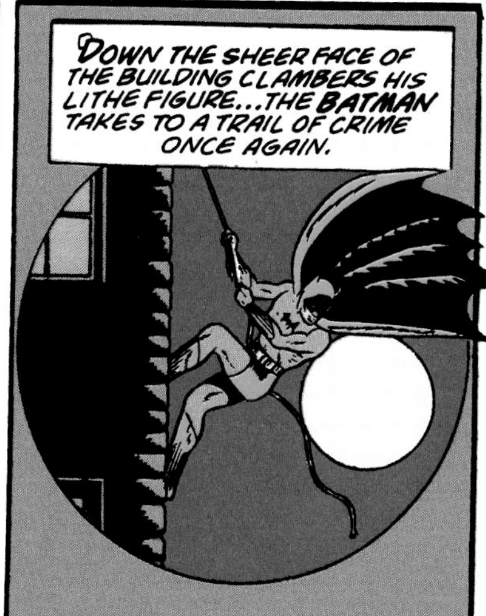
DOWN THE SHEER FACE OF THE BUILDING CLAMBERS HIS LITHE FIGURE... THE BATMAN TAKES TO A TRAIL OF CRIME ONCE AGAIN.

A POLICE CAR! CARTER HAS VISITORS!
MOMENTS LATER THE PERFECTLY TRAINED BODY CLEARS THE HIGH FENCE SURROUNDING THE CARTER HOME.

INSIDE THE HOUSE.....
YOU CAN'T ARREST ME! WHAT SORT OF TRUMPED UP CHARGE HAVE...
YOU BEEN SHOOTIN' YOUR MOUTH OFF AGAINST THE MAYOR!
YEAH, THAT'S LIBEL!

.....THEN A MOCKING VOICE...
WE'RE TAKIN' YOU TO JAIL AND... HUH?
SPEAKING OF JAIL--- HOW LONG HAVE YOU BEEN OUT?
WHA?
IT'S... IT'S THE BATMAN!

YOU'LL HAVE TO BE QUICKER THAN THAT!
WITH THE SWIFTNESS OF THOUGHT, A HAND REACHES OUT FOR THE NEARBY FLOOR LAMP, AND..
GET HIM! GET-UGH!

BEFORE THE MEN CAN RECOVER, THE BATMAN IS TWISTING AMONG THEM LIKE AN ANGRY CYCLONE!
MUCH BETTER THAN SLEEPING POWDER AND GETS THE SAME EFFECT!

I DON'T THINK THEY'LL BOTHER US FOR A WHILE!
THE BATMAN! JUST THE MAN I'VE BEEN LOOKING FOR TO CLEAN UP THIS TOWN! THE BATMAN— THE ONLY MAN!

NOW, CARTER, SUPPOSE YOU TELL ME WHY THUGS LIKE THAT PARADE AROUND IN POLICE UNIFORMS?
GLADLY! IT BEGAN WHEN OUR MAYOR SUDDENLY DIED IN OFFICE! THE NEXT MAN IN LINE TO FILL HIS PLACE WAS OF COURSE THE PRESIDENT OF THE CITY COUNCIL!

HARLISS GREER WAS THAT MAN! A CRAFTY POLITICIAN WHO TOOK ORDERS FROM OUR NUMBER 1 RACKETEER, "BUGS" NORTON! AS SOON AS HE GOT INTO OFFICE IT ALL STARTED...

GREER FIRED EVERY HONEST OFFICIAL, HE DISCHARGED ALL POLICEMEN AND REPLACED THEM WITH "BUGS" NORTON'S THUGS! WHEN CITY COUNCIL PROTESTED...
I CAN ANSWER THAT— THEY WERE BEATEN UP AND THREATENED! THE USUAL THING!

NOW, GAMBLING DENS HAVE SPRUNG UP, NEW TAXES BEEN LEVIED THAT PUT MONEY IN THE POCKETS OF GREER AND NORTON! OUR CITY HAS BECOME A RACKETEER'S PARADISE.
WHY NOT CALL THE GOVERNOR? CALL FOR AN INVESTIGATING COMMITTEE

THAT CALL MUST COME FROM THE MAYOR AND LOCAL AUTHORITIES, ACCORDING TO THE LAWS OF THIS STATE..... WE'RE LICKED!
NOT YET! IF YOU CAN'T BEAT THEM "INSIDE" THE LAW, YOU MUST BEAT THEM "OUTSIDE" IT-- AND THAT'S WHERE I COME IN!

FIRST, YOU GET TO SOMEPLACE WHERE YOU'LL BE SAFE FROM NORTON'S MEN! GET GOING!

AFTER CARTER HAS GONE....
NOW, AFTER TYING YOU UP AND HIDING YOU IN THE CELLAR, I'LL GET TO WORK ON MAYOR GREER AND "BUGS" NORTON!

THE NEXT NIGHT... THE OFFICE OF MAYOR GREER!
NORTON SAYS YOU GOTTA...
WHAT IS IT, BLACKIE?
SOME KID JUST GAVE ME THIS PACKAGE FOR YA!

WHEN THE BOX IS OPENED....
LOOK! A BAT!
WHAT? WHOSE IDEA OF A JOKE IS THIS?
JOKE?- IT AIN'T NO JOKE-NOT WITH THE BATMAN AROUND, IT AIN'T!
AND IN THE BOX... A NOTE...
Better get out of town Greer while you're able! To-morrow it may be too late!

AND AT THAT MOMENT AT "BUGS" NORTON'S PALATIAL HOME...
I TELL YA, BOSS, I'M WORRIED! CARTER AND THE BOYS HAS DISAPPEARED!
SHUT UP! I'LL DO ALL THE WORRYING AROUND HERE!

THEN, A GIGANTIC SHADOW IS THROWN ON THE WALL.....
WHAT TH'....
A BAT! A GIANT BAT!
HOLY CATS! THE BATMAN!

THERE IS A SUDDEN TINKLE OF BROKEN GLASS AS SOMETHING WHIZZES THROUGH THE WINDOW..
BOSS, LOOK OUT! HE'S THROWIN' SOMETHIN'!
5.

... A BIZARRE SIGHT GREETS THE GUNMEN'S EYES......
A BAT!
THE SIGN OF THE BATMAN!

THE BATMAN'S IN TOWN! WHAT'LL WE DO NOW, "BUGS"?
DO? NOTHING! HE CAN'T TOUCH US! WE OWN THIS TOWN!
THERE GOES THE TELEPHONE!
NORTON, THE BATMAN'S IN TOWN! I JUST GOT A......
YEAH, WE GOT ONE TOO! TAKE IT EASY! IF THE BATMAN COMES LOOKING FOR TROUBLE, HE'S GONNA GET IT!
IT'S GETTING LATE, BOYS, GET OVER TO HIGHWAY 4 AND MEET THE TRUCK WITH THE NARCOTICS SHIPMENT.
UNKNOWN TO THE RACKETEERS, A SMALL FIGURE HAS BEEN PERCHED OUTSIDE LISTENING-ROBIN, THE BOY WONDER!
NARCOTICS! -THAT'S DOPE! --BETTER TELL BATMAN RIGHT AWAY!
SOMETIME LATER, AS A TRUCK RUMBLES UNDER A LOW ARCH, TWO FIGURES LEAP OFF AND DROP TO ITS ROOF AS SILENTLY AND LIGHTLY AS TWO CATS...
TRAVELING ONWARD, THE TRUCK FINALLY HALTS BEFORE A PARKED CAR.
HYA! GOT A LOAD FOR YA!
BUGS IS ONE SMART GUY! THOSE STATE POLICE WOULD NEVER THINK A BIG TRUCK WOULD BE CARRYING A SMALL TRUNK OF DOPE WORTH A FORTUNE!
THEN, AS IF DROPPING FROM THE SKY, TWO FIGURES PLUMMET DOWNWARD.
JUST DROPPED IN TO PLAY A RETURN ENGAGEMEN
HOLY CATS! IT'S THE BATMAN-AND THAT ROBIN KID!

BROTHER-YOU'RE GOING ON A MERRY-GO-ROUND RIDE--- AND YOU DON'T KNOW IT!

ALWAYS OUTNUMBERED BUT NEVER OUTFOUGHT-THIS IS THE CODE OF THE BATMAN AND ROBIN-AND, AT THE MOMENT THEY ARE CERTAINLY LIVING UP TO IT...

THIS RIDE'S ON THE HOUSE, BOYS?!!

LATER THAT NIGHT AT "BUGS" NORTON'S HOME...
WELL, DID YA FIND OUT WHAT'S HOLDING UP THE BOYS AND THE SHIPMENT?
AND HOW! THE BOYS AND THE DOPE IS GONE, DISAPPEARED!
YEAH! AND LOOK WHAT WE FOUND STICKIN' TO THE TRUCK!
THE BATMAN!
AT THAT MOMENT, ON A LONELY COUNTRY ROAD... TWO WEIRD FIGURES ARE FRAMED AGAINST THE MOON.
THAT'S THAT! NOW FOR OUR NEXT STEP IN OUR "FRIGHT" CAMPAIGN AGAINST GREER AND NORTON!
I NOTICED A LOT OF KI SPENDIN MONEY ON SLOT-MACHIN IN TOWN! WHY NOT...
NOT A BAD IDEA! TO-MORROW I'LL GET TO WORK ON NORTON'S EVIL SLOT-MACHINES! - WITH A VENGEANCE!
NEXT DAY..... IN A SMALL CANDY STORE..
IT'S NOT RIGHT.... THESE BOYS SPENDING MONEY GAMBLING! I THINK..
NOBODY'S ASKIN' YOU TO THINK! YOU JUST KEEP YOUR MOUTH CLOSED!
KEEP IT CLOSED OR WE'LL SHUT IT FOR YA-- FOR GOOD!
WHERE'S OUR TAKE? WE WANT WHAT'S COMIN' TO US!
AND YOU'RE GOING TO GET IT!
I ALWAYS DID SAY TWO HEADS WERE BETTER THAN ONE!

YES! AND IF YOU WANT TO KEEP MY RESPECT YOU'LL STOP PLAYING THE MACHINES! ROBIN DOESN'T, SO WHY SHOULD YOU?
GEE, IF ROBIN THE BOY WONDER DON'T, I GUESS THAT'S GOOD ENOUGH FOR US! WE'LL TELL ALL THE KIDS!

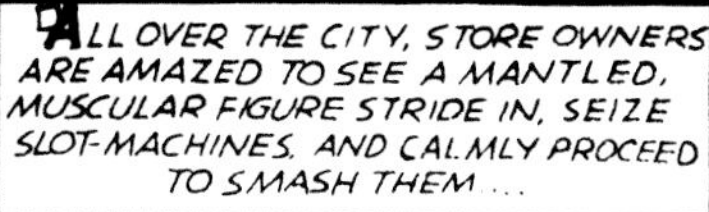
ALL OVER THE CITY, STORE OWNERS ARE AMAZED TO SEE A MANTLED, MUSCULAR FIGURE STRIDE IN, SEIZE SLOT-MACHINES, AND CALMLY PROCEED TO SMASH THEM....

WHEN YOU SEE NORTON'S MEN TELL THEM THE BATMAN DECIDED TO PLAY THE MACHINES HIS OWN WAY!
TH-THE BATMAN!

BOSS, THE BATMAN'S RUNNIN' ALL AROUND THE TOWN WRECKIN' OUR SLOT-MACHINES
THERE AIN'T ONE LEFT IN GOOD CONDITION!
THE BATMAN AGAIN!

THEN A SERIES OF STRANGE EVENTS TAKE PLACE.....MAYOR GREER'S "POLICEMEN" START TO DISAPPEAR.... A "POLICEMAN" MIGHT BE WALKING HIS BEAT WHEN....

...A COWLED SHADOW MIGHT DROP UPON A MAN.

OR A SMALL AGILE FIGURE MIGHT SUDDENLY FLASH THROUGH THE AIR..

THE DISAPPEARANCES BEGIN TO TAKE EFFECT
I CAN'T UNDERSTAND IT! TWENTY OF OUR MEN HAVE VANISHED DURING A FEW NIGHTS! WHO....
IT'S THE BATMAN! — THAT'S WHO! I DON'T LIKE IT! THE TOWNSPEOPLE ARE BEGINNING TO LAUGH AT US!.... A MAN AND A BOY AGAINST OUR "MOB" ... BAH!

AT THAT MOMENT, THAT "MAN AND BOY" ARE PLANNING THE LAST BATTLE IN THEIR CAMPAIGN....
OUR PLAN IS WORKING! THE PEOPLE ARE BEGINNING TO LAUGH AT GREER'S MEN!
GOOD! I KNEW THEY WOULD LOSE THEIR FEAR ONCE THOSE HOODLUMS WERE MADE TO LOOK LIKE FOOLS! NOW WE'RE READY! LISTEN!
NEXT DAY A GROUP OF BOYS ARE ASTONISHED TO SEE A FAMILIAR FIGURE APPEAR BEFORE THEM....
WH-WHY, YOU'RE ROBIN THE BOY WONDER!
YES! I'M ROBIN! I UNDERSTAND YOU FELLOWS HAVE A SMALL PRINTING PRESS! HOW WOULD YOU LIKE TO USE IT TO FIGHT RACKETEERS?
IT'S HIM, ALL RIGHT, JUST LIKE THE PICTURES OF HIM IN THE MAGAZINE! GEE WHIZ!
SURE! SWELL!
UNDER ROBIN'S INSTRUCTION, THE TINY PRESS POURS OU SHEAVES OF LEAFLETS.
MAYOR GREER MAY CONTROL THE BIG NEWSPAPER PRESSES, BUT NOT THIS SMALL ONE!
I'LL ROUND U A GANG TO HAN OUT THE PAPERS TO THE PEOPLE!
A VERITABLE HORDE OF YOUNGSTERS DISTRIBUTE LEAFLETS TO THE ASTOUNDED TOWNSPEOPLE
HERE'S SOME MORE FOR YA!
LOOK AT THIS!
HERE YA ARE! GET A COPY OF "THE TINY PRESS" FREE! ABSOLUTELY FREE!
HURRY UP! THEY'RE GOING LIKE HOT-CAKES!
CANDY STOR
BY NIGHTFALL, THE ENTIRE TOWN HAS READ AND HAS BEEN STIRRED BY A LEAFLET! THIS LEAFLET...
TINY
CITIZENS AWAKE!
RID YOURSELVES OF CORRUPT CITY OFFICIALS! FIGHT AGAINST RACKETEERS AND KILLERS! MEETING TO-NIGHT AT THE MUSIC HALL! ALL WELCOME!
A TYPICAL SCENE IN THE HOME OF ANY HONEST POLICEMAN FIRED BY MAYOR GREER..
BILL! WHY ARE YOU TAKING OUT YOUR OLD SERVICE REVOLVER?
A SMALL BOY STOPPED HERE BEFORE AND TOLD ME TO CARRY IT TO THE MASS MEETING TO-NIGHT! LOOKS LIKE THERE'S GOING TO BE SOME ACTION!
THAT NIGHT THE CROWDED MUSI HALL SEES A STARTLING SIGHT WHEN THE BATMAN MOUNTS TH SPEAKER'S PLATFORM!........ SKILLFULLY, THE BATMAN URGES THE PEOPLE TO BATTLE AGAINST THE RACKETEERS WHO HAVE ENSLAVED THEM.....
....AND CRIMINALS, LIKE THOSE WHO ARE DICTATORS OF YOUR OWN CITY!.... ARE YOU WITH ME?
YES! HE'S RIGHT!
LET'S GET RID OF THE RATS!
FIGHT!
YES LET'S FIGHT!

THE RETIRED POLICEMEN ARE ORGANIZED INTO SQUADS WHICH TAKE OVER GREER'S THUGS IN POLICE UNIFORM...
RAISE YOUR HANDS, RATS... WE DON'T WANT TO SHOOT UNLESS WE HAVE TO!
OKAY, OKAY, THEY'RE RAISED!
DON'T SHOOT! DON'T SHOOT!

IN A SHORT WHILE THE CITY HAS BEEN TAKEN OVER IN ORDERLY FASHION BY THE PEOPLE!
WELL, THE CITY IS IN OUR HANDS! WHAT DO WE DO NEXT?
YOU DON'T, BUT ROBIN AND I DO! WE'RE GOING TO GET MAYOR GREER AND "BUGS" NORTON!

AS ROBIN ENTERS GREER'S APARTMENT BY A BACKDOOR.....
GREER'S GONE!...I.... SAY, THERE HE IS NOW!
I'M NOT STAYING HERE TO BE PUT IN JAIL!

LIKE AN ARROW SHOT FROM A TAUT BOW, ROBIN'S BODY HURTLES INTO SPACE..
GOT TO TAKE THIS LONG CHANCE IF I EXPECT TO GET GREER!

STRONG HANDS CLUTCH THE LAMP-POST AND BREAK HIS FALL...
COME TO POPPA!

RELEASING HIS HOLD, THE WONDER BOY DROPS TO THE BACK OF THE FLEEING MAN!
NOT THINKING OF GOING ANYWHERE WERE YOU, GREER?
OOOF!

SMACK!
STICK AROUND--, WE'VE GOT THINGS TO TALK OVER!

AT THAT MOMENT NORTON PREPARES TO MAKE HIS EXIT....
BOSS, WE BETTER SCRAM! THAT MOB WILL BE HERE IN A MINUTE!
YOU'RE TELLING ME! C'MON!

THEN-A VOICE...
WERE YOU THINKING OF GOING AWAY WITHOUT SAYING GOOD-BYE TO ME? TSK! TSK!
IT'S HIM AGAIN!
WITH PLEASURE!
GET HIM!
DON'T TELL ANYBODY, FELLA, BUT YOU WERE FRAMED!
GRASPING A PICTURE, THE BATMAN SENDS THE FRAME SCALING ACROSS THE ROOM, WHERE...
AAWK

AS A SHOT WHISTLES OVER HIM, THE BATMAN CATAPULTS FORWARD IN ONE LIGHTNING MOVE...
YOU'RE NEXT!

... AND NOW, NORTON- LET'S SEE IF YOU CAN REALLY TAKE IT!

NO-NO! DON'T TOUCH ME!

HAVE YOU EATEN LATELY- OR DON'T YOU CARE TO ANSWER?
PPHFFT!

AND WITH THIS, I END THE NORTON-GREER COMBINE!
LATER, A GRATEFUL PEOPLE GATHER BEFORE TWO HEROIC FIGURES----
HURRAH FOR THE BATMAN AND ROBIN!
ONE THING PUZZLED US, BATMAN.... WHAT HAPPENED TO THE THUGS THAT VANISHED?
THEY'RE TIED AND GAGGED IN MR CARTER'S CELLAR! YOU'LL FIND THEM THERE ALL READY FOR JAIL!

NEXT DAY FINDS BRUCE WAYNE AND YOUNG DICK GRAYSON AGAIN SPEEDING UP A WINDING ROAD...
WELL, DICK, WE DIDN'T HAVE MUCH OF A VACATION IN THAT TOWN, BUT MAYBE WE'LL HIT A QUIET PLACE NEXT!
YEAH! MAYBE!- BUT I HAVE MY DOUBTS! WHEREVER WE GO WE FIND TROUBLE

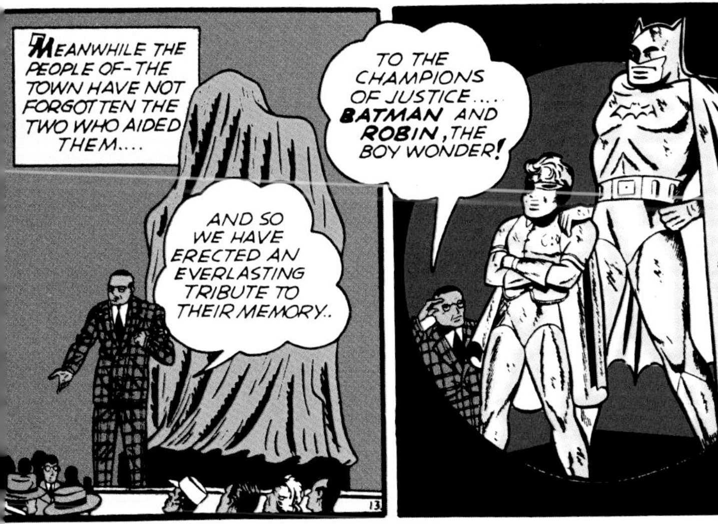
MEANWHILE THE PEOPLE OF-THE TOWN HAVE NOT FORGOTTEN THE TWO WHO AIDED THEM....
AND SO WE HAVE ERECTED AN EVERLASTING TRIBUTE TO THEIR MEMORY..
13
TO THE CHAMPIONS OF JUSTICE.... BATMAN AND ROBIN, THE BOY WONDER!
BOB KANE

AMERICA'S GREAT ADVENTURE STRIP CHARACTERS.
BATMAN AND ROBIN THE BOY WONDER
Original
WILL ASTOUND YOU IN THE NEXT ISSUE WITH THEIR MOST AMAZING ADVENTURE.
DON'T MISS IT!!!

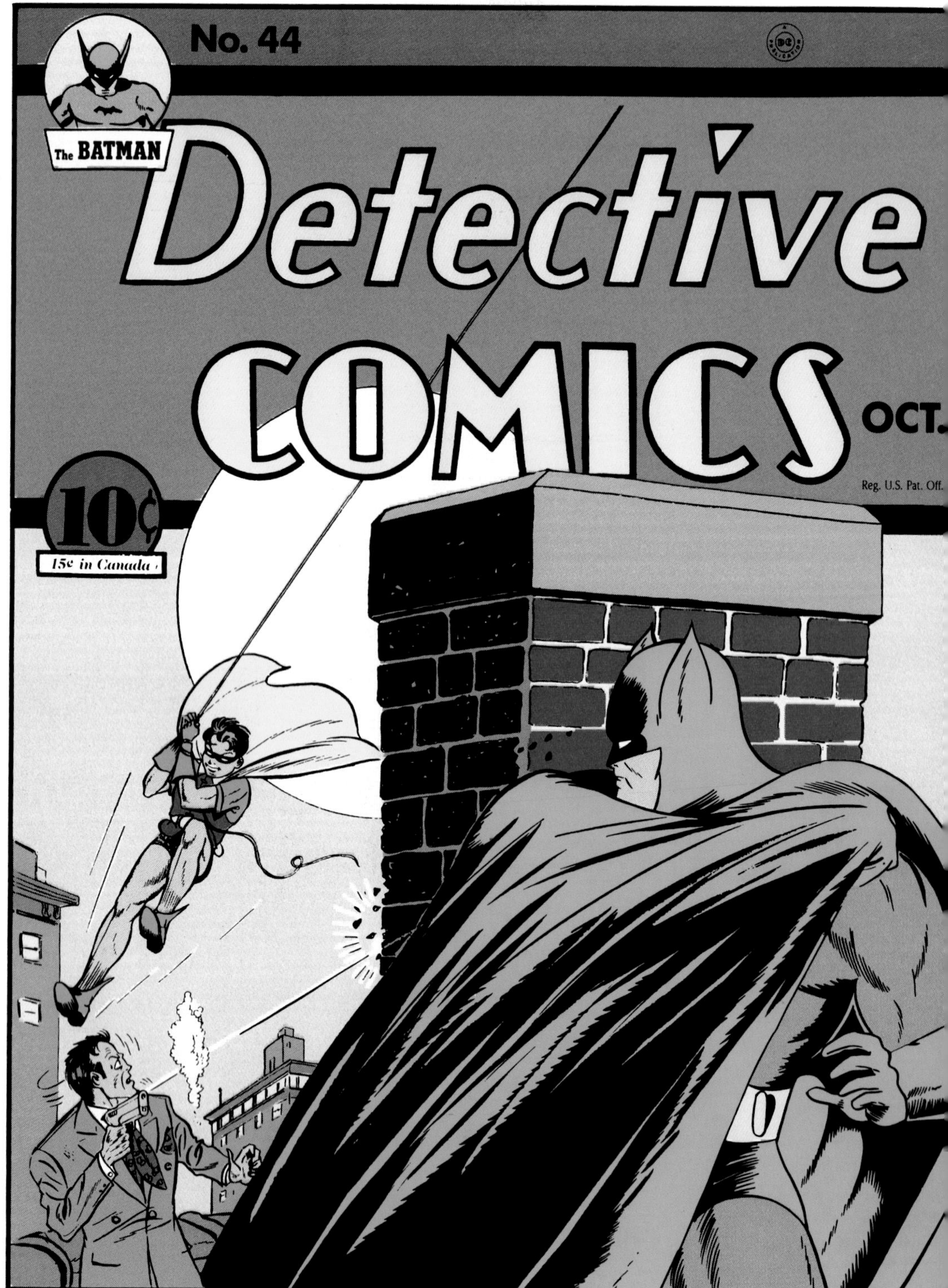
No. 44
The BATMAN
Detective
COMICS
OCT.
Reg. U.S. Pat. Off.
10¢
15¢ in Canada

BATMAN
WITH Robin -THE BOY WONDER-
BY BOB KANE
FANTASTIC ADVENTURE IN THE ALIEN WORLD, THIS IS WHAT AWAITS THE BATMAN AND ROBIN, THE BOY WONDER, AS THEY ENTER THE STRANGEST LAND THAT MAN COULD EVER DREAM OF ... A LAND OF BIG AND SMALL ...... A LAND SO BIZARRE AS TO BE BEYOND BELIEF.... THIS WAS "THE LAND BEHIND THE LIGHT!"
LATE ONE NIGHT YOUNG DICK GRAYSON, WHO IS IN REALITY ROBIN THE BOY WONDER, SITS UP READING AS HE AWAITS THE RETURN OF THE BATMAN....
THE CLOCK SUDDENLY TOLLS THE HOUR....
TWELVE O'CLOCK! -- GETTING LATE! WISH THE BATMAN WOULD GET BACK SOON!

GOSH! I'VE READ SO MUCH I'M GETTING GROGGY, SLEEPY! OH WELL, I'LL STAY UP A LITTLE LONGER.... MAYBE HE'LL COME SOON!

AS THE TIME CREEPS BY ON SILENT FEET, SUDDENLY....
BATMAN! YOU'RE LATE! WHAT TOOK YOU SO LONG!?
THAT CLUE I'VE BEEN FOLLOWING UP! IT LEAD ME STRAIGHT TO THE DOOR OF A DR. MARCO!

I'VE COME BACK FOR YOU! WE'RE GOING TO PAY A VISIT TO DR. MARKO AND FIND OUT JUST WHAT SORT OF MADMAN HE IS!
JUST A SEC. AND I'LL PUT MY COSTUME ON!

MOMENTS LATER, TWO MANTLED FIGURES WALK OUT INTO THE NIGHT... A MAN AND A BOY..... BATMAN AND ROBIN, THE BOY WONDER......

...ON AND ON...THROUGH THE DENSE FOG.....WALK THE TWO....UNTIL...
JUST LOOK AT THAT FOG! CAN HARDLY SEE A THING!
LOOK! THAT'S THE HOUSE THERE!

13 BLEAK STREET! THIS IS IT!
THAT NUMBER AND STREET JUST FIT THE HOUSE!

AS THE BATMAN TURNS THE KNOB THE DOOR OPENS SOFTLY, SILENTLY...
WELL..... WE MIGHT AS WELL GO IN!
SURE, WHY NOT? WE'VE GOT NOTHING TO LOSE...EXCEPT OUR LIVES!

ENTERING, THEY SUDDENLY STAND STOCK-STILL AS A MAN APPEARS BEFORE THEM.
COME IN! I HAVE BEEN EXPECTING YOU!

I SAW YOU SNOOPING AROUND HERE EARLIER THIS EVENING! CURIOUS, AREN'T YOU?
CURIOUS IS RIGHT!-CURIOUS TO FIND OUT WHAT SORT OF MAD SCHEME YOU'RE UP TO!

MAD SCHEME?! IS IT MADNESS TO HAVE DISCOVERED THE SECRET OF THE FOURTH DIMENSION?
THE FOURTH DIMENSION?

YES, AND I CAN PROVE IT-PROVE THAT I AM THE ONLY LIVING MAN TO HAVE SEEN THE LAND THAT LIES IN THE FOURTH DIMENSION!

THE BATMAN AND ROBIN ARE LED INTO THE HIGH VAULTED INTERIOR OF A LARGE ROOM.....
I PUT THE SWITCH SO, AND LIGHT IS FORMED... A VEIL OF LIGHT BEYOND WHICH IS THE FOURTH DIMENSION!
THAT STILL DOESN'T PROVE ANYTHING!

YOU CAN FIND NO BETTER PROOF THAN THIS!
LOOK!
AS DR. MARKO WALKS INTO THE LIGHT, A STARTLING THING HAPPENS... HIS BODY BEGINS TO DISAPPEAR!

IN A MOMENT THE FIGURE OF DR. MARKO HAS VANISHED, AS IF IN THIN AIR!
GONE! IT'S UNBELIEVABLE!
RIGHT IN FRONT OF OUR EYES!

I DON'T KNOW WHERE MARKO HAS GONE, BUT THERE'S ONE SURE WAY OF FINDING OUT.... I'M GOING TO WALK INTO THE LIGHT!
THEN I'M GOING WITH YOU!

WITHOUT A MOMENT'S HESITATION THE TWO DAUNTLESS FIGURES WALK INTO THE VEIL OF LIGHT! WHAT SORT OF LAND... WHAT SORT OF DANGERS WILL THEY FIND?? WHAT LIES BEYOND?

IT'S JUST LIKE WALKING THROUGH A CURTAIN INTO ANOTHER WORLD!
THIS IS ANOTHER WORLD.. THE WORLD OF THE FOURTH DIMENSION
JUST LOOK AT THE SIZE OF THOSE TREES
I WONDER WHERE DR. MARKO IS? HE ISN'T AROUND!
SUDDENLY.....
3
HMM! THIS IS A STRANGE PLACE....A VERY STRANGE PLACE..
BOY, I'LL SAY..
BATMAN AND ROBIN GAZE UPON A STAGGERING SIGHT
HEY! A MAN! ..A GIANT!
WHY, HE MUST BE AT LEAST THIRTY FEET TALL!
SO THE "SMALL ONES" NOW TRESPASS ON THE KING'S PROPERTY! .. THAT MEANS DEATH!
THE TOWERING COLOSSUS HOLDS THE BATMAN AND ROBIN IN HIS HUGE HANDS AS IF THEY WERE TOYS.
5
STRANGE! YOU ARE BIGGER THA THE "SMALL ONE VERY STRANGE THINK I WILL PUT YOU IN CELL AN INFORM T KING!

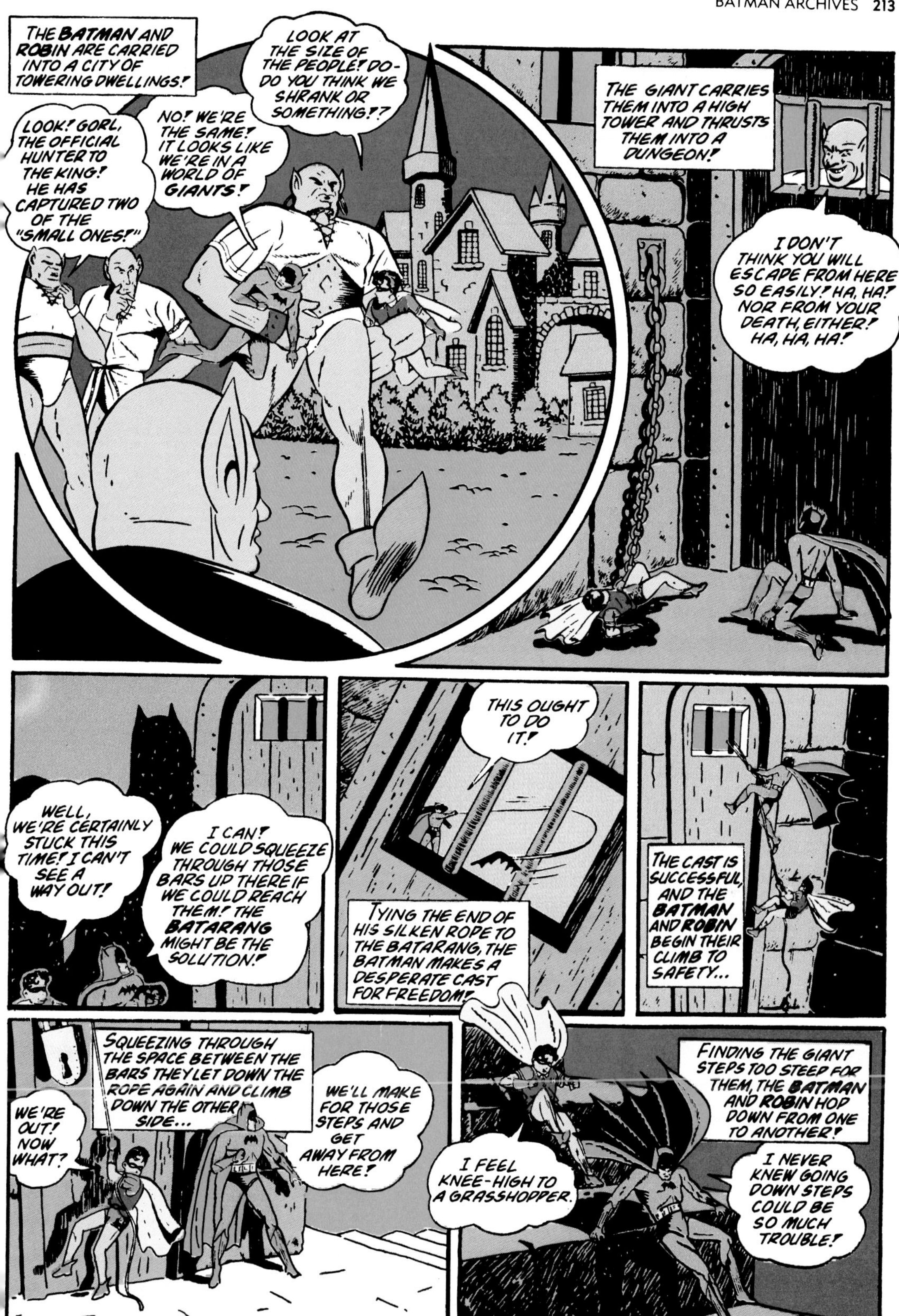
THE BATMAN AND ROBIN ARE CARRIED INTO A CITY OF TOWERING DWELLINGS!
LOOK! GORL, THE OFFICIAL HUNTER TO THE KING! HE HAS CAPTURED TWO OF THE "SMALL ONES!"
NO! WE'RE THE SAME! IT LOOKS LIKE WE'RE IN A WORLD OF GIANTS!
LOOK AT THE SIZE OF THE PEOPLE! DO-DO YOU THINK WE SHRANK OR SOMETHING!?
THE GIANT CARRIES THEM INTO A HIGH TOWER AND THRUSTS THEM INTO A DUNGEON!
I DON'T THINK YOU WILL ESCAPE FROM HERE SO EASILY! HA, HA! NOR FROM YOUR DEATH, EITHER! HA, HA, HA!
WELL, WE'RE CERTAINLY STUCK THIS TIME! I CAN'T SEE A WAY OUT!
I CAN! WE COULD SQUEEZE THROUGH THOSE BARS UP THERE IF WE COULD REACH THEM! THE BATARANG MIGHT BE THE SOLUTION!
THIS OUGHT TO DO IT!
TYING THE END OF HIS SILKEN ROPE TO THE BATARANG, THE BATMAN MAKES A DESPERATE CAST FOR FREEDOM!
THE CAST IS SUCCESSFUL, AND THE BATMAN AND ROBIN BEGIN THEIR CLIMB TO SAFETY...
SQUEEZING THROUGH THE SPACE BETWEEN THE BARS THEY LET DOWN THE ROPE AGAIN AND CLIMB DOWN THE OTHER SIDE...
WE'RE OUT! NOW WHAT?
WE'LL MAKE FOR THOSE STEPS AND GET AWAY FROM HERE!
FINDING THE GIANT STEPS TOO STEEP FOR THEM, THE BATMAN AND ROBIN HOP DOWN FROM ONE TO ANOTHER!
I FEEL KNEE-HIGH TO A GRASSHOPPER.
I NEVER KNEW GOING DOWN STEPS COULD BE SO MUCH TROUBLE!
5

TWO DOORS!
YOU LOOK THROUGH ONE AND I THE OTHER AND WE'LL SEE IF ANYONE IS ABOUT!
AS ROBIN WALKS CAUTIOUSLY TOWARD THE DOOR, A CAT SOFTLY, SILENTLY, STALKS BEHIND A NORMAL SIZE HOUSE-CAT... BUT NOW AS LARGE AS A TIGER!
EVEN AS THE CAT LEAPS, SOME INSTINCT WARNS ROBIN OF IMPENDING DANGER, AND HE SWERVES TO THE SIDE!
HUH?
FURIOUS, THE CAT MAKES ANOTHER BOUND TO ITS INTENDED VICTIM, WHEN A MANTLED FIGURE LAUNCHES FORWARD TO LAND UPON ITS BACK... BATMAN!
NOT SO FAST PUSSY!
FLAILING OUT WITH SHARP CLAWS THE CAT TRIES TO SHAKE HIM OFF, BUT THE BATMAN HOLDS ON LIKE GRIM DEATH....
NOW'S MY CUE TO SING "HOLD THAT TIGER!"
..... HIS MUSCLES BUNCHING FROM THE STRAIN, THE BATMAN DRAWS HIS ARM TIGHTER...TIGHTER... UNTIL HE FEELS THE BODY GO LIMP BENEATH HIM.
6
NOW I KNOW HOW A MOUSE FEELS! THE SIZE OF THAT CAT!
DON'T FORGET WE'RE IN A LAND OF GIANTS, SO THAT EVERYTHING IS LARGE COMPARED TO US!

TWO GIANT HANDS SUDDENLY SCOOP UP THE TWO FIGURES!
TRYING TO ESCAPE, EH? THE KING SHOULD KNOW OF THIS!
BATMAN AND ROBIN ARE TAKEN TO THE KING!
I HAVE CAPTURED TWO OF THE "SMALL ONES" YOUR MAJESTY! IT SEEMS TO ME THAT THEY ARE SPIES.
GORL, YOU ALWAYS DISTURB ME WHEN I'M EATING! WHAT IS IT NOW?
THEN, THEY MUST KNOW WE PLAN TO WAR UPON THEM TO-MORROW! BUT, THEY SEEM MUCH LARGER THAN THE "SMALL ONES"?
PERHAPS THE "SMALL ONES" ARE TRYING TO BREED A RACE OF GIANTS!
THEN WE ARE IN DANGER! KILL THEM! ACT AT ONCE!
EXACTLY MY SENTIMENTS! NOTHING LIKE QUICK ACTION!
WITH STARTLING SUDDENNESS THE BATMAN PICKS UP A SHAKER OF PEPPER AND....
SPICY STUFF, EH, KING, OLD BOY!
PEPPER!! OH, MY EYES! MY EYES! THEY'RE BURNING!
ATCHOO! KILL THEM! ATCHOO! ATCHOO!
I'LL SMASH YOU FLAT!
THANKS FOR THE SPRING BOARD, PAL!
MISSED!

OH! MY NOSE!
THAT'S WHAT YOU GET FOR BEING TOO NOSY!
AS THE GIANT TRIES TO CATCH ROBIN, THE BOY SCURRIES THROUGH HIS LEGS....
FIRST I'LL ATTEND TO THIS TROUBLESOME BRAT....WH---?
CRASH!
LOOKS LIKE I'VE STRUCK THE SEAT OF YOUR TROUBLE, CHUM
THE BATMAN TAKES ADVANTAGE OF GORL'S PECULIAR STANCE, AND HURTLES THROUGH THE AIR TO LAND WITH AMAZING RESULTS...
AS A GUARD RUSHES UP, ROBIN PREPARES TO BATTLE AS ONCE DID DAVID WITH GOLIATH..WITH THE SLING!
COME ON, FELLA, THE BIGGER THEY ARE, THE HARDER THEY FALL!
WITH UNERRING ACCURACY THE STEEL PELLET ZIPS THROUGH THE AIR AND SLAMS INTO THE GIANT'S TEMPLE!
HOW DID THAT STRIKE YOUR FANCY?
SEIZING THE OPPORTUNITY, THE BATMAN AND THE BOY WONDER SUDDENLY SEND THEIR ROPES FLYING ABOUT THE GUARD'S TREMENDOUS HULK.
BRAINS OVER BRAWN, ROBIN, EH?
YOU SAID IT!
8.

BEFORE THE GIANT CAN RECOVER, THEY SUDDENLY JERK ON THE ROPES.... HARD!
AH... AHHH... AHHH!!
ATCHOO! GUARDS! GUA.... (SPLUB)
COULDN'T GO WITHOUT GIVING YOU A PRESENT - HERE'S A NICE SOFT FRUIT!
C'MON, THE GUARDS WILL BE HERE IN A MINUTE!
BETTER TAKE THIS, WE MIGHT NEED WEAPONS!
THE BATMAN AND ROBIN TAKE TO THE WINDOW FOR MEANS OF ESCAPE....
WE CAN'T GET DOWN THIS WAY! - AND I CAN HEAR THOSE GUARDS COMING!
PARDON ME, BUT I'VE JUST HAD A BRAIN STORM!
THAT'S AN UMBRELLA! WHAT....?
WRONG, ROBIN! THIS IS NO UMBRELLA, THIS IS OUR PARACHUTE!
A MOMENT LATER, THE HUGE UMBRELLA UNFURLED, THE INTREPID DUO HOP OFF INTO SPACE!...
NOTHING LIKE PREPARING FOR A RAINY DAY, I ALWAYS SAY!
...AND ALIGHT SAFELY!
MADE IT!
YES, AND NOW I SUGGEST WE SEE HOW FAR AWAY FEET CAN TAKE US FROM THIS CHARMING LOCALE!

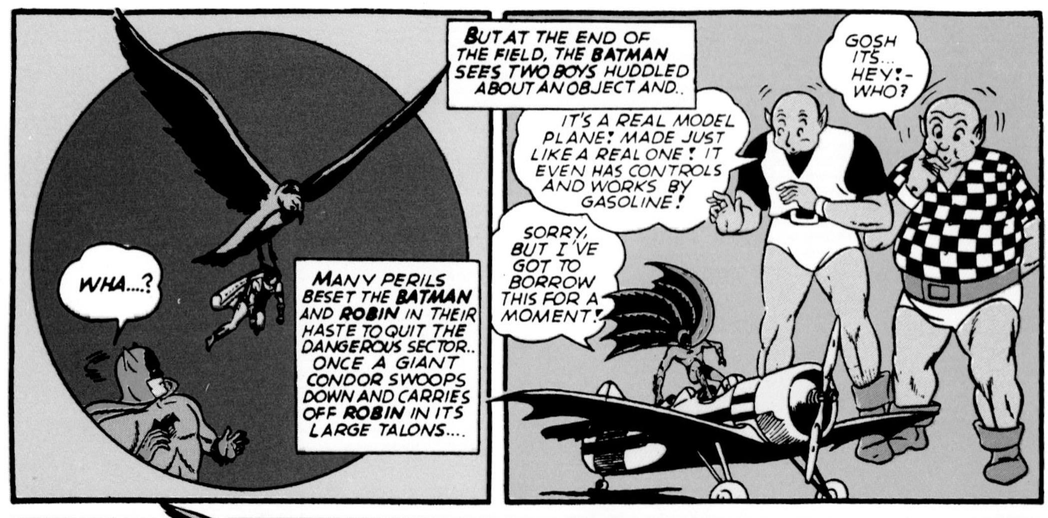
WHA...?
MANY PERILS BESET THE BATMAN AND ROBIN IN THEIR HASTE TO QUIT THE DANGEROUS SECTOR.. ONCE A GIANT CONDOR SWOOPS DOWN AND CARRIES OFF ROBIN IN ITS LARGE TALONS....
BUT AT THE END OF THE FIELD, THE BATMAN SEES TWO BOYS HUDDLED ABOUT AN OBJECT AND..
IT'S A REAL MODEL PLANE! MADE JUST LIKE A REAL ONE! IT EVEN HAS CONTROLS AND WORKS BY GASOLINE!
GOSH ITS... HEY!- WHO?
SORRY, BUT I'VE GOT TO BORROW THIS FOR A MOMENT!

IN A BIZARRE BATTLE, THE MODEL PLANE OVERTAKES THE GIANT CONDOR, AND THE BATMAN HURLS HIS KNIFE WITH UNCANNY SKILL...

AS ROBIN PLUMMETS DOWN, THE PLANE DIVES UNDER HIM IN PERFECT TIMING AND....
GOOD CATCH, EH, ROBIN?
NOT BAD!

LATER...
WE WOULD RUN OUT OF GAS!
LOOK! LOOK!
10.

SWERVING PAST THE GAPING JAWS, THE BATMAN THRUSTS THE FORK FORWARD IN ONE LITHE MOVE...
THIS HAD BETTER WORK ..OR WE'RE GONERS!
A CROCODILE! HE'S ABOUT AS BIG AS A DRAGON!

BELLOWING WITH PAIN AS THE FORK PIERCES HIS EYE, THE BEAST TURNS TAIL.....
YOU'VE DONE IT! YOU'VE BEATEN HIM!
SHADES OF ST. GEORGE!!
IMMEDIATE DANGER AVERTED, THE TWO DRIFT DOWN STREAM UNTIL..
ROBIN, DID YOU NOTICE HOW SMALL EVERYTHING HAS GOTTEN? QUEER, THAT.... A CITY.... -- A TINY CITY
LOOK OVER THERE! DR. MARKO!
YOU!- YOU ARE SAFE!
DR. MARKO EXPLAINS
SO YOU ESCAPED TO THESE PEOPLE WHEN YOU SAW US CARRIED OFF BY THE GIANT?
YES! THESE ARE GOOD PEOPLE! THIS IS THE LAND OF THE "SMALL ONES"!!
SMALL IS RIGHT!
QUEER, ISN'T IT? BY SOME FREAK OF NATURE THIS WORLD IS DIVIDED INTO A LAND OF GIANTS AND MIDGETS!
THEY'RE JUST LIKE SMALL, HAPPY CHILDREN!
WE WOULD BE MUCH HAPPIER IF IT WEREN'T FOR THE GIANTS! THEY ARE VERY EVIL! VERY EVIL!
HEP.. HEP...HEP
WHAT CAN WE DO? THEY WILL TRAMPLE US DOWN! THEY ARE SO HUGE! WE CAN NEVER HOPE TO SURVIVE! WOE IS US.. OH WOE!!
I WONDER.... I WONDER? I THINK I HAVE A PLAN THAT MAY WORK!...AT LEAST I HOPE SO..... LISTEN..
THE BATMAN HASTILY INFORMS THE KING OF THE INTENDED INVASION BY THE GIANTS.....
THE NEXT DAY THE TINY DWELLINGS SHAKE AS WITH EARTH-TREMBLING STEPS THE GIANTS STRIDE INTO VIEW!
D..DO...N-NOT B-BE..A...FRAID! ATTACK THE ENEMY!!
THE GIANTS
THE GIANTS ARE COMING!

1
DEATH TO THE SMALL ONES!
INEXORABLY THE GIANTS ADVANCE, TRAMPLING DOWN EVERYTHING IN THEIR PATH
DEATH!
DESPERATELY, THE TINY DEFENDERS BRING THEIR OUTMODED CANNON INTO PLAY..
FIRE!
2
FUNNIES
3
BUT THE MOCKING GIANTS HIT THE CANNON-BALLS BACK TO THE TINY ARMY!
HA HA! WE PLAY BALL!
4
FEARLESSLY THE TINY PEOPLE FIGHT THE GIANTS HAND TO HAND IN THEIR DETERMINATION TO SAVE THEIR LAND FROM THE INVADERS!
I'LL MAKE A HOME RUN!
1..... 2....2½ ...3 FIRE!
5
THE LITTLE PEOPLE LET GO OF THE BEAN SHOOTER AND......
12

SUDDENLY A SQUADRON OF TINY PLANES APPEAR AND TOSS OBJECTS THAT HIT THE GROUND AND BURST OPEN! BEES, HORNETS, GNATS, MOSQUITOES EMERGE AND DESCEND IN A SWARM UPON THE VAST AREAS OF SKIN SO BRAZENLY EXPOSED BY THE GIANTS..
I'M STUNG! OUCH!
OUCH!
OUCH!
IT WORKED! YOUR PLAN OF PUTTING THOSE INSECTS IN BAGS THAT BURST WHEN THEY HIT THE GROUND WORKED!
AS MORE INSECTS SWARM TOWARDS THEM, THE GIANTS SUDDENLY LOSE THEIR TASTE FOR BATTLE AND FLEE IN MORTAL TERROR....
THE GIANTS ARE FLEEING! WE HAVE WON, WE HAVE WON!
BUT ONE GIANT DOES NOT FLEE, FOR HE SUDDENLY SPIES AND SPRINGS AFTER ROBIN... GORL!
YOU! I'LL FIX YOU NOW! I'LL CRUSH YOU TO BITS!
OH OH! TROUBLE!
WITH GIANT STRIDES HE COMES NEARER ..NEARER... EVER CLOSING THE GAP... NEARER, UNTIL....
HA! I'VE GOT YOU NOW!
NO NO!
WAKE UP! .. WAKE UP!
NO...N.. ..HUH? ..WHA ...
IT DIDN'T HAPPEN! IT WAS A DREAM! ...A DREAM!
SAY, WHAT'S THE MATTER WITH YOU? WHAT'RE YOU MUMBLING ABOUT?
WHAT WERE YOU READING, ANYWAY? OH, OH!
GIANTS AND DWARFS IN MYTH AND FABLE
THAT'S POTENT STUFF, KID!.. LIKE AS NOT TO GIVE YOU BAD DREAMS..... NIGHTMARES!
YOU'RE TELLING ME!
NEXT MONTH BACK TO REALITY ..THE REALITY OF THE BATMAN AND ROBIN THE BOY WONDER IN THEIR CEASELESS FIGHT AGAINST Crime IN A NEW BREATH-TAKING Adventure

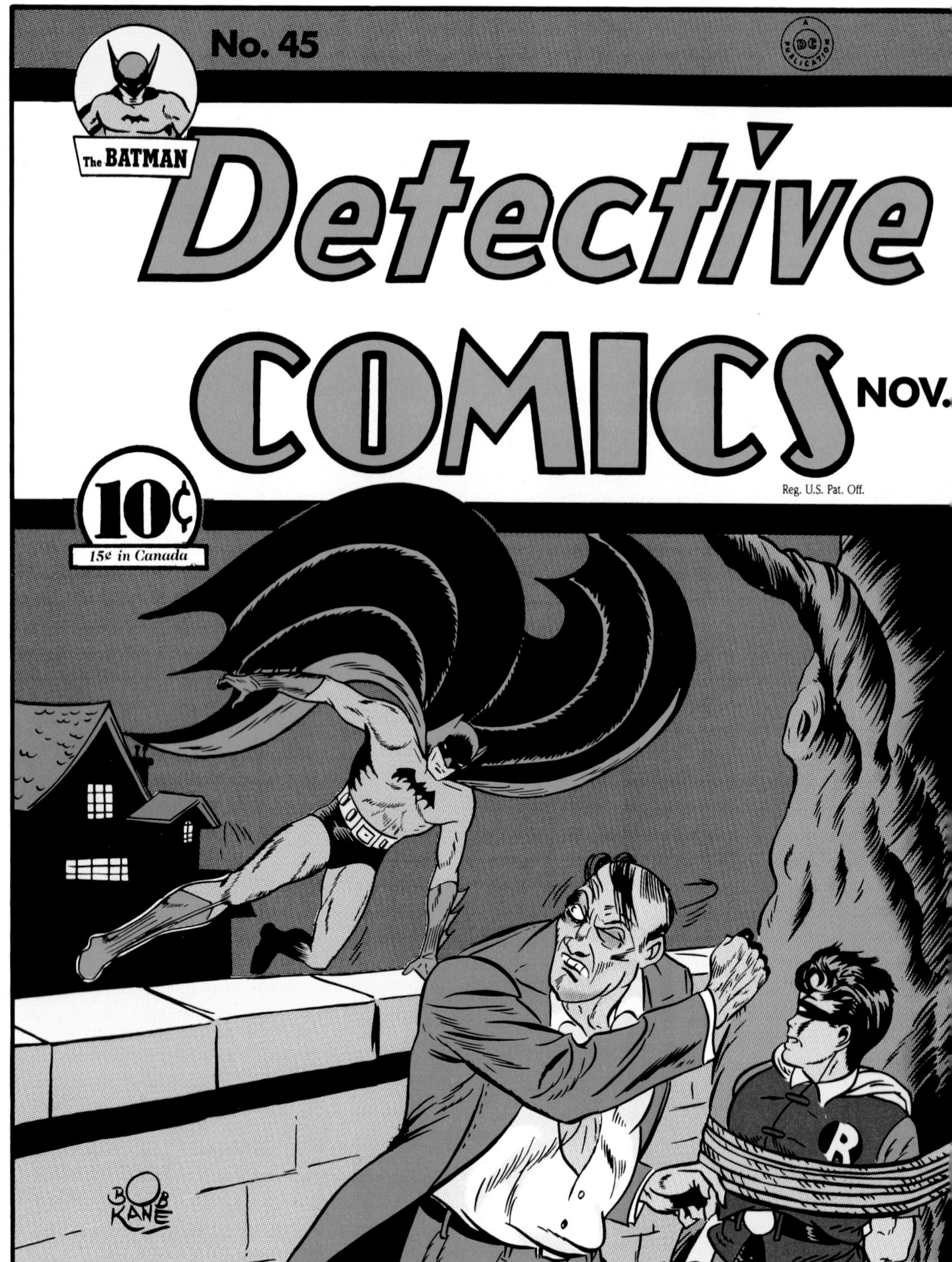
No. 45
A DC PUBLICATION
The BATMAN
Detective
COMICS
NOV.
Reg. U.S. Pat. Off.
10¢
15¢ in Canada
BOB KANE

BATMAN
WITH Robin
-THE BOY WONDER-
BY BOB KANE
THE JOKER - WHAT MAN OR WOMAN DOES NOT TREMBLE AT THE SOUND OF THAT DREADFUL NAME? WHAT NEW TERROR WILL HE BRING UPON THEM? - WHERE WILL HE STRIKE NEXT? - SOON, ONLY TOO SOON, WILL THEY KNOW! AND SOON THE COURAGEOUS BATMAN AND PLUCKY ROBIN, THE BOY WONDER, WILL OPPOSE THIS MAD HARLEQUIN OF HATE AS THEY ENTER UPON "THE CASE OF THE LAUGHING DEATH!"
Symphony in Murder
#1
NIGHTFALL, AND AS THE SHADOWS LENGTHEN, A HOODED FIGURE WATCHES A GROUP OF FIVE MEN SKULK TOWARD THE BUILDING THAT IS THE PRIVATE MUSEUM OF JOSHUA SLADE.........

AS THE CARETAKER OPENS THE DOOR IN ANSWER TO INSISTENT RINGING OF THE DOORBELL
WHAT'S THE IDEA OF... ...UGH!
THAT GOT 'IM!
SWIFTLY, THE COWLED FIGURE OF THE BATMAN GOES INTO ACTION
I FELT THERE WAS SOMETHING SUSPICIOUS ABOUT THEIR ACTIONS, AND NOW I KNOW IT!
INSIDE THE MARAUDERS GO ABOUT THEIR CHOSEN TASKS
OKAY, BOYS, LET'S GET TO WORK! FRANKIE, YOU TAKE CARE O' THE BURGLAR ALARM!
THIS JOB IS GONNA BE A CINCH!
SORRY, GENTLEMEN! BUT I DON'T THINK YOU'RE GOING TO DO MUCH OF YOUR WORK TO-NIGHT!
THEN LIKE A DARK THUNDER CLOUD, THE BATMAN STORMS INTO THE ROOM!
THE BATMAN!
NO GUNS! IT MIGHT DRAW THE COPS! CLUB 'IM DOWN!
AS THE DESPERATE THUGS RACE TOWARD HIM, THE BATMAN SEIZES A LANCE.....
HAVEN'T DONE THIS SINCE MY COLLEGE DAYS, BUT...
IT SEEMS I HAVEN'T FORGOTTEN HOW TO POLE-VAULT!
WHAT TH'
HUH?
AND STREAKING FORWARD, PLUNGES THE POINT INTO THE FLOOR--- AND VAULTS OVER THE ASTOUNDED GANGSTERS!
AS HIS LITHE BODY CLIMBS UPWARD, THE BATMAN RELEASES HIS HOLD UPON THE LANCE AND REACHES FOR THE CHANDELIER.

GET
HAT
UY!
THE WAY THAT GUY FLIES AROUND, YOU'D THINK HE WAS A BIRD!
...SWINGING IN A TREMENDOUS ARC, THE DARK KNIGHT RELEASES HIS HOLD AND HURTLES TO THE STAIRWAY....
NOTHING LIKE AN ACTIVE LIFE TO KEEP YOU IN GOOD SHAPE!
EVEN AS THE MEN RACE FORWARD, THE THE BATMAN LEAPS AGAIN.... THIS TIME FOR A HANGING DRAPERY...
SWAYING LIKE SOME GIANT PENDULUM, HIS OUTSTRETCHED LEGS ENCOUNTER A TOWERING STATUE....
LIKE A FALLING TREE, THE HUGE MASS OF SCULPTURE PLUNGES DOWN TO PIN THE FLEEING MEN....
NEXT TIME TAKE OFF YOUR HATS VHEN YOU'VE GOT COMPANY!
HAPPY NIGHTMARES!
POWERFUL BLOWS SEND THE MEN TO DREAMLAND!

THE WHINE OF A POLICE SIREN FILLS THE AIR....
POLICE!.. ..OH,OH! ONE OF THE MEN IS GETTING AWAY!

THINK I'LL TRAIL THIS BIRD... MAYBE I'LL BAG BIGGER GAME!

LOOKS LIKE THIS IS THE SPOT, ALL RIGHT!
THE TRAIL ENDS...
PAWN BROKER

ALLOWING A FEW MOMENTS TO ELAPSE, THE BATMAN CROSSES THE STREET AND ENTERS THE MYSTERIOUS DWELLING!

THE PLACE IS BARE!....YET, SOMEONE CAME IN HERE! MUST BE SOME SORT OF SECRET ENTRANCE THAT LEADS SOMEWHERE ABOUT!

PUSHING AGAINST THE BRICKS, THE BATMAN SEARCHES IN VAIN FOR THE HIDDEN ENTRANCE
NOT A TRACE!..I'D GIVE A PRETTY PENNY TO FIND OUT HOW THAT BIRD DISAPPEARED, AND WHERE HE IS NOW!

..AND AT THAT MOMENT THE ANSWER TO THE BATMAN'S LAST QUERY IS TO BE FOUND IN THE MUSIC STORE OF A. REKOJ!
YOU FOOLS!-YOU BUNGLING FOOLS!
BUT WE COULDN'T HELP IT, BOSS. IT WAS THE BATMAN THAT DID IT!

THE BATMAN!
I SHOULD HAVE KNOWN! FATE ALWAYS SEES TO IT THAT OUR PATHS CROSS!

BRING WHAT'S LEFT OF THE MOB DOWN TO-MORROW NIGHT. WE'VE GOT A JOB TO DO!
OKAY, BOSS!

LOCKING THE DOOR BEHIND THE DEPARTING HOODLUM, THE OLD MAN SHUFFLES TO THE REAR OF THE STORE, AND LIFTING A STRIP OF CARPET, EXPOSES A TRAP DOOR.

DESCENDING TO A ROOM THAT SEEMS TO OVERFLOW WITH ART TREASURES, THE OLD MAN PROCEEDS TO PEEL OFF CLOTHING AND REMOVE MAKEUP...

..TO REVEAL DEAD-WHITE, ASK-LIKE FACE WITH COLD, LACK EYES... HILE THE MOUTH S DRAWN INTO REPELLENTLY ERRIBLE SMILE ...THE SMILE OF.... THE JOKER!
EVEN MY HOODLUMS DON'T SUSPECT THAT OLD WICKED REKOJ-MUSIC DEALER, IS - THE JOKER!
NOW, TO COMPLETE MY REVENGE UPON MY ENEMIES. TO DISTRICT ATTORNEY CARTER, I SEND THE RECORD OF MUSIC.... AND DEATH!!

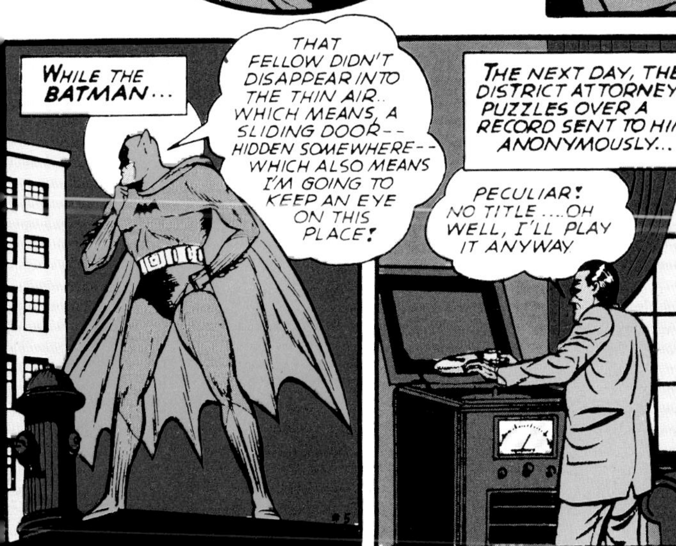
WHILE THE BATMAN...
THAT FELLOW DIDN'T DISAPPEAR INTO THE THIN AIR.. WHICH MEANS, A SLIDING DOOR-- HIDDEN SOMEWHERE-- WHICH ALSO MEANS I'M GOING TO KEEP AN EYE ON THIS PLACE!
THE NEXT DAY, THE DISTRICT ATTORNEY PUZZLES OVER A RECORD SENT TO HIM ANONYMOUSLY...
PECULIAR! NO TITLE ....OH WELL, I'LL PLAY IT ANYWAY

AS THE RECORD REVOLVES, A VIOLIN IS HEARD PLAYING STRANGE, UNEARTHLY MUSIC...
WHAT EERIE, FORBIDDING MUSIC THAT IS!

ABRUPTLY, THE MUSIC STOPS, AND A VOICE IS HEARD... A MOCKING, DRONING VOICE...
DISTRICT ATTORNEY CARTER, EVEN AS I SPEAK THE NEEDLE BITES INTO THE RECORD, RELEASING A DEADLY GAS SPRAYED ON ITS SURFACE! IT BRINGS YOU DEATH FROM- THE JOKER!
THE JOKER!.. WHA...I-I FEEL SO QUEER! I---
A SECOND LATER A STILL FORM SLUMPS IN HIS CHAIR..THE FACE SET IN A CLOWN'S GRIN WHILE WILD HYSTERICAL LAUGHTER COMES FROM THE RECORD!
...DEATH FROM THE JOKER! HA HA HA HA...
HA..HA..HA
AS THE NEEDLE REMAINS IN THE LAST GROOVE, THE MACABRE LAUGH IS REPEATED OVER AND OVER..
LISTEN! SOMEBODY'S LAUGHING LIKE A MANIAC! SOUNDS CRAZY!
THAT'S THE D.A.'S HOUSE.... SOMETHING'S WRONG! COME ON!
THE POLICEMEN BREAK DOWN THE DOOR!
CARTER...WITH THE JOKER GRIN ON HIS FACE!... AND THAT NUTTY LAUGH COMING FROM THAT RECORD!
I'LL TURN IT OFF! - IT GIVES ME THE CREEPS!
THE PUBLIC IS SOON AWARE OF THE JOKER'S RETURN..
BUT, BRUCE, HOW COME THE POLICE DIDN'T DIE WHEN THEY WALKED IN OR WHEN THEY PLAYED THE RECORD OVER AGAIN AT THEIR HEADQUARTERS!?
THE GAS PROBABLY DISSIPATED RAPIDLY AFTER ONLY ONE PLAYING! THE JOKER - ALIVE! I WONDER WHAT HE'S PLANNING NEXT?
THAT NIGHT....
OKAY.... YOU'VE ALL GOT YOUR INSTRUMENT CASES! YOU KNOW WHAT TO DO!
YOU'VE GOT NOTHING TO WORRY ABOUT! WE'RE ALL SET!
AS THE MEN EXIT, A MANTLED FIGURE WATCHES: THE BATMAN!
GOOD THING I DECIDED TO TAKE A LOOK HERE TO-NIGHT! ALL THOSE MEN CARRYING INSTRUMENT CASES! WONDER WHAT'S UP!
THE MEN PAY A CALL UPON TERRY MANNERS AND HIS BAND!
WHA- WHAT'S THE IDEA?
IT'S VERY SIMPLE! YOU'RE SUPPOSED TO PLAY AT THE SCHUYLER BALL TO-NIGHT.... ONLY WE'RE GOING TO TAKE YOUR PLACE!
OKAY, MEN- TIE 'EM UP!

POSING AS PERRY MANNERS' ORCHESTRA, THE HOODLUMS GAIN ENTRANCE TO THE SCHUYLER MANSION....
I DON'T SEE MR. MANNERS ABOUT! WHERE IS HE?
OH, HE'LL BE ALONG! HE'S A LITTLE TIED UP AT THE MOMENT!
SUDDENLY THE MEN OPEN THEIR CASES AND PULL OUT THEIR "INSTRUMENTS!"...
WHY- WHY YOU'RE NOT MUSICIANS!
CERTAINLY WE ARE. THIS CAN PLAY AS PRETTY A TUNE AS YOU'D WANT TO HEAR!
OKAY! LINE UP, EVERYBODY!
OKAY! WE GOT IT ALL! LET'S GET GOING AND ...WHA?..
THAT BAG MUST BE RATHER HEAVY FOR YOU... I'LL HELP YOU CARRY IT!
THE LOOT IS QUICKLY GATHERED AND PLACED IN A SMALL BAG, WHEN A MOURNFUL VOICE IS HEARD.....
YOU KNOW MY REPUTATION... I'M NOT JOKING WHEN I SAY THAT THE FIRST MAN WHO MOVES WILL DIE! DROP YOUR GUNS! GIVE ME THAT BAG!
S-SURE, JOKER- SURE!
THE JOKER AND THE HOODLUMS SUDDENLY WHEEL ABOUT TO FACE THEIR COMMON ENEMY ---THE BATMAN!
THE BATMAN!
FIRST THE JOKER, AND NOW THIS GUY!
LUCKY I TRAILED THESE BIRDS!
THE BATMAN BECOMES A VERITABLE HUMAN TORNADO OF ACTION!
CAN'T LET HIM GET AWAY!
A SUDDEN LEAP THROUGH THE WINDOW CARRIES THE BATMAN IN THE WAKE OF THE FLEEING JOKER!

A FLYING TACKLE STOPS THE JOKER....

SOMETHING I LEARNED IN COLLEGE, JOKER!

BUT AS THE TWO MEN RISE, THE JOKER SWINGS THE HEAVY SATCHEL LOADED WITH JEWELS....

THEN PERHAPS THIS MIGHT TEACH YOU SOMETHING ALSO!...

AGAIN THE LOADED BAG DESCENDS WITH CRUSHING FORCE...

... TEACH YOU NOT TO CROSS MY PATH AGAIN! HA HA HA!

A FEW MOMENTS LATER AS THE **BATMAN** RISES SHAKILY TO HIS FEET...

JOKER'S GONE.... THERE GO THOSE THUGS.. I'VE GOT TO FOLLOW THEM!

INSIDE THE BRICK INTERIOR, ONE OF THE MEN INSERTS A STEEL BLADE INTO A CRACK, AND A PORTION OF THE WALL SLIDES BACK
NO WONDER I COULDN'T FIND THE SECRET DOOR BEFORE!
MAKING THEIR WAY THROUGH A SMALL TUNNEL, THE MEN ENTER THE REAR OF THE MUSIC STORE-- TO A REKOJ!
...SO THAT'S IT, BOSS! THE JOKER GOT AWAY WITH THE JEWELS WHILE THE BATMAN WAS GIVING US THE WORKS!
FOOLS! YOU'VE BLUNDERED AGAIN! I'M DISGUSTED WITH YOU! GET OUT!-GET OUT!
AS THE MEN LEAVE BY THE DOOR OF THE SHOP, REKOJ DESCENDS TO HIS SECRET ROOM AND ONCE MORE HE REMOVES HIS MAKEUP.
THE IDIOTS! I MAKE THEM DO ALL THE DIRTY WORK, GATHER ALL THE JEWELS TO-GETHER...
WAX!
...THEN I STEP IN AND TAKE IT AWAY FROM THEM! NOW I DON'T HAVE TO DIVIDE IT WITH THEM! HA HA! THE FOOLS! THE UTTER FOOLS! HA HA HA HA HA
THEN A VOICE..... THE BATMAN'S VOICE!
SO, YOU EVEN DOUBLE-CROSS YOUR OWN MEN, EH JOKER?
YOU! HOW DID YOU FIND ME!
AS THE BATMAN STEPS FORWARD CAUTIOUSLY, THE JOKER FURTIVELY PRESSES A FLOOR BUTTON WITH HIS FOOT AND A GLASS CYLINDER BEGINS TO DESCEND
I'LL MAKE SURE YOU DON'T GET AWAY THIS TIME, JOKER!
DON'T FORGET, THERE IS ALWAYS A HIDDEN TRICK WHEN YOU PLAY THE GAME OF CHANCE WITH THE JOKER!
THE BATMAN IS IMPRISONED IN A GLASS TOMB!
WHA-?
THE HIDDEN TRICK, BATMAN! A BIT DRAMATIC, PERHAPS, BUT EFFECTIVE! THE GLASS IS SHATTER-PROOF, AND YOU'LL SUFFOCATE TO DEATH QUITE SLOWLY AS YOUR AIR SUPPLY GIVES OUT!

NOW, WHILE YOU DIE I'LL BE ON MY WAY ACROSS THE OCEAN TO GATHER SOME MORE TREASURE! $500,000 WORTH! HA HA HA HA! ADIEU BATMAN, ADIEU! HA HA HA HA HA
WHEN THE JOKER LEAVES, THE BATMAN DRAWS A CERTAIN VIAL FROM HIS UTILITY BELT
THE JOKER UNDERESTIMATES ME! THE ACID IN THIS VIAL OUGHT TO LET ME OUT OF HERE QUICKLY ENOUGH!
THE POWERFUL ACID EATS AWAY THE SHATTER-PROOF GLASS!
$500,000 WORTH OF TREASURE ON THE OCEAN! I WONDER WHAT HE MEANT?
FREE, THE BATMAN SEARCHES FOR A POSSIBLE CLUE TO THE JOKER'S CRYPTIC WORDS, WHEN HE FINDS.....
S.S. ORIENTAL TO BRING $500,000 JADE BUDDHA TO U.S.
MINIATURE JADE BUDDHA ENCRUSTED WITH VALUABLE GEMS, TO BE SOLD TO BUY FOOD, CLOTHES AND MEDICAL SUP-
THIS IS WHAT HE MEANT! HE'S GOING TO STEAL THAT BUDDHA! THOSE POOR CHINESE ARE NOT GOING TO BE DONE OUT OF NECESSITIES IF I CAN HELP IT!
SOME TIME LATER.... ABOARD THE S.S. ORIENTAL ON THE HIGH SEAS....
WHAT HAPPENED?
THAT MAN'S PLANE CRACKED UP AND LANDED IN THE SEA. THE SHIP SENT OUT A RESCUE PARTY!
MUST BE A MUSICIAN! SURE IS CLUTCHING THAT VIOLIN CASE TIGHT ENOUGH!
WHEN THE RESCUED MAN IS LEFT TO REST IN A STATE-ROOM, HE SMILES... THE FRIGHTFUL SMILE – OF THE JOKER!
IT WORKED PERFECTLY! I'M ON THE BOAT WITH THE $500,000 JADE BUDDHA! THE BUDDHA THAT WILL SOON BE MINE!
AT THAT MOMENT A FORM LIKE A MAMMOTH BAT WINGS TOWARD THE SHIP THE BATPLANE!

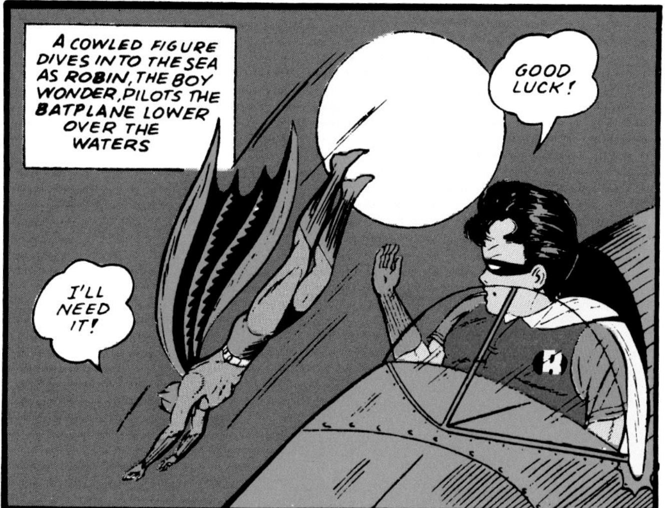
A COWLED FIGURE DIVES INTO THE SEA AS ROBIN, THE BOY WONDER, PILOTS THE BATPLANE LOWER OVER THE WATERS
GOOD LUCK!
I'LL NEED IT!

SWIMMING TO THE SHIP THE BATMAN CLAMBERS UP ITS SIDE

AT THAT VERY INSTANT, THE JOKER IS ALREADY AT WORK WITH HIS GAS-GUN!
THIS WILL PUT THEM TO SLEEP FOR A LITTLE WHILE!
WHA..
GAS!

THE JOKER TAKES AN ACETYLENE TORCH FROM THE VIOLIN CASE AND PLAYS ITS FLAME UPON THE STEEL DOOR...
SINCE THE CAPTAIN HAS THE KEY, I'LL HAVE TO RESORT TO OTHER METHODS TO GET THIS DOOR OPEN!

A MOMENT LATER THE JOKER HOLDS THE JADE BUDDHA IN HIS HANDS
MINE! ALL MINE! AND NO ONE CAN TAKE IT AWAY FROM ME!

AREN'T YOU FORGETTING ABOUT ME, JOKER?
BATMAN!

THE JOKER'S TRY FOR HIS GAS-GUN IS UNSUCCESSFUL AS THE BATMAN KNOCKS IT FROM HIS HAND!
I'LL--
YOU'LL NOTHING!

THE JOKER MAKES FOR THE OPEN DOORWAY....
YOU'LL NEVER TAKE ME, BATMAN!
I'M GOING TO TRY!
SUDDENLY WHIRLING, THE JOKER SEIZES A FIRE-AXE FROM THE WALL AND STABS OUT AT THE BATMAN, WHO NIMBLY STEPS ASIDE, AND...
HOLDING THE END OF THE AXE, THE BATMAN PIVOTS SWIFTLY..
IT LOOKS LIKE I'VE SORT OF SWEPT YOU OFF YOUR FEET, EH, JOKER?
TO SEND THE JOKER FLYING INTO THE WALL!
AS THE BATMAN LEAPS FORWARD TO FOLLOW UP HIS ADVANTAGE, THE JOKER FLAILS OUT WITH BOTH FEET, CATCHING HIM OFF GUARD...
NOT YET, BATMAN, NOT YET!
HE MUST BE A THIEF!
THE JADE BUDDHA!
A MASKED MAN!
AS THE JOKER RACES OUT ON DECK PURSUED BY THE BATMAN, THE CHINESE DELEGATION SEES THE JADE BUDDHA AND MISUNDERSTANDS THE SITUATION...
MY COMING TO HELP THE BATMAN WASN'T A BAD IDEA AFTER ALL!
THE OTHER IS TRYING TO SAVE THE BUDDHA!

AS THE GROUP CONVERGE ON HIM, A SMALL, COMPACT FRAME PLOWS INTO THEM LIKE A HUMAN BATTERING RAM-ROBIN THE BOY WONDER!
JUST LIKE IN FOOTBALL! "TAKING YOU OUT" SO THE BATMAN CAN GO THROUGH!
AS THE JOKER SPEEDS AWAY, THE BATMAN FLINGS HIS BODY UPWARD TO GRASP A BAR.....
SWINGING LIKE A PENDULUM, HIS BODY FLIES OUT AND UP..
UP CATAPULTS THE LITHE FIGURE TO LAND ON THE UPPER DECK UPON THE FLEEING JOKER!
A SMASHING BLOW, AND THE JOKER GOES STAGGERING BACK TO THE SHIP'S RAIL AND...
DOWN...DOWN PLUMMETS THE JOKER TO HIT THE WATER AND REMAIN BELOW!
I WONDER IF THIS IS REALLY THE END OF THE JOKER AT LAST! I WONDER!
THE BATMAN SOON SETS THINGS RIGHT WITH THE CHINESE..
WE APOLOGIZE DEEPLY FOR OUR MISTAKE! FORGIVE US!
YOU HAVE DONE OUR PEOPLE A GREAT SERVICE!
IT'S EVERYONE'S DUTY TO MAKE THINGS EASIER-FOR WAR-STRICKEN PEOPLE! I HOPE YOU SELL THIS, THE PROCEEDS WILL DO MUCH TO REMEDY THEIR PLIGHT!
OUT INTO THE NIGHT SOARS THE BATPLANE, CARRYING A MAN WHO HAS HAD THE SATISFACTION OF SEEING A JOB WELL DONE!
JUST THINK! THERE GOES A MAN WHO PLACES HIS VERY LIFE IN DANGER SO THAT OTHERS MAY LIVE IN GREATER SECURITY!
NO MAN CAN MAKE A GREATER SACRIFICE FOR HIS PEOPLE! HE IS TRULY A GREAT MAN, THIS BATMAN!
BOB KANE

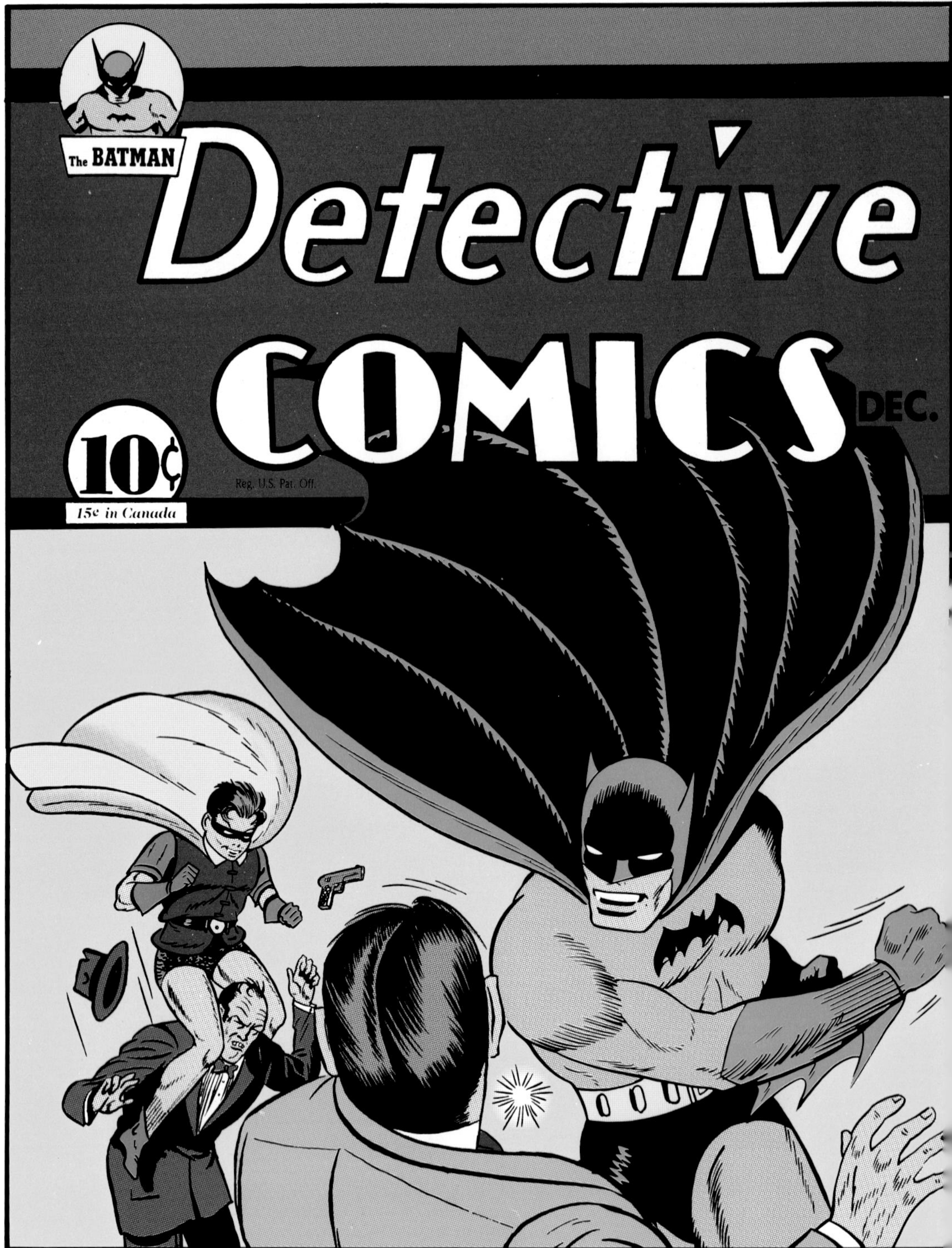
The BATMAN
Detective
COMICS
DEC.
10¢
15¢ in Canada
Reg. U.S. Pat. Off.

BATMAN
WITH Robin -THE BOY WONDER-
BY- BOB KANE
ONCE AGAIN CRIME REARS ITS UGLY HEAD TO PREY UPON SOCIETY..... AND ONCE AGAIN EMERGES THAT SUPER-FOE OF CRIME — THE BATMAN! GARBED IN THE HUES OF NIGHT ITSELF, HE HOVERS ABOVE THE HORDES OF EVIL LIKE IMPENDING DOOM.... AND ALWAYS AT HIS SIDE, LIKE A STRONG RIGHT ARM, IS GRINNING, RECKLESS ROBIN, THE BOY WONDER, WHO IS SOMETHING OF A CRIME-BUSTER IN HIS OWN RIGHT!
ETCHER SILVER CO.
AS THE THIEVES BEGIN TO LOOT A WAREHOUSE, SUDDENLY A BAT-CLOAKED SHAPE SWINGS OVER THEIR HEADS...
...TO PLUMMET DOWN LIGHTLY ATOP THE WAREHOUSE STEPS!

1 WITH A CHALLENGING MOCKING SMILE ON HIS LIPS, THE COWLED INVADER STANDS THERE LIKE SOME TERRIBLE FIGURE OF VENGEANCE...

GOOD EVENING, GENTLEMEN!

IT-IT'S THE **BATMAN!** PLUG 'IM! PLUG 'IM!

YA NUT! WANNA DRAW THE COPS! COME ON...LET'S RUSH HIM ALL AT ONCE!

AS ONE THUG ADVANCES UP THE STAIRS, THE HEEL OF A BOOT SMACKS AGAINST HIS CHIN...

2

HEEL MEETS HEEL!

3 UNDAUNTED BY OVERWHELMING ODDS, THE **BATMAN** STANDS HIS GROUND!

BET YOU GO DOWN FASTER THAN YOU CAME UP!

As the thugs shakily pick themselves up!...
OW! MY HEAD!
WHAT HIT ME?
'MUSTA BEEN A HURRICANE PASSING BY!

.... THE BATMAN CATAPULTS FORWARD... AND DOWN THEY GO AGAIN!
ZORN'S CANDY SHOP

MOVING EASILY, DECEPTIVELY SWIFT AS A STRIKING SNAKE, THE BATMAN WEAVES ABOUT THE MEN, HIS FISTS INDUCING QUICK SLEEP!
OKAY.... YOU CAN RELAX NOW!

AS HIS HAND CLOSES ABOUT A SURVIVING HOODLUM....
D..DON'T HIT ME! PLEASE DON'T HIT ME!
WHA TH'...! A KID... A KID NO MORE THAN SEVENTEEN AT MOST!

OKAY, KID, I WON'T HIT YOU- BUT YOU'RE GOING TO JAIL LIKE THE REST OF YOUR PALS!
JAIL! DON'T SEND ME TO JAIL! IT WOULD KILL MY MOTHER! SHE DOESN'T KNOW ABOUT THIS!

I SHOULD THINK SHE WOULDN'T, BUT JUST THE SAME, I ...
DON'T SEND ME TO JAIL!... PLEASE! I'LL DO ANYTHING! I'LL EVEN TELL YOU ABOUT SOMETHING, SOMETHING BIG!

"SOMETHING BIG!" WHAT ARE YOU TALKING ABOUT? SPILL IT!
YOU GOTTA PROMISE TO PROTECT ME! IF THEY EVER KNEW, MY LIFE WOULDN'T BE WORTH TWO PINS!

THESE MEN CAN'T HEAR A THING! THEY'RE BLISSFULLY UNCONSCIOUS OF EVERYTHING! TALK!
WELL.... CARSTAIRS, THE RACKETEER, IS PLANNING SOMETHING, 'CAUSE HE GOT A BIG GANG TOGETHER LAST NIGHT!... HE SAYS WE'RE GONNA BE MILLIONAIRES IF WE STRING ALONG WITH HIM!

HE SAYS THE PEOPLE AND THE COPS WON'T PUT UP ANY FIGHT WHEN WE DO OUR JOBS! HE'S WORKING WITH SOME PROFESSOR THAT PLANNED THE WHOLE THING!
ALL OF US GOT A VIAL OF THESE PILLS. THEY'RE SUPPOSED TO MAKE US IMMUNE TO THE PROFESSOR'S STUFF IF WE SWALLOW ONE!
IN THAT CASE, I'LL TAKE A FEW PILLS WITH ME. THEY MIGHT COME IN HANDY AT THE RIGHT MOMENT! NOW... WHEN IS THE NEXT MEETING OF CARSTAIRS' MEN?

ER SILVE CO.
WE'RE SUPPOSED TO GO TO ONE TONIGHT!... BUT IT LOOKS LIKE THESE GUYS WON'T BE ABLE TO GO.... IF YOU'RE GONNA TURN 'EM IN!
BOTH YOU AND THESE MEN WILL GO! IT WILL BE WORTH IT IF I CAN FIND OUT A WAY TO COMBAT THE PROFESSOR'S MENACE TO THE PEOPLE.

YOU'RE GOING TO THAT MEETING TONIGHT! I'LL MEET YOU HERE TOMORROW NIGHT AT TWELVE SHARP! YOU'RE TO TELL ME ALL THAT WENT ON! UNDERSTAND?
(GULP!) OKAY, IF YOU SAY SO!

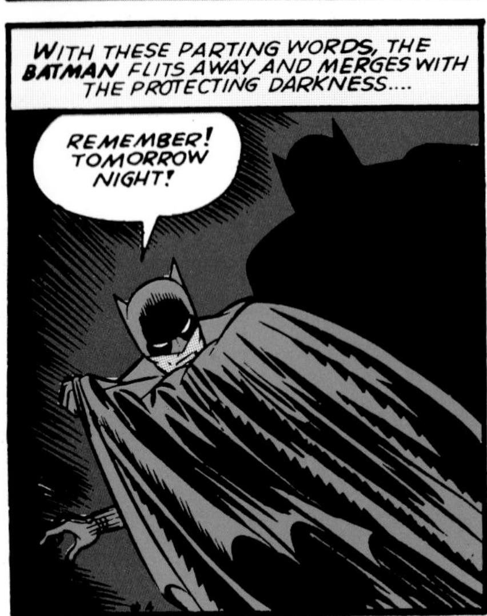
WITH THESE PARTING WORDS, THE BATMAN FLITS AWAY AND MERGES WITH THE PROTECTING DARKNESS....
REMEMBER! TOMORROW NIGHT!

GONE! ...IT'S... IT'S AS IF HE DISAPPEARED IN THE SHADOWS -- LIKE - LIKE A GHOST!

SOMETIME LATER THE HOODLUMS AWAKEN, AND RISE ON SHAKY LEGS.....
GOSH! ME JAW FEELS AS IF IT'S BROKE!
THE BATMAN! HE AIN'T HERE! WADAYA SUPPOSE HAPPENED?
IT'S A BREAK FER US, ANYWAY C'MON, LET'S GET GOIN' T'THAT MEETIN'! ---BUT QUICK!

THE MEN SPEED IN THEIR CAR TO AN OLD HOUSE ON THE OUTSKIRTS OF TOWN.....
HURRY-WE CAN'T BE LATE FOR THE MEETING! YEAH...CARSTAIRS WILL BE HERE, SURE...

INSIDE, THEIR LEADER ADDRESSES THEM
BOYS....IT LOOKS LIKE WE GOT THE RIGHT NUMBER OF MEN IN OUR LITTLE ORGANIZATION AT LAST! WE'RE READY TO START! THE PROFESSOR WILL TELL YOU ALL ABOUT IT!

INTO THE ROOM WALKS A MAN ONCE THOUGHT DEAD-- THE CRAFTY, DIABOLICAL, ARCH-CRIMINAL, PROFESSOR HUGO STRANGE!
I WILL GIVE YOU YOUR INSTRUCTIONS NOW. FOR TOMORROW WE STRIKE! TOMORROW AT NOON-TIME! NOW, LISTEN CAREFULLY...

NOON TOMORROW! AND I'M TO MEET THE BATMAN AT NIGHT! BY THAT TIME IT WILL BE TOO LATE! TOO LATE!

NOONTIME.... IN ONE OF THE GREAT CITY BANKS...ARMED MEN SUDDENLY APPEAR....
OKAY. EVERYBODY.. RAISE 'EM!
THIS IS A STICKUP!
ROBBERS! GUARDS! GUARDS!

AS THE GUARDS RUN UP PULLING AT THEIR REVOLVERS, CARSTAIRS' THUGS SUDDENLY SQUEEZE THE TRIGGERS OF THEIR STRANGE GUNS, AND A FINE SPRAY EMANATES.....
THROW DOWN THOSE..... WHA...?
HA...HA.. HA...!

....AS THEY BREATHE THE SPRAY, A WEIRD THING HAPPENS....THE GUARDS DROP THEIR GUNS AND COWER BEFORE THE HOODLUMS IN UTTER TERROR...
D-DON'T SHOOT US! PLEASE DON'T SHOOT!
IT WORKED! LOOK AT THEM! IT WORKED!

THE BANK LOOTED, THE THUGS RACE OUTSIDE TO MEET POLICEMEN WHO WERE ATTRACTED BY THE TELLER'S SHOUT....
GIVE IT TO 'EM!
WHAT?
S BANK

TREMBLING WITH FEAR, THE POLICE QUAIL BEFORE THE BANDITS...ICY TERROR CLUTCHES THEIR HEARTS.....

D-DON'T HIT ME!

HAW, HAW! LOOK AT HIM!... SCARED STIFF! HAW HAW!

FIRST TIME I EVER SAW A POLICEMAN SCARED BEFORE! SURE IS A NOVELTY!

FEAR!! FEAR!! FEAR!

AND ALL OVER THE CITY IT IS THE SAME! BANDITS LOOT BANKS, WAREHOUSES, STORES, AS A STRANGE MALADY SEIZES THE PEOPLE... FEAR...FEAR HAS BECOME MASTER OF THE CITY!

AND LATER THAT DAY, WHEN THE BANDITS BRING THEIR PLUNDER, THAT MASTER OF VILLAINY, PROFESSOR STRANGE, IS JUBILANT!

THAT STUFF OF YOURS IS A SUCCESS, PROFESSOR! AND WHAT A SUCCESS! THERE'S THE PROOF ON THE TABLE!

I KNEW MY "FEAR" DUST WOULD BE! AND I HAVE A BIGGER PLAN FOR IT! AT TONIGHT'S MEETING I'LL TELL YOU ALL ABOUT IT!

AS THE MEN PREPARE TO LEAVE, PROFESSOR STRANGE'S SHREWD EYES GROW HARD...

AT LAST NIGHT'S MEETING THAT BOY THERE LOOKED NERVOUS, STRAINED! I'VE A FEELING HE'S UP TO SOMETHING.

YEAH... HE DOES AT THAT! I'LL HAVE A FEW OF THE BOYS TAIL HIM!

THAT NIGHT, AS A COWLED FIGURE DARTS ACROSS SHADOWY STREETS, THE CLOCK TOLLS MIDNIGHT HOUR.... IS THIS TOLLING THE DEATH-KNELL OF THE BATMAN? DOES THE BATMAN KEEP A RENDEZVOUS WITH DEATH?

BUT THE BATMAN IS NEVER TO HEAR THE ANSWER TO THAT QUESTION, FOR AT THAT MOMENT A CRUSHING BLOW RENDERS HIM SENSELESS!

... AND WHEN THE BATMAN AWAKENS, HE SEES BEFORE HIM A FACE HE HAD HOPED NEVER TO SEE AGAIN....

GREETINGS, BATMAN,... IT SEEMS THAT FATE HAS SEEN TO IT THAT WE SHOULD MEET AGAIN! FATE HAS BEEN UNKIND THIS TIME... TO YOU!

1
OLD ENEMIES, CRIMINAL AND CRIME-SMASHER STAND BEFORE EACH OTHER!
I SAY UNKIND BECAUSE THIS TIME I SHALL VENT MY FULL HATRED UPON YOU! YOU SHALL FEEL IT SLOWLY. SLOWLY BUT SURELY!
DO YOUR WORST! YOU DON'T SCARE ME WITH YOUR MELODRAMATIC THREATS!
2
AT A SIGNAL FROM THE MADMAN, THE BATMAN'S ARMS ARE SUDDENLY PINIONED TO HIS SIDES AND A HULKING THUG SPRINGS FORWARD!
NOW GO TO IT!
3
AS THE BATMAN SAGS UNDER THE EFFECT OF THE CRUEL FOUL BLOW. THE OTHER THUGS IN THE ROOM SPRING FORWARD AND DIRECT BLOWS AT HIM AS HE VALIANTLY TRIES TO FIGHT AGAINST OVERWHELMING ODDS!
GIVE IT TO HIM! KILL HIM!
THIS IS FOR WHAT HE DID TO ME ON THE PIER!
4
AS THEIR NEMESIS SLUMPS HELPLESSLY BEFORE THEM, THE COWARDLY THUGS SUBJECT HIM TO A TERRIBLE BEATING!
5
..UNTIL FINALLY HIS SENSES SWIM AND HE IS DROWNED IN WELCOME OBLIVION!
BOY, CAN HE TAKE IT!
YEAH! I THOUGHT HE WOULD NEVER DROP!
TAKE HIM IN TO THE NEXT ROOM!
6
TIME CREEPS BY, AND UNDER THE BLESSED SLEEP, THE BATMAN'S BODY SLOWLY GAINS REST AND RECOUPS ITS STRENGTH
GOT TO GET UP!... MUST! AH. THAT'S BETTER!... I ACHE ALL OVER! HEAR A VOICE!
..AND WITH MY "FEAR" DUST WE CAN TAKE OVER THE COUNTRY! IF WE SPRAY IT OVER THE CITY, THE COUNTRY, EVEN THE CAPITOL ITSELF, WHO WILL OPPOSE US?
7
ALL THE HIGH MEN IN PUBLIC OFFICE WILL BE AFRAID OF US! THEY WILL LET ME TAKE OVER THE REINS OF THE GOVERNMENT! I CAN BE DICTATOR OF AMERICA! UNDER THE INFLUENCE OF MY "FEAR DUST" THE WORLD WILL BOW!

FIRST WE MUST PUT "FEAR" DUST INTO THE PEOPLE. THEY MUST BE AFRAID TO BUY, BE AFRAID OF INVASION,.... SO AFRAID THAT ALL WILL BE CHAOS! THEN IS THE TIME TO STRIKE!
HERE ARE PAPERS GIVING YOU ALL INSTRUCTIONS WHERE TO SPRAY THE "FEAR" DUST! I MYSELF WILL GET MY PLANE AND DISCHARGE DUST OVER THE CITY!
CAN'T TRUST MYSELF TO RUSH THEM YET, TILL I GET MY FULL STRENGTH BACK! MUST WAIT!
SOMETIME LATER THE THREE MEN LEFT AS GUARDS SUDDENLY SEE THE DOOR OPEN AND A SLUMPING FIGURE STAND WEAKLY ON THE THRESHOLD!
OH.... STILL HERE!... I...... THOUGHT...
WELL-WELL! LOOK WHO'S UP!
C'MON- LET'S GET TO WORK ON HIM AGAIN AND PUT HIM BACK TO SLEEP.
SUDDENLY THE SLUMPING FORM STRAIGHTENS, SMOOTH MUSCLES RIPPLE, SUGGESTING HIDDEN STRENGTH, AS THE GIGANTIC FRAME OF THE BATMAN STANDS TOWERING IN THE LIGHT!
SO YOU THINK IT'S FUNNY, EH?....
ULP!
HUH!
.....WELL, THIS OUGHT TO PUT YOU IN STITCHES!
YEARS OF RIGOROUS ATHLETIC TRAINING HAVE ENABLED THE BATMAN NOT ONLY TO RESIST BUT TO RECOVER FROM THE BRUTAL BEATING THAT WOULD HAVE MORTALLY INJURED MOST MEN!
WHY DON'T YOU KICK ME NOW, YOU BRAVE MAN!
RIFLING THE PROFESSOR'S PAPERS, THE BATMAN FINDS THE LIST OF INSTRUCTIONS AND THEN HASTILY CONTACTS HIS YOUNG AIDE, ROBIN, THE BOY WONDER!
OH, IT'S YOU, BATMAN! WHERE HAVE YOU BEEN THE WHOLE NIGHT? I'VE BEEN WANDERING ALL AROUND TOWN LOOKING FOR YOU!
CAN'T STOP TO EXPLAIN NOW, BUT TAKE ONE OF THOSE PILLS I GAVE YOU LAST NIGHT AND LISTEN CAREFULLY! COPY THIS DOWN.

AT BREAKNECK SPEED, THE BATMAN STREAKS OUT INTO THE NIGHT.......
IT'S STILL POSSIBLE FOR ROBIN AND ME TO STOP STRANGE'S THUGS. FIRST STOP.... FORTY-SECOND STREET STATION!

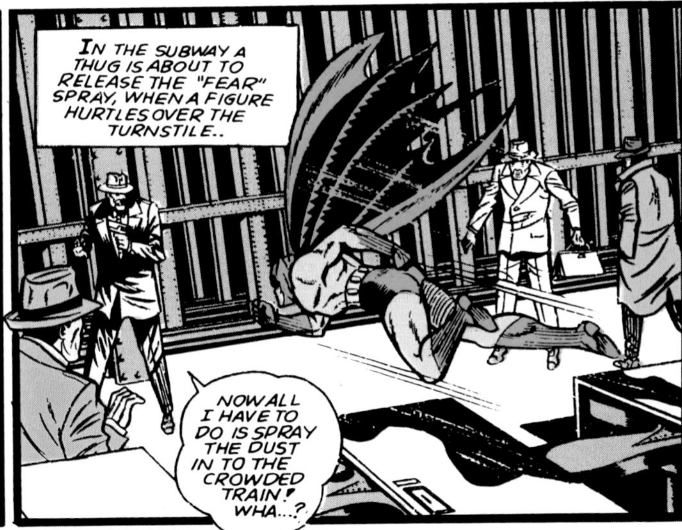
IN THE SUBWAY A THUG IS ABOUT TO RELEASE THE "FEAR" SPRAY, WHEN A FIGURE HURTLES OVER THE TURNSTILE..
NOW ALL I HAVE TO DO IS SPRAY THE DUST IN TO THE CROWDED TRAIN! WHA...?

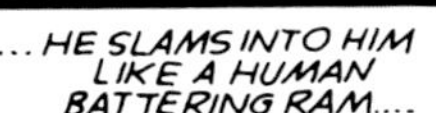
... HE SLAMS INTO HIM LIKE A HUMAN BATTERING RAM....

... AND SENDS HIM SAILING WITH A WELL-PLACED BLOW!

THE BATMAN!
HE'S GONE.... QUICK AS HE CAME!
SAID TO TURN THIS GUY OVER TO THE POLICE!

WHILE AT THAT MOMENT ROBIN, THE BOY WONDER, IS BUSILY ENGAGED IN CLIMBING A TELEGRAPH POLE NEAR THE CITY RESERVOIR....
I SEE THOSE MEN THE BATMAN TOLD ME WERE GOING TO EMPTY "FEAR" SPRAY INTO THE RESERVOIR!

GOOD THING I DID THIS SORT OF THING WHEN I WORKED WITH MOTHER AND DAD IN THE CIRCUS!

1
....REACHING HIS QUARRY HE DIVES IN A SUICIDE PLUNGE....
THE THUGS QUICKLY DRAW THEIR SPRAY GUNS AND THROW "FEAR" DUST AT THE BOY WONDER.
2
...TO LAND WITH AMAZING RESULTS!
...ROLL OUT THE BARREL
3
THAT'S THAT ROBIN KID!
THE "FEAR" DUST DOESN'T EVEN AFFECT HIM!
WOULD THEY BE SURPRISED TO KNOW I SWALLOWED AN ANTIDOTE PILL JUST AS THEY DID!
4
5 THEN, BEFORE THEY CAN RECOVER, HE POUNCES UPON THEM, BOTH FISTS FLYING!
YOU LOOK TIRED....WHY DON'T YOU LIE DOWN!?
6 MOMENTS LATER....ON A THEATRE MARQUEE ABOVE A CROWDED CITY STREET CORNER....
NOW FOR A LITTLE "FEAR" DUST FOR THE CROWD!
REX
MELODY OF 1941
Starring
TYRONE TAYLOR
and
MYRNA ROGERS
7 WHEN SUDDENLY AS IF FROM NOWHERE, A LITHE FIGURE FLASHES ABOVE THE CROWD, DIRECTLY FOR A DANGLING SIGN!
DR. H. ROBINS DENTIST

1 WITH THE TRAINED SKILL OF AN ACROBAT, THE BOY WONDER SWINGS UP ONTO THE MARQUEE.
REX
MELODY OF 1941 Starring TYRONE TAYLOR and MYRNA ROGERS
DR. H. ROBINSON DENTIST
2 .....AND DROPS THE HOODLUM WITH A PARALYZING PUNCH!
COMB THIS OUT OF YOUR WHISKERS!
3 ANOTHER TREMENDOUS LEAP CARRIES ROBIN OFF THE MARQUEE TO THE SIGN, AND THEN TO THE SIDEWALK!
DID YOU SEE WHAT I SEE--?
IT AIN'T NO MIRACLE, BROTHER! THAT'S THAT KID THE WHOLE COUNTRY'S TALKING ABOUT! ROBIN THE BOY WONDER!
IN THE MEANTIME THE BATMAN HAS QUESTIONED ONE OF STRANGE'S THUGS AND LEARNED THE LOCATION OF HIS AIRPLANE HANGAR....
4 AT PROFESSOR STRANGE'S SECRET HANGAR
...PLANE WOULD ACT UP AT A TIME LIKE THIS!... I.....THAT SHADOW!... THE BATMAN!
5 I'LL KILL YOU ONCE AND FOR ALL!
WITH A CRY OF RAGE, THE MAD PROFESSOR WHIRLS SO SUDDENLY THAT HE TAKES EVEN THE BATMAN BY SURPRISE....
6 ...THOUGH HIS SHOULDER IS NUMB WITH SUDDEN SHOCK AND PAIN, THE BATMAN LOCKS GRIPS WITH THE MANIAC!
7 .....THE BATTLE BECOMES A GRIM ONE, WITH DEATH WAITING TO CLAIM THE LOSER!

ABRUPTLY, THE ARCH-CRIMINAL MANAGES TO LOOSEN HIS HAND, AND LASHES OUT AT THE BATMAN....
BLAST YOU!
MISSED! TSK, TSK!

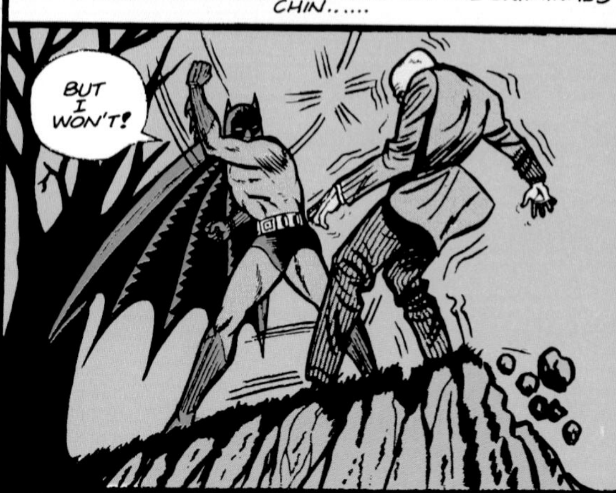
....BUT THE NIMBLE BATMAN IS NOT TO BE CAUGHT NAPPING A SECOND TIME. THERE IS A CRACK LIKE THAT OF A RIFLE SHOT AS HIS FISTS LAND ON THE CRIMINAL'S CHIN......
BUT I WON'T!

...FOR A MOMENT HE TEETERS ON THE EDGE, CLAWING FOR BALANCE, AND THEN WITH A TRAILING SHRIEK TOPPLES TO HIS DOOM!
WELL....THIS TIME IT REALLY LOOKS AS IF IT IS THE END OF THE EVIL CAREER OF PROFESSOR HUGO STRANGE!
YAAAAAAA-A-A-A......

THAT NIGHT, AS THE MOON SHEDS ITS LIGHT OVER A NOW PEACEFUL CITY, TWO FIGURES STAND ON A LONELY ROAD....
WELL...I GUESS WE CLEANED OUT THE "FEAR" GANG! NOW WHAT DO WE DO?
NOTHING MUCH LEFT TO DO BUT TO SET FREE THE KID THAT HELPED ME BREAK THIS CASE. HE'S TIED UP IN STRANGE'S HOUSE!

YOU KNOW...IT MUST HAVE BEEN A PECULIAR SIGHT TO SEE POLICEMEN AFRAID FOR THE FIRST TIME....
THEY COULDN'T HELP BEING AFRAID UNDER THE INFLUENCE OF THAT "FEAR" DUST ANYMORE THAN YOU COULD HELP CATCHING A COLD!

WHAT ABOUT THE PEOPLE THE "FEAR" DUST AFFECTED? WHAT CAN BE DONE ABOUT THEM!
I'LL GIVE THE PILLS TO A RESEARCH LABORATORY. THEY'LL FIND OUT WHAT THEY'RE MADE OF AND MAKE ENOUGH ANTIDOTE FOR THOSE POOR UNFORTUNATES!

THANKS FOR BEING WITH US AGAIN THIS MONTH! ROBIN AND I LOOK FORWARD TO THESE LITTLE GET-TOGETHERS WITH ALL YOU READERS EVERY MONTH IN DETECTIVE COMICS! LET'S MAKE IT A STANDING DATE!
BOB KANE

No. 47
The BATMAN
Detective
JAN.
COMICS
10¢
Reg. U.S. Pat. Off.
BOB KANE

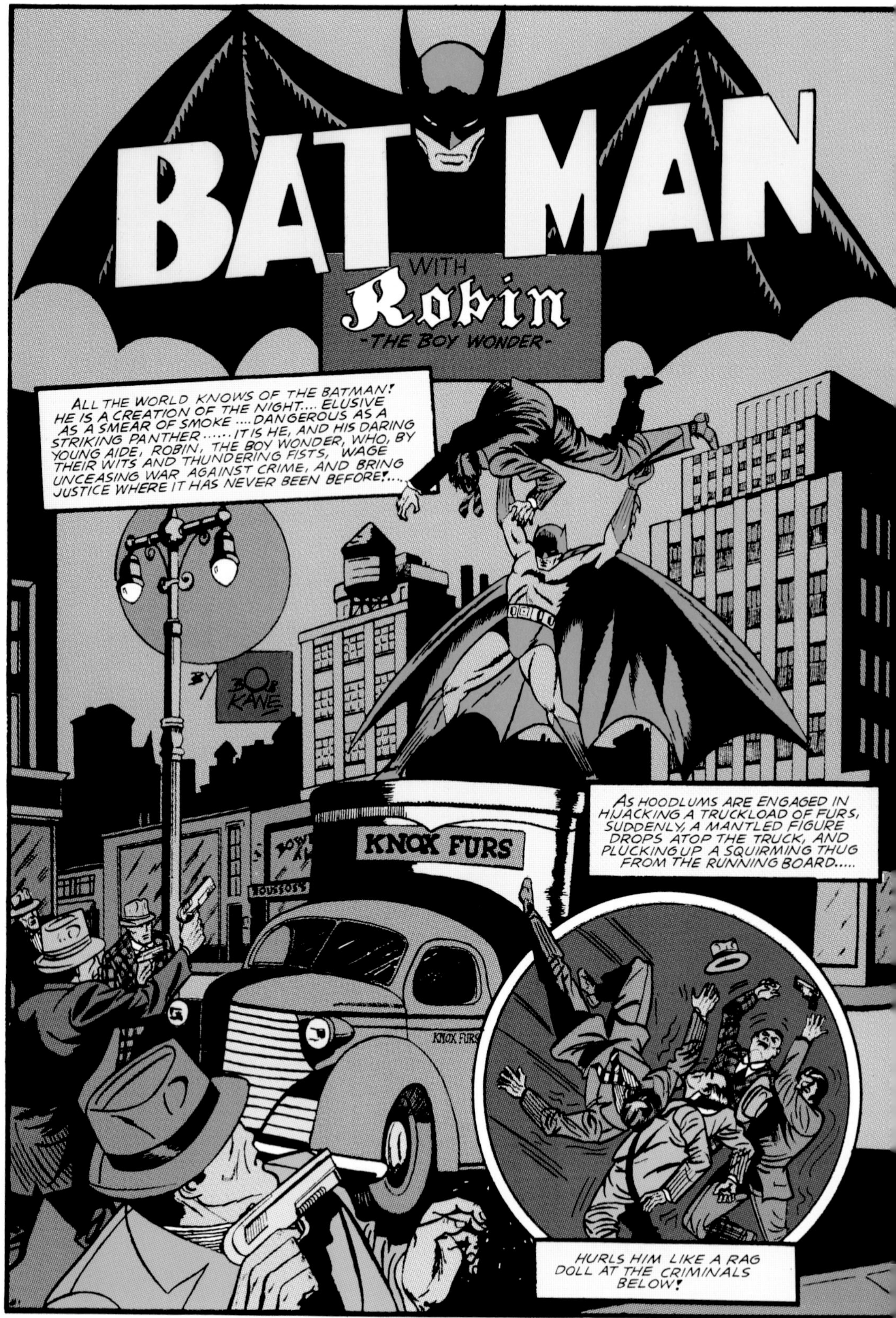
BATMAN
WITH
Robin
-THE BOY WONDER-
ALL THE WORLD KNOWS OF THE BATMAN! HE IS A CREATION OF THE NIGHT.... ELUSIVE AS A SMEAR OF SMOKE ....DANGEROUS AS A STRIKING PANTHER ......IT IS HE, AND HIS DARING YOUNG AIDE, ROBIN, THE BOY WONDER, WHO, BY THEIR WITS AND THUNDERING FISTS, WAGE UNCEASING WAR AGAINST CRIME, AND BRING JUSTICE WHERE IT HAS NEVER BEEN BEFORE!....
BY BOB KANE
KNOX FURS
AS HOODLUMS ARE ENGAGED IN HIJACKING A TRUCKLOAD OF FURS, SUDDENLY, A MANTLED FIGURE DROPS ATOP THE TRUCK, AND PLUCKING UP A SQUIRMING THUG FROM THE RUNNING BOARD.....
KNOX FURS
HURLS HIM LIKE A RAG DOLL AT THE CRIMINALS BELOW!

CRIME FIGHTER...... SUPERFOE OF EVIL.... THE BATMAN HAS STRUCK AGAIN!
AU REVOIR, GENTLEMEN.... I TRUST I'VE NOT INTRUDED!

SUDDENLY, THE BLAST OF A POLICE WHISTLE CUTS THROUGH THE AIR..... THERE IS THE SOUND OF EXCITED VOICES.....
THE SHOT CAME FROM AROUND THE CORNER!
POLICE! —MY EXIT CUE!

WHEELING ABOUT SWIFTLY, THE DARK KNIGHT SPRINGS OFF THE TRUCK.....
COME TO PAPA!

...HIS OUTSTRETCHED HANDS CLOSE VISE-LIKE AROUND THE LOWER RUNG OF A NEARBY FIRE-ESCAPE LADDER....
JONES Cafe

PERPLEXED POLICE ARRIVE ON THE SCENE....
WHA..? THESE GUYS LOOK LIKE THEY WERE STRUCK BY A HURRICANE!
THEY CERTAINLY WEREN'T FIGHTING THEMSELVES! I WONDER WHAT HIT THEM?

....AND UNOBSERVED, IS THE ANSWER TO THAT QUESTION.... THAT MYSTERIOUS PERSONALITY...DUBBED BATMAN!

UP OVER THE ROOFTOPS HE FLITS...... DIZZY HEIGHTS HOLD NO TERROR FOR THE BATMAN!

SOMETIME LATER, HE ENTERS WHAT SEEMS TO BE A DESERTED BARN ON A BARREN FIELD.....

UPON PRESSING A BUTTON, A SECTION OF THE BARN'S FLOOR SLIDES AWAY, REVEALING A FLIGHT OF STEPS...

.... HE PADS SILENTLY THROUGH THE TUNNEL BELOW.....

... HE ASCENDS ANOTHER FLIGHT OF STEPS AT THE END OF THE LONG TUNNEL.....

....AND STEPS THROUGH ANOTHER PANEL INTO A LUXURIOUSLY FURNISHED ROOM!
H'YA DICKEY, M'LAD!
THE SECRET LABYRINTH HAS LED TO THE LAIR OF THE BATMAN!

...JUST A MINOR SKIRMISH WITH THE CRIMINAL ELEMENT! ANYONE PHONE WHILE I WAS GONE?
YOUR BANKER, HARVEY MIDAS, SAID TO CALL IN THE MORNING FOR THE ANNUAL REPORT ON YOUR HOLDINGS!

..IN THE MORNING, HE STEPS FROM THE DOORWAY OF HIS PRIVATE HOME,... NOT AS THE EERIE BATMAN.... BUT AS THE SPENDTHRIFT, PLEASURE-LOVING SOCIETY PLAY BOY..... BRUCE WAYNE!
HMM! NICE DAY FOR A BIT OF POLO!

LATER, HE ENTERS THE SUMPTUOUS OFFICE OF HARVEY MIDAS, MULTI-MILLIONAIRE BANKER.
HELLO MIDAS! HOW'S THE MARKET BEEN TREATING YOU LATELY?
ARRUMPH! NOT BAD, BRUCE... NOT BAD! NOW LET'S GET DOWN TO BUSINESS CAN ONLY SPARE A MOMENT OR TWO! PRESSED FOR TIME, YOU KNOW!

SUDDENLY, THE DOOR BURSTS OPEN....
HI, BRUCE! HELLO, DAD! ARE YOU ALL SET TO GO TO THE OPENING FOOTBALL GAME WITH ME?
ROGER MY BOY..... I'M SORRY, BUT, I CAN'T MAKE IT-TOO BUSY!

ARRUMPH! AFTER ALL, ROGER, IF I DIDN'T ATTEND TO MY BUSINESS, YOU WOULDN'T BE ABLE TO POSSESS ALL THE MONEY YOU HAVE NOW!
(BLAST THE MONEY!)

I THOUGHT I HEARD YOU SAY SOMETHING, ROGER?
NOTHING IMPORTANT... JUST TALKING TO MYSELF.
BUT, ONE PERSON DID HEAR! BRUCE'S KEEN EARS HAVE CAUGHT THOSE WORDS!

WHEN ROGER GOES.....
PERHAPS, BUT I WOULDN'T LET IT INTERFERE WITH THE COMRADE-SHIP OF MY OWN SON!
WISH I COULD BE MORE OF A COMPANION TO THE BOY, BUT, AFTER ALL.... BUSINESS BEFORE PLEASURE!

THAT NIGHT, A SOLITARY FIGURE CLIMBS THE VINE-COVERED TRELLIS OF THE MIDAS MANSION.....
THIS CASE INTERESTS ME STRANGELY! I SHOULD LIKE TO KNOW A LITTLE MORE ABOUT THE MIDAS FAMILY!
ONCE MORE, BRUCE WAYNE HAS REVERTED TO HIS OTHER SELF.. ...THE BATMAN!

HE PEERS INTO A LIGHTED ROOM...
MOTHER, SOME OF THE GIRLS FROM SCHOOL ARE HAVING A LITTLE TEA PARTY TOMORROW AFTERNOON. THEY'RE BRINGING THEIR MOTHERS! WILL YOU COME TOO?
YOU KNOW I CAN'T! WE'RE HAVING OUR CLUB LUNCHEON TOMORROW! NOW, PLEASE DON'T BOTHER ME! I'VE GOT THESE INVITATIONS TO GET OUT!

MR. BROWN ON THE TELEPHONE, MISS DIANE!
IT'S JOHNNY! I'LL TAKE IT, JUPKINS.
JOHNNY BROWN AGAIN! DIANE, I THOUGHT I TOLD YOU NOT TO SEE HIM!

WHY? WHAT'S THE MATTER WITH JOHNNY? JUST BECAUSE HE'S NOT RICH AND...
I WILL NOT HAVE MY DAUGHTER GOING OUT WITH A MERE CLERK IN HER FATHER'S BANK! YOUR FATHER WILL HEAR OF THIS! AFTER ALL, YOU MUST THINK OF YOUR SOCIAL POSITION, MY DEAR!

IN THE ENSUING DAYS, BRUCE WAYNE IS SEEN IN MANY NIGHT SPOTS.....
I SEE BRUCE WAYNE IS OUT AGAIN TONIGHT. DOESN'T HE EVER GO HOME?
THAT FELLOW'S CHIEF OCCUPATION SEEMS TO BE JUST RUNNING AROUND THE NIGHTCLUBS!

BUT THEY ARE WRONG, FOR BRUCE WAYNE'S CHIEF OCCUPATION AT THE MOMENT IS KEEPING A WATCHFUL EYE ON YOUNG ROGER MIDAS!
THAT KID HAS BEEN HITTING IT UP QUITE A BIT THESE NIGHTS!

YOUNG ROGER IS SEEN AT THE GAMBLING TABLES, NIGHT AFTER NIGHT....BUT, ALWAYS LURKING IN THE BACKGROUND, IS BRUCE WAYNE!
BETS, PLEASE!
100 ON 18 RED.

ONE NIGHT, BRUCE IS SURPRISED WHEN ROGER PICKS UP A CLARINET FROM ONE OF THE MEN OF THE NIGHTCLUB BAND AND PLAYS ALONG WITH THEM...
...SAY– THAT BOY'S GOOD!

...AND WHEN BRUCE CALLS ROGER TO HIS TABLE AND ASKS HIM ABOUT IT...
SAY, ROG..... YOU CAN REALLY PLAY THAT THING, CAN'T YOU?
YOU NEVER KNEW I WANTED TO LEAD MY OWN ORCHESTRA, DID YOU? FATHER WOULDN'T HEAR OF IT!..SAID IT WOULD NEVER DO FOR THE SON OF HARVEY MIDAS TO BE A MERE ORCHESTRA LEADER!

IT IS NOT SO LONG AFTER, THAT DIANE MIDAS MAKES HER DEBUT INTO SOCIETY..... AND WHAT A DEBUT IT IS.....
Society
by Jerry Robinson
DIANE MIDAS MAKES DEBUT
DEB'S COMING OUT PARTY COSTS $50,000
MOST LAVISH OF ALL DEBUTS

...AND UNDER THE STRONG INFLUENCE OF HER SOCIAL-MINDED FATHER AND MOTHER MARRIES NOT JOHNNY BROWN, BUT A DEFUNCT EUROPEAN COUNT!
DARLING! NOW, YOU ARE MINE!
YES, AND SO'S MY MONEY!

AND AT HIS HOME, BRUCE WAYNE PONDERS...
FATHER AND MOTHER MIDAS HAVE CERTAINLY MADE A WRECK OF THEIR CHILDREN'S LIVES! IF THERE WERE ONLY SOMETHING I COULD DO.....IF ONLY SOMETHING WOULD HAPPEN....
BUT, SOMETHING WILL HAPPEN..... EVENTS HAVE ALREADY SHAPED THEMSELVES SO THAT BRUCE WAYNE MAY DISCARD THE ROLE OF IDLE PLAYBOY, AND BECOME THE EERIE BATMAN.

IN THE ENSUING MONTHS, ROGER IS SEEN CONSTANTLY WITH EVIL COMPANIONS...ONE NIGHT AS GAMBLERS AND HE PREPARE FOR A GALA EVENING....

C'MON, ROGER... LET'S GO DOWN TO AL'S PLACE!
SURE... AL'S PLACE! YIPPEE! HIC!

AS IF OUT OF THE EMPTY SKY, A WEIRD FIGURE PLUMMETS DOWN!

STRANGE COMPANY YOU KEEP, ROGER -TIN HORN GAMBLERS!
GET THIS CAR GOIN'! GET OUTTA HERE!
THE BATMAN!

AS THE CAR DARTS FORWARD, THE TIPSY BOY IS UNABLE TO CONTROL THE WHEEL, AND IT CAREENS MADLY..
HEY.... TAKE IT EASY! LOOK OUT.... THE NEWSBOY!
Q714

LIKE A JUGGERNAUT, THE CAR HURTLES TOWARD THE HELPLESS BOY.

...THE CAR SPEEDS AWAY, LEAVING BEHIND A STILL FORM SPRAWLED IN THE GUTTER!
I-I HIT HIM! I OUGHT TO TAKE HIM TO A HOSPITAL!
KEEP GOIN', YOU FOOL! DO YOU WANT TO GET ARRESTED?

YOU FELLOWS WON'T TELL ANYBODY ABOUT THIS, WILL YOU? MY FATHER WOULDN'T LIKE IT!
YEAH! I GUESS HE WOULDN'T WANT IT KNOWN THAT HIS SON WAS A HIT AND RUN DRIVER!
SURE! THAT WOULDN'T BE SO NICE FOR THE SON OF HARVEY MIDAS!

THE NEXT DAY SHOCKING NEWS HEADLINES THE PAPERS...
DAILY BUGLE
NEWSBOY CRIPPLED BY SPEEDING CAR
"HIT AND RUN" DRIVER SPEEDS FROM SCENE OF CRIME...
THE COWARDLY DRIVER OF THE CAR THAT CRIPPLED POOR DANNY MOORE, A NEWSBOY, OUGHT TO BE

....AND THAT VERY NIGHT,....IN THE MIDAS HOME.....
...AND YOU MEAN TO SAY THESE MEN WANT $5000 FROM ME TO KEEP THEM QUIET ABOUT THIS UNFORTUNATE ACCIDENT--OR ELSE THEY WILL TELL THE NEWSPAPERS?
YES! THEY SAID YOU WOULD PAY ANYTHING TO KEEP SOME MUD FROM SMEARING THE FAMILY NAME! WHAT CAN WE DO?

ABRUPTLY.....
-DO NOTHING AND TAKE YOUR PUNISHMENT!' DO YOU THINK THAT ONE PAYMENT WILL STOP THESE MEN? THEY'LL BLACKMAIL YOU ALL YOUR LIFE!
HUH?
WHA? WHO ARE YOU?
THE BATMAN-- AT YOUR SERVICE...AND GIVING YOU SOME SOUND ADVICE. DO NOT GIVE IN TO THE BLACKMAILERS' DEMANDS!
BATMAN, EH? WELL, MR. BATMAN, I'LL DO AS I SEE FIT. PLEASE MIND YOUR OWN BUSINESS AND GET OUT OF MY HOUSE!

MIDAS, YOU THINK YOUR MONEY CAN BUY ANYTHING? ONE THING IT CAN'T BUY IS YOUR SON'S SELF-RESPECT!
GET OUT! ...GET OUT!

...AND ON THE FLOOR BELOW, IS ANOTHER COSTUMED FIGURE....ROBIN, THE BOY WONDER!
I'M SORRY, ALEXIS. I DON'T LOVE YOU! I ONLY MARRIED YOU BECAUSE OF MOTHER AND DAD! I'M LEAVING FOR RENO IN THE MORNING!
YOU CAN'T DIVORCE ME....YOU CAN'T!

IF SHE DIVORCES ME, I WON'T HAVE ANY INCOME TO LIVE ON! HM! THINK I'LL HAVE TO DO AS I DID WITH MY FIRST WIFE!
SLAM

AS ALEXIS LEAVES AND SPEEDS AWAY IN HIS CAR, A SMALL FIGURE IS SEEN CLINGING TO THE TIRE-RACK....IT IS THE BOY WONDER, ROBIN!
GOOD THING THE BATMAN TOLD ME TO KEEP AN EYE ON THIS BIRD! HE'S UP TO NO GOOD!

ALEXIS QUICKLY CONTACTS TWO HOODLUMS. AS THEY PLOT, THEY ARE UNAWARE THAT THEIR TALK IS HEARD BY THE WONDER BOY!
THE SAME JOB WE DID FOR YA ONCE BEFORE, EH?
YES! I WILL LEAVE THE SIDE DOOR OPEN. WHEN YOU ENTER I WILL TELL YOU WHERE THE FAMILY JEWEL SAFE IS!
PRETTY SMOOTH. WE SPLIT FIFTY-FIFTY AND THE FAMILY DOESN'T EVER KNOW YOU'RE IN ON THE JOB! SMOOTH!

LATER,... ROBIN REPORTS...

...AND THE COUNT IS OPENING THE DOOR TOMORROW NIGHT AT EXACTLY EIGHT O'CLOCK!
HMMM.... AND MIDAS IS PAYING OFF THE BLACKMAILERS AT TEN O'CLOCK! LOOKS LIKE WE'RE GOING TO BE QUITE BUSY TOMORROW!

THE NEXT NIGHT... AT A FEW MOMENTS BEFORE EIGHT O'CLOCK!

U-UUHH! THAT SHADOW... WHO?...

GREETINGS FROM THE BATMAN, MY DEAR COUNT!

LOOKS LIKE THE COUNT IS DOWN FOR THE COUNT!
H!ST! THEY'RE COMING! BETTER HIDE!

A MOMENT LATER... A BANDIT CAUTIOUSLY POKES HIS HEAD INTO THE HOUSE..
HEY- WHERE ARE YOU?

RIGHT HERE, SWEETHEART!
AWK!

THE BATMAN'S FIST SHOOTS OUT JUST ONCE MORE AND THAT'S QUITE SUFFICIENT!
THE B-BATMAN! THIS IS NO PLACE FOR ME!

LATER THAT EVENING, MIDAS' CAR DRAWS UP TO THE APPOINTED DWELLING DESIGNATED BY THE BLACKMAILERS....
SURE THIS IS THE PLACE, ROGER?
YES, THAT'S THE NUMBER, ALL RIGHT!

AS MIDAS AND ROGER ENTER THE DWELLING, TWO MANTLED FIGURES LEAP OFF THE CAR-ROOF....THEY ARE THE BATMAN AND ROBIN!
WHETHER MIDAS LIKES IT OR NOT, WE'RE GOING TO STOP THOSE DIRTY BLACKMAILERS!

GOT THE FIVE GRAND, MIDAS?
YES, IN FIVES AND TENS, AS YOU REQUESTED.

SUDDENLY, THERE IS THE SOUND OF SPLINTERING WOOD-AND A PAIR OF BROAD SHOULDERS CRASHES THROUGH THE DOOR.....
SORRY-BUT I DON'T THINK I'LL BOTHER TO KNOCK!
OH, MAMA! IT'S THE BATMAN!

GUNPLAY ALWAYS DID BOTHER ME!
O-OH!

PHFFT!
HOW'S THAT FOR USING MY HEAD!

PANIC-STRICKEN, THE REMAINING BLACKMAILERS RETREAT......
C'MON, WE'LL SPLIT UP! I'LL GO UP THE FIRE-ESCAPE AND YOU GO DOWN!
BE WITH YOU IN A SEC! I WANNA DO SOMETHIN' FIRST!

SIC THE BATMAN ON US, WILLYA... TAKE THIS!
ROGER! LOOK OUT!

ROBIN - YOU TAKE THE RAT GOING TO THE ROOF! I'LL GET THE ONE THAT FIRED THE SHOT!
ROGER -SHOT!

WELL-KNOWING HIS DANGER, THE BOY WONDER DOESN'T EVEN HESITATE, BUT SCRAMBLES UP THE FIRE-ESCAPE AFTER THE FLEEING BLACKMAILER!

HE IS JUST IN TIME TO SEE THE ESCAPING MAN LEAP ACROSS TO THE NEXT ROOF...
I'LL NEVER CATCH THAT GUY UNLESS... THAT POLE-THAT MIGHT DO IT!

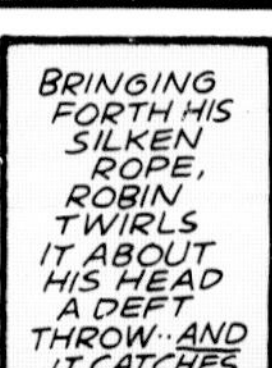
BRINGING FORTH HIS SILKEN ROPE, ROBIN TWIRLS IT ABOUT HIS HEAD A DEFT THROW.. AND IT CATCHES HOLD....

THAT DOES IT!

..TAKING A SHORT RUN, THE BOY WONDER SPRINGS.. HIS BODY SWINGS LIKE A PENDULUM OVER SHEER AND DIZZY HEIGHTS...

...IT SWINGS OVER TO THE NEXT ROOF.... AND AS THE BOY LETS GO OF THE ROPE, DROPS WITH STUNNING FORCE ONTO THE BLACKMAILER!!
SURPRISE!

HE MEANS BUSINESS!
MEANWHILE, THE BATMAN HAS BEEN HAVING QUITE A TIME PURSUING HIS CHOSEN MAN.... A BULLET FANS HIS CHEEK...

AS THE MAN LEAPS INTO HIS OPEN CAR, THE BATMAN DECIDES TO STAKE ALL ON A RISKY TRY....

...A DEATH-DEFYING LEAP INTO SPACE....
HERE GOES NOTHING!

....AND THE BATMAN'S PLUNGING BODY DROPS INTO THE REAR SEAT OF THE CAR!
I COULD SHAKE THE MEASLES EASIER THAN THIS GUY!
MADE IT! WHEW!

BROTHER.... YOUR RIDE IS OVER RIGHT NOW!

WITH NO-ONE TO HOLD THE WHEEL, THE CAR VEERS INTO A POLE, JUST AS THE BATMAN LEAPS IN THE NICK OF TIME!...

THE BLACKMAILERS QUICKLY TRUSSED, THE BATMAN AND ROBIN TURN TO THE BUSINESS AT HAND....
WH-WHAT ARE YOU DOING?
HE'LL BLEED TO DEATH HERE! I'M TAKING HIM TO YOUR DOCTOR. THERE MAY BE STILL A CHANCE!

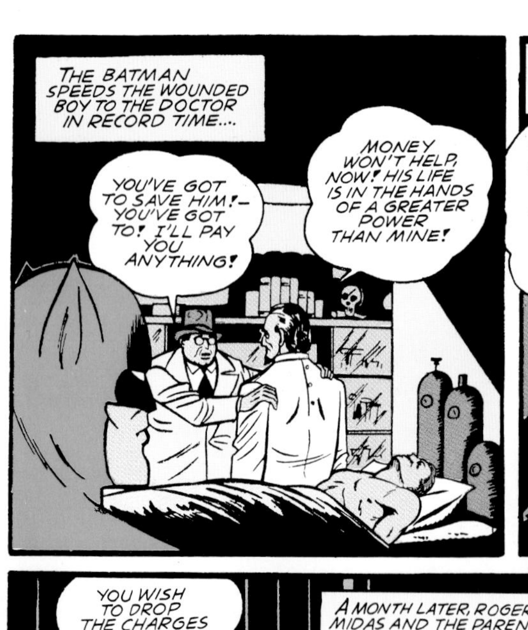
THE BATMAN SPEEDS THE WOUNDED BOY TO THE DOCTOR IN RECORD TIME....
YOU'VE GOT TO SAVE HIM!— YOU'VE GOT TO! I'LL PAY YOU ANYTHING!
MONEY WON'T HELP, NOW! HIS LIFE IS IN THE HANDS OF A GREATER POWER THAN MINE!

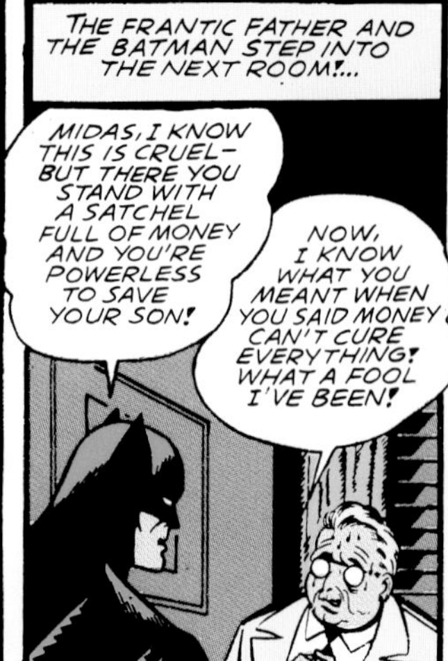
THE FRANTIC FATHER AND THE BATMAN STEP INTO THE NEXT ROOM!...
MIDAS, I KNOW THIS IS CRUEL— BUT THERE YOU STAND WITH A SATCHEL FULL OF MONEY AND YOU'RE POWERLESS TO SAVE YOUR SON!
NOW, I KNOW WHAT YOU MEANT WHEN YOU SAID MONEY CAN'T CURE EVERYTHING! WHAT A FOOL I'VE BEEN!

TO THE ANXIOUS PAIR, MINUTES SEEM TO CLING LIKE FLYPAPER......THEN, AT LONG LAST, THE DOOR SWINGS OPEN...
DOCTOR, WILL HE...?
IT'S A MIRACLE, BUT HE'LL PULL THROUGH! HE WILL LIVE!

YOU WISH TO DROP THE CHARGES AGAINST THIS YOUNG MAN. ! WHY?
A MONTH LATER, ROGER MIDAS AND THE PARENTS OF THE INJURED NEWSBOY STAND BEFORE A JUDGE...
HE HIRED SPECIALISTS TO OPERATE ON MY BOY, SO THAT HE MAY WALK AGAIN!
HE HAS ALSO PUT ASIDE A TRUST FUND SO MY BOY CAN GO TO COLLEGE -- AND HAS GIVEN ME A JOB. HE HAS BEEN VERY KIND, AND VERY HUMBLE!
I KNOW THAT MY MONEY CAN'T ATONE FOR MY CRIME! I'M READY TO STAND TRIAL AND TAKE MY PUNISHMENT!
YOUNG MAN-- YOU'VE MADE RESTITUTION... BUT, WHAT'S MORE IMPORTANT IS THAT YOU'VE LEARNED YOUR LESSON! CASE IS DISMISSED!

LATER THAT DAY..... BRUCE WAYNE VISITS THE MIDAS HOME....
JUST CAME FROM YOUR OFFICE, MIDAS! THOSE STATEMENTS ON MY HOLDINGS....
SORRY, BRUCE! YOUR BUSINESS WILL HAVE TO WAIT! I'M GOING TO A FOOTBALL GAME WITH MY SON!
INCIDENTALLY, BRUCE, LISTEN TO ME ON THE AIR TONIGHT.... "ROGER MIDAS AND HIS MELODEERS".
HURRY, DIANE.... WE CAN'T KEEP JOHNNY BROWN WAITING ALL DAY!
WILL WONDERS NEVER CEASE?
COMING, MOTHER DEAR!
LATER... THE WAYNE HOME..
LOOKS LIKE MRS. MIDAS HAS FORGOTTEN HER SOCIAL PREJUDICES, EH?
YES... AND MR. MIDAS HAS DECIDED TO TAKE A LITTLE TIME OFF FROM BUSINESS AND BECOME A REAL PAL TO HIS SON! OTHER PARENTS CAN TAKE A TIP FROM THIS CASE! IT'S WELL WORTH THINKING ABOUT!

No. 48
A DC PUBLICATION
The BATMAN
Detective
COMICS
FEB.
Reg. U.S. Pat. Off.
10¢
BOB KANE

BATMAN
WITH Robin THE BOY WONDER
BY BOB KANE
WHEN CRIMINALS PLOT TO ROB THE GREAT VAULT HOUSING THE NATION'S GOLD RESERVE, THEN IT IS THAT THE CLOAKED BATMAN AND YOUNG, LAUGHING ROBIN THE BOY WONDER, STEP IN TO NULLIFY CRIME'S THRUST AND DRAW BACK THE CURTAIN THAT VEILS THE MYSTERY OF
THE SECRET CAVERN
OUR STORY BEGINS IN KENTUCKY, WHEN A MAN IDLY ROWING ON A STREAM, SUDDENLY DRIFTS INTO A GASH IN THE SIDE OF A MOUNTAIN.....
WONDER WHERE THIS LEADS TO?

THE MAN IS STUNNED BY THE VASTNESS AND STRANGENESS OF THE WORLD HE HAS ENTERED INTO.....
WHA....? A CAVERN.... A GREAT LIMESTONE CAVERN!

AS HE ROWS, THE GREAT NATURAL WONDERS STRETCH BEFORE HIM MILE UPON MILE.....
I'VE DISCOVERED IT! I'VE DISCOVERED A LIMESTONE CHAMBER THAT IS EVEN GREATER THAN THE MAMMOTH CAVE OR THE CARLSBAD CAVERNS! IT'S MAGNIFICENT!

TAKING OUT HIS SURVEYING INSTRUMENTS, THE MAN STEPS ON THE CAVE'S FLOOR, AND SOON HAS MORE CAUSE FOR EXCITEMENT...

WHY..., FROM MY CALCULATIONS, THIS CAVERN PASSES DIRECTLY UNDER THE GREAT GOLD TREASURY VAULT OF FORT STOX!

WHEN THE MAN GETS BACK TO TOWN, HE CAN HARDLY CONTROL HIS EXCITEMENT.....
IF I DON'T TELL SOMEONE, I'LL BUST! LISTEN TO ME, MEN.....
WHAT'S GOT YOU ALL HOPPED UP, MISTER?

HE TELLS OF HIS GREAT DISCOVERY.....
SO YOU FOUND A BIG LIMESTONE CAVE! SO WHAT?
BUT IT GOES DIRECTLY BENEATH THE GOVERMENT GOLD VAULT AT FORT STOX!

WHAT?.... THE GOLD VAULT?.... ARE YOU KIDDIN'?
SAY-WHERE-ABOUTS IS THIS PLACE, MISTER?
AH-I-ER-DOUBT IF I CAN FIND IT AGAIN! AH-GOOD DAY!
AT THE GLITTER OF GREED IN THE STRANGERS' EYES, THE MAN REALIZES THE SIGNIFICANCE OF HIS DISCOVERY.....

HE SHUT UP LIKE A CLAM! HE KNOWS WHERE THAT PLACE IS!
GOOD THING WE DECIDED TO COME TO THIS BURG TO HIDE OUT FROM THE COPS!
YEAH-LOOKS LIKE WE STUMBLED ONTO SOMETHING BIG!

THE CRIMINALS FIND OUT THE MAN, HENRY LEWIS, IS ROUGHING IT ALONE IN A LOG CABIN IN THE WOODS AND.....THE NEXT MORNING.....
WHA..... WHAT IS THIS?
TAKE IT EASY, LEWIS! WE DECIDED TO SEE IF WE COULD PERSUADE YA TO TELL US WHERE THE OPENING TO THE CAVE IS!

WHEN LEWIS REFUSES, HE IS BEATEN, TORTURED.... BUT HE STOUTLY MAINTAINS HIS SILENCE...
HE'S OUT AGAIN! I WONDER IF HE'D TALK IF WE PROMISED TO GIVE HIM A SHARE OF THE HAUL?
NAW! THIS GUY IS A MILLIONAIRE. HIS HOBBY IS SURVEYIN'! HE'S WORTH PLENTY!

SAY, AIN'T THIS GUY LEWIS GOT A KID NAMED LINDA, SINGIN' IN RENALDO'S TOP HAT CLUB?
YE-AH! THEY BILL HER AS A SOCIETY SINGER!
SAY-IT OUGHTA BE A CINCH FOR US TO COOK UP A WAY FOR LEWIS TA TALK NOW!

TWO NIGHTS LATER.... GOTHAM CITY.... IN A PRIVATE OFFICE OF THE TOP HAT CLUB.
LISTEN, RENALDO.... THIS CLUB OF YOURS AIN'T DOING SO HOT. NOW, HOW WOULD YOU LIKE A CHANCE TO MAKE SOME DOUGH- BIG DOUGH?
YOU INTEREST ME STRANGELY, NICK.... KEEP TALKING!

LATER THAT EVENING..... AS LINDA LEWIS WALKS TO THE BAND PLATFORM, SHE STOPS FOR A WORD WITH A WEALTHY, SOCIETY PLAYBOY NAMED BRUCE WAYNE.....
HOW ABOUT A MOVIE AFTER YOU FINISH YOUR NUMBER, LINDA?
ALL RIGHT, BRUCE. WAIT FOR ME!

...AND LATER, WHEN SHE HAS FINISHED, AND HAS CHANGED CLOTHING.... SUDDENLY....
WHO..?
I HAVE BEEN WAITING FOR YOU! COME WITH ME!

WITH THE INSTINCT FOR SELF PRESERVATION STRONG, THE GIRL DIPS HER HAND IN HER DRESSER DRAWER AND BRINGS OUT A SMALL PEARL-HANDLED REVOLVER...
YOU'RE MAD! STAY AWAY FROM ME! STAY AWAY OR I'LL SHOOT!
COME WITH ME!
3

AS THE MAN NEARS HER, LINDA AUTOMATICALLY PULLS THE TRIGGER .....THERE IS A SHOT!
I-I WAS ONLY FOOLING! YOU SHOULDN'T HAVE.... OHHH!

THE DOOR IS THRUST OPEN.....
THAT SHOT!... NICK!
I DIDN'T MEAN TO- HE....HE WAS CRAZY! HE WOULD HAVE KILLED ME!
SHE SHOT 'IM!

YOU LITTLE FOOL! NICK WAS ONLY HAVING SOME FUN-HE'S A PRACTICAL JOKER! THE THREE OF US WERE IN ON IT!
I KILLED HIM! I KILLED A MAN! OH-WHAT AM I GOING TO DO?
HE'S DEAD! GOT IT RIGHT THROUGH THE HEART!

NOBODY HEARD THE SHOT. THE BAND WAS PLAYING TOO LOUD!
GIVE ME THAT GUN. YOU GET OUT OF THE CITY-TO YOUR FATHER IN KENTUCKY! WE'LL TAKE CARE OF THIS. NO ONE WILL KNOW!

BLINDLY, THE DISTRACTED, BEWILDERED GIRL FOLLOWS INSTRUCTIONS.... AND WHEN SHE LEAVES....
OKAY, NICK - YOU CAN GET UP NOW!
BOY-DID SHE FALL FOR OUR LITTLE ACT!

FOR A MINUTE I WAS WORRIED IF SHE HAD REAL SLUGS IN THAT GUN!
I SHOVED THE BLANKS IN WHILE SHE WAS OUT SINGIN'!
NOW, ALL I HAVE TO DO IS SHOW LEWIS THIS GUN WITH THE GIRL'S PRINTS ON IT, AND HE'LL SPILL EVERYTHING!

AFTER WAITING IN VAIN FOR LINDA, BRUCE WAYNE QUESTIONS RENALDO.....
SHE'S GONE? BUT SHE HAD AN APPOINTMENT WITH ME!
AH-ER-I ALMOST FORGOT! SHE SAID SHE COULDN'T MAKE IT TONIGHT-SOME OTHER TIME, PERHAPS!

FUNNY SHE DIDN'T COME TO TELL ME THAT HERSELF! LINDA'S NOT LIKE THAT! WONDER IF ANYTHING IS WRONG?
4

A STREAKING EXPRESS TRAIN ROARS TOWARD KENTUCKY CARRYING LINDA LEWIS...

WHEN LINDA REACHES HER FATHER'S SECLUDED CABIN....
RENALDO! YOU-HERE?
YOU TOOK A TRAIN...I CAME BY PLANE, AND BEAT YOU BY A FEW HOURS!

FATHER-THESE MEN-THOSE GUNS AT YOUR BACK? WHY?
NEVER MIND THAT! RENALDO HERE TELLS ME YOU KILLED A MAN! IS IT TRUE? TELL ME!

YES, FATHER, I DID.... BUT IT WAS IN SELF-DEFENSE! I SWEAR IT! YOU'VE GOT TO BELIEVE ME!
I BELIEVE YOU, LINDA!

THE BATMOBILE FLASHES THROUGH THE STREETS WITH BULLET SPEED....

HEY- DID YOU SEE THAT?
SURE I SAW IT- BUT THAT DON'T SAY I HAVE TO BELIEVE IT!
Z-I-N-G

THE CAR COMES TO A STOP IN THE BACK ALLEY OF RENALDO'S APARTMENT HOUSE.....
THAT'S RENALDO'S APARTMENT. YOU STAY HERE. I'LL CALL YOU IF I NEED HELP!

SWIFTLY AND NOISELESSLY, THE BATMAN MOVES UP THE FIRE ESCAPE!

YEAH, NICK- RENALDO IS DOWN IN KENTUCKY, TAKIN' CARE O' LINDA LEWIS AND HER OLD MAN! YOU STAY HID- REMEMBER, YOU'RE SUPPOSED TO BE DEAD!
6

AS THE BODYGUARD HANGS UP A SHADOW SEEMS TO CREEP ALONG THE FLOOR....
HUH? THAT SHADOW- LIKE A BAT- THE BATMAN! HE'S HERE!

WHIRLING IN TERROR, THE THUG WHIPS OUT A GUN, AND FIRES.....

A WEIRD FIGURE SPRINGS FROM THE SHADOWS....
I'M NOT THERE... HERE I AM!

LINDA LEWIS AND HER FATHER ARE IN TROUBLE...

....AND YOU KNOW WHY!

DON'T HIT ME LIKE THAT AGAIN! DON'T-
TALK, YOU WHIMPERING WRETCH-TALK! WHAT ABOUT RENALDO AND LEWIS? TALK!

THE COWARDLY THUG BABBLES AS THE BATMAN STARES AT HIM GRIMLY....
SO THAT'S THE SCHEME, IS IT?.... AND WHERE IS NICK HIDING OUT? TELL ME OR I'LL....
I'LL TELL... HE'S HIDING ON MARKER PLACE IN AN OLD GARAGE. IT'S SUPPOSED TO BE A GARAGE... BUT IT'S REALLY A GAMBLING JOINT.

I'VE ALREADY MET NICK BEFORE- HE'S A FIRST CLASS RAT WITH A THIRD RATE CONSCIENCE! IT'LL BE A PLEASURE TO NAB HIM!

MOMENTS LATER, AS THE BATMOBILE WHIZZES TOWARD ITS DESTINATION...
SOMETHING ON YOUR MIND?
I JUST REMEMBERED THAT I DIDN'T TIE THAT HOODLUM UP. I'LL BET HE'S ON THE PHONE RIGHT NOW, SPEAKING WITH NICK!

THE BATMAN'S HUNCH IS CORRECT!
I HADDA TALK, HE WOULD A KILLED ME. HE'S ON HIS WAY OVER!
YOU DIRTY SQUEALER! OKAY.....THE BOYS AND I WILL TAKE CARE O' HIM!

HOODLUMS, EAGER TO SETTLE OLD SCORES WITH THEIR NEMESIS, TAKE THEIR PLACES AT WINDOWS.....WHEN.......
WE'LL GET 'IM WHEN... HEY-WHAT'S, THAT COMIN THIS WAY?
IT'S-IT'S THE BATMOBILE..... AND IT'S COMIN' STRAIGHT AT THE GARAGE!

THERE IS A SUDDEN RENDING, SMASHING OF WOOD AS THE BATMOBILE CRASHES THROUGH THE BARRED GARAGE DOORS!
CRACK!

I'M COMING FOR YOU, NICK!
DON'T LET 'IM GET ME! PLUG 'IM! GIVE 'IM ALL THE BULLETS YOU'VE GOT!

WITH A SUDDEN LITHE MOVEMENT, THE BATMAN SCOOPS UP THE HEAVY TABLE.....

8

....AND BEARS IT FORWARD LIKE A BATTERING RAM!
YOU GAMBLED ON THE TABLE, BUT I'LL BET YOU DIDN'T GAMBLE ON THIS!

THE BATMAN'S STEEL FISTS LASH OUT IN PILE-DRIVER BLOWS!
KEEP SCORE FOR ME ROBIN!

C'MON-LET'S GET THAT KID!
GANGING UP ON ME, EH?

TIME TO RE-TIRE, EH, BOYS?
OOF!!!

PANIC-STRICKEN AT THE SUDDEN DEFEAT OF HIS MOBSTER PALS, NICK FLEES IN TERROR.....
THEY AIN'T GONNA GET ME! NOT ME!
NICK DOESN'T WANT TO PLAY ANYMORE!

A QUICK TWIRL, AND A ROPE WHISTLES OUT AT NICK....
HE WANTS TO LEAVE US....
9

...BUT I THINK HE CHANGED HIS MIND!

AFTER PHONING THE POLICE AND TELLING THEM TO PICK UP THE GANGSTERS, THE BATMAN BLINDFOLDS NICK AND SPEEDS BACK TO THE SECRET BARN.....
WH-WHERE ARE YOU TAKING ME?
TO KENTUCKY, NICK-TO KENTUCKY!

MOMENTS LATER A WEIRD SHAPE RISES IN THE AIR..... IT IS THE BATPLANE!

LIKE SOME ANCIENT, FABLED BIRD, IT WINGS THROUGH THE SKY..

MILES ARE COVERED IN MOMENTS AS THE BATPLANE DASHES THROUGH THE HEAVENS, UNTIL AT LAST THE BATPLANE FLUTTERS DOWN TO A STOP A SHORT DISTANCE AWAY FROM THE LEWIS CABIN..
WE'RE HERE! — KENTUCKY!

LATER AS A GUARD STANDS BEFORE THE CABIN, A MUSCULAR ARM ENCIRCLES HIS THROAT..

INSIDE THE CABIN, A SECOND GUARD STARTS AT THE SOUND OF A KNOCK AT THE DOOR....
MUST BE BLACKIE! WONDER WHAT HE WANTS?

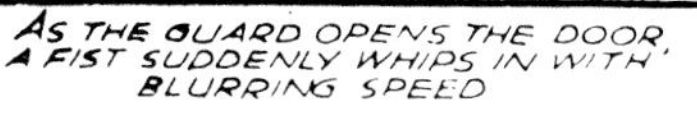
AS THE GUARD OPENS THE DOOR, A FIST SUDDENLY WHIPS IN WITH BLURRING SPEED

UGH!

SAY "HELLO" TO THE LADY, NICK!
WHY-WHY, IT'S THE MAN I KILLED..... ONLY HE ISN'T DEAD! HE'S ALIVE!
WHA-AT?

THE BATMAN FREES LEWIS AND ACQUAINTS THEM WITH THE TRUE FACTS
THEN, IT WAS ALL A SCHEME SO DAD WOULD REVEAL THE LOCATION OF THE CAVERN?
FRAME MY DAUGHTER, WOULD THEY?
YES... AND INCIDENTALLY, I THINK WE HAD BETTER GET THERE RIGHT AWAY!

MOMENTS LATER, A BOAT SLIPS ALONG THE WATER THAT WINDS THROUGH THE TWISTING LABYRINTH OF THE GREAT CAVERN...
WHAT A SOLEMN, AWESOME PLACE!
SO MAJESTIC AND SO SOMBRE!
HOW DEADLY QUIET IT IS!

BETTER HURRY-- RENALDO AND HIS MEN MUST BE DIGGING INTO THE VAULT BY NOW!

WHILE FURTHER ON, RENALDO'S MOBSTERS DIG LIKE MOLES THROUGH THE ROCK......UNTIL
RENALDO! THIS IS IT! WE'RE THROUGH!
OKAY! WE'LL GO UP NOW!

NOISELESSLY, THE MOBSTERS SCAMPER UP THE LADDER INTO FORT STOX ITSELF....
VAULT

THOSE BATS GIVE ME THE CREEPS. THEY REMIND ME TOO MUCH OF THE BATMAN! LIKE HE WAS HERE!
YOU NUTS? I SUPPOSE YOU EXPECT THE BATMAN TO STEP OUT OF THE SHADOWS AND SAY....

....GOOD EVENING, GENTLEMEN!
I-I'M SEEIN' THINGS! I MUST BE!
AWK!

AS ROBIN USES AN OAR, WITH A PURPOSE OTHER THAN THAT FOR THE ONE IT WAS INTENDED, THE BATMAN SPRINGS FORWARD TOWARD THE UPRIGHT LADDER...
NOW, YOU'RE SEEING THINGS... STARS!

DOWN COMES THE LADDER, AND THE GUNMEN WITH IT!
JUST LIKE HUMPTY DUMPTY-YOU HAD A GREAT FALL!

THE MEN RISE SHAKILY TO THEIR FEET.....

....ONLY TO GO DOWN AGAIN!
YOU CERTAINLY DO HAVE YOUR UPS AND DOWNS, DON'T YOU?

MEANWHILE, THE BOY WONDER GIVES A GOOD ACCOUNTING OF HIMSELF.....
A LITTLE SOMETHING FOR YOU, BUDDY!
12

....AND YOU'RE NO EXCEPTION, HORSEFACE!

AN UNTHINKING GUNMAN IN THE VAULT TAKES A POT SHOT AT THE DYNAMIC DUO....
I'LL GET THAT BATMAN YET!
I HEARD A SHOT!
LOOK! OVER THERE!
YOU NUTS? WANTA BRING THE SOLDIERS OUT?

THEIR RETREAT CUT OFF THE GUNMEN FALL BEFORE THE WITHERING GUNFIRE OF THE NATION'S SOLDIERS! IT MARKS THE END OF THE PLOT TO LOOT THE VAULT!

.....WHILE BELOW, AS RENALDO TRIES TO FLEE, A MANTLED FIGURE SEEMS TO WIND ITSELF AROUND HIS BODY...
TAKE IT EASY, RENALDO...

YOU'RE NOT GOING ANYWHERE.... FOR MAYBE TWENTY YEARS OR SO.

WHEN THE BATMAN TURNS TO FIND MR. LEWIS, HE DISCOVERS THE GENTLEMAN IS QUITE BUSY.....
WHAT ?
THESE ARE THE MUGGS THAT TIED ME UP AND BEAT ME! NOW, LET'S SEE HOW THEY LIKE IT FOR A CHANGE!

WHEN ALL IS EXPLAINED TO THE FORT STOX COMMANDER, THE BATMAN AND ROBIN PREPARE TO TAKE LEAVE OF LEWIS AND LINDA......
YOU'VE DONE YOUR COUNTRY A GREAT SERVICE! I'LL SEE THAT THE PRESIDENT HEARS OF THIS AND GIVES YOU BOTH A SUITABLE AWARD!
THAT'S NOT NECESSARY. BEING AMERICANS IS ENOUGH OF AN AWARD!

I SALUTE TWO GREAT AMERICANS!
OUTLINED AGAINST THE MOON IS A CRAFT CARRYING TWO FIGURES. THE BATMAN AND ROBIN, THE BOY WONDER!
BOB KANE

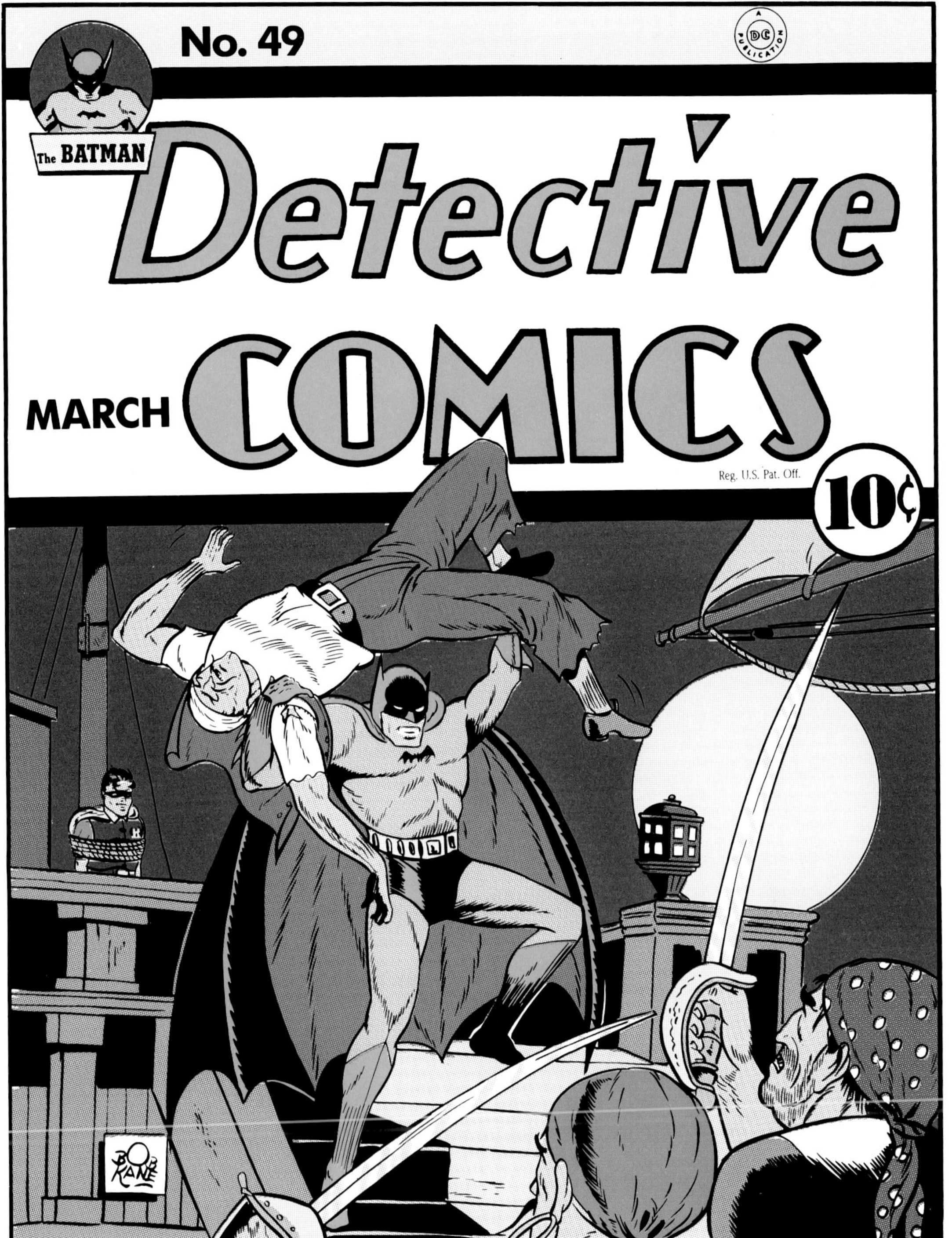
No. 49
A DC PUBLICATION
The BATMAN
Detective
MARCH
COMICS
Reg. U.S. Pat. Off.
10¢
BOB KANE

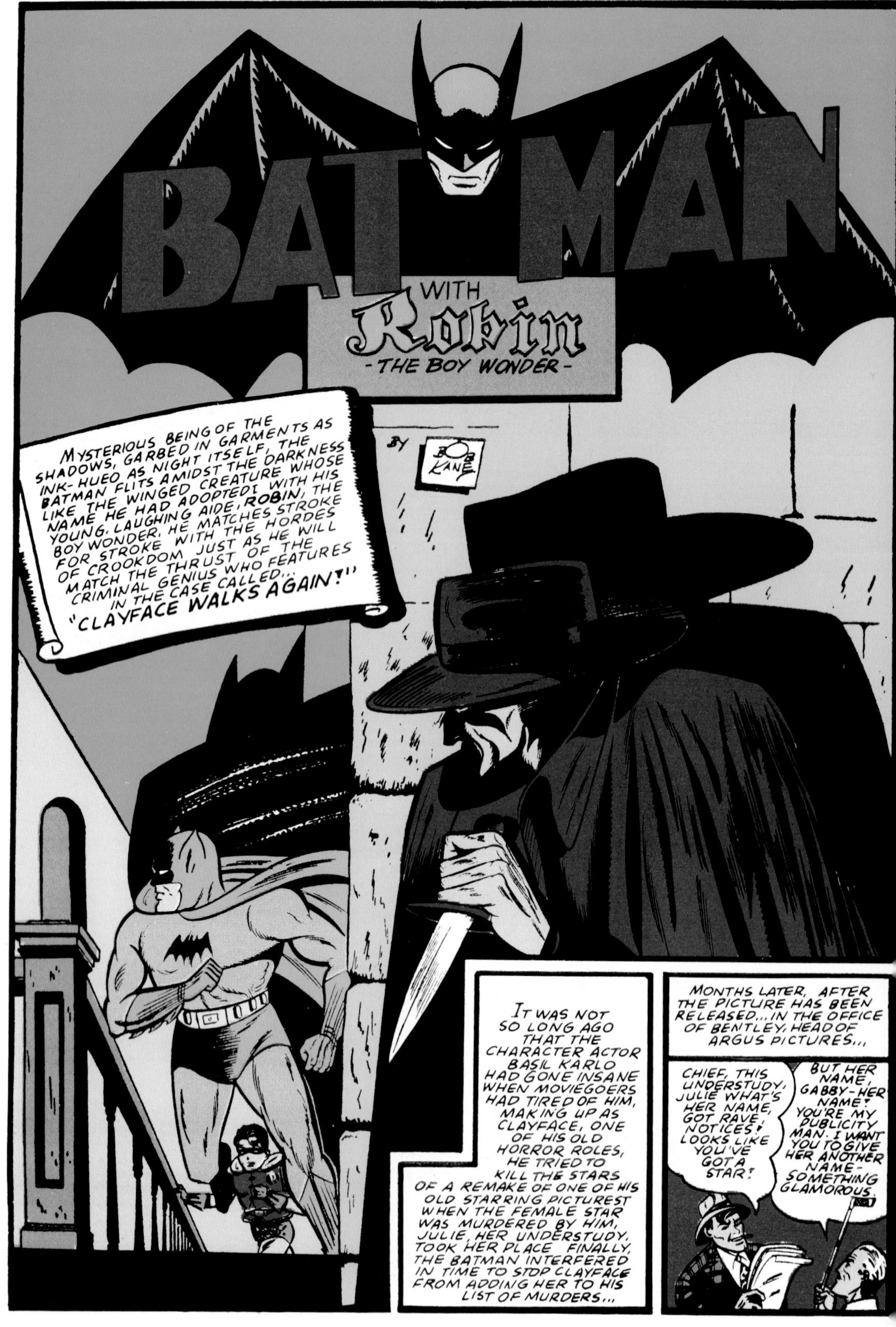
BATMAN
WITH
Robin
-THE BOY WONDER-
MYSTERIOUS BEING OF THE SHADOWS, GARBED IN GARMENTS AS INK-HUED AS NIGHT ITSELF, THE BATMAN FLITS AMIDST THE DARKNESS LIKE THE WINGED CREATURE WHOSE NAME HE HAD ADOPTED! WITH HIS YOUNG, LAUGHING AIDE, ROBIN, THE BOY WONDER, HE MATCHES STROKE FOR STROKE WITH THE HORDES OF CROOKDOM JUST AS HE WILL MATCH THE THRUST OF THE CRIMINAL GENIUS WHO FEATURES IN THE CASE CALLED... "CLAYFACE WALKS AGAIN!"
BY BOB KANE
IT WAS NOT SO LONG AGO THAT THE CHARACTER ACTOR BASIL KARLO HAD GONE INSANE WHEN MOVIEGOERS HAD TIRED OF HIM, MAKING UP AS CLAYFACE, ONE OF HIS OLD HORROR ROLES, HE TRIED TO KILL THE STARS OF A REMAKE OF ONE OF HIS OLD STARRING PICTUREST WHEN THE FEMALE STAR WAS MURDERED BY HIM, JULIE, HER UNDERSTUDY, TOOK HER PLACE. FINALLY, THE BATMAN INTERFERED IN TIME TO STOP CLAYFACE FROM ADDING HER TO HIS LIST OF MURDERS...
MONTHS LATER, AFTER THE PICTURE HAS BEEN RELEASED... IN THE OFFICE OF BENTLEY, HEAD OF ARGUS PICTURES...
CHIEF, THIS UNDERSTUDY, JULIE WHAT'S HER NAME, GOT RAVE NOTICES! LOOKS LIKE YOU'VE GOT A STAR!
BUT HER NAME, GABBY-HER NAME! YOU'RE MY PUBLICITY MAN. I WANT YOU TO GIVE HER ANOTHER NAME-SOMETHING GLAMOROUS.

SHE TOOK THE PUBLIC BY STORM, AND ...
"STORM" THAT'S IT! —BUT LET'S SPELL IT "S-T-O-R-M-E!"
SNAP!

"STORME"- NOT BAD! NOW A FIRST NAME- ONE THAT WILL BE IN CONTRAST! SOMETHING GENTLE, KIND, SWEET!
WHO WAS IT IN BOOKS THAT WAS GENTLE, KIND!

"PORTIA"? SHAKESPEARE'S "PORTIA!" HOW DO YOU LIKE THIS? "PORTIA STORME!"
ITS A NATURALY A NATURAL! CALL UP THE NEWSPAPERS, THE MOVIE MAGS! SPREAD THAT NAME FROM HERE TO TIMBUCTOO!
SNAP!

A STAR IS BORN!
GOTHAM GAZETTE
PORTIA STORME
SCREEN STARS
NEWS
PORTIA STORME
MOVIE MAG
10¢
PORTIA STORME
A STAR IS BORN
PORTIA STORME
Starring PORTIA STORM

A FEW DAYS LATER, JULIE, NOW PORTIA STORME, TALKS WITH HER FIANCE, BRUCE WAYNE...
YOU'RE ON YOUR WAY UP, A NEW STAR, A NEW NAME!
...AND A NEW CAREER! OH, BRUCE, IF ONLY YOU WOULD DO SOMETHING!

...IF ONLY YOU'D FIND YOURSELF A CAREER INSTEAD OF BEING THE PUBLIC'S NUMBER ONE PLAYBOY!
SORRY, HONEY. I'M HAVING TOO GOOD A TIME TO BE BOTHERED WITH ANYTHING REMOTELY CONNECTED WITH WORK! (YOU'D BE MIGHTY SURPRISED IF YOU KNEW I HAD A CAREER- AS THE BATMAN!)

THEN I'M SORRY, BRUCE. UNTIL YOU DECIDE TO MAKE SOMETHING OF YOURSELF, I'M AFRAID OUR ENGAGEMENT IS OFF!
I-I SEE.

I'M NOT WALKING OUT ON YOU, BRUCE. ANYTIME YOU DECIDE TO CHANGE YOUR WAYS, I'LL COME BACK TO YOU GLADLY!
I UNDERSTAND! IT'S ALL RIGHT!

IN CASE YOU EVER NEED ME FOR ANYTHING, JUST HOLLER. IF EVER THERE'S ANYTHING I CAN DO...
THANK YOU, BRUCE, BUT I DON'T THINK I'LL EVER BE IN MUCH TROUBLE.

BUT PORTIA IS WRONG.
SHE WILL NEED BRUCE WAYNE SOON.... BUT AS HIS OTHER SELF... THE BATMAN!

THAT VERY NIGHT, AS THUNDER YELLS OUT IN BASS, AND LIGHTNING GLITTERS IN THE HEAVENS, A PRISON AMBULANCE ROLLS SLOWLY ALONG A WET ROAD...
WHO IS THAT GUY IN THE BACK?
BASIL KARLO, THAT HORROR MOVIE ACTOR! WHAT A NIGHT TO BE TRANSFERRING HIM TO THE STATE ASYLUM! SORTA FITS DOESN'T IT?

AS THE RAIN RUSHES DOWN WITH INCREASING FORCE, THE TRUCK SUDDENLY SKIDS MADLY ON THE SLIPPERY ROAD AND PLUNGES OFF THE EMBANKMENT...

THERE IS A CRASH - A SUDDEN STILLNESS! MINUTES PASS. THEN, A LONE FIGURE RISES SHAKILY FROM THE TWISTED MASS OF STEEL AND WOOD...

A FLASH OF JAGGED LIGHTNING MOMENTARILY ILLUMINATES THE MACABRE SCENE, AND REVEALS THE FACE OF THE SURVIVOR... BASIL KARLO, THE PRISONER!
YOU SEE? IT'S ME-KARLO! AND I'M FREE! FRE-EE-EEE!

MOMENTS LATER, THE OWNER OF A MOVIE MAKE-UP SUPPLY STORE FALLS BACK IN UTTER TERROR AS A TERRIBLE FIGURE NEARS HIM...
WHO-WHAT DO YOU WANT?

THERE IS A STRANGLED SCREAM, THE FALL OF A BODY! THEN KARLO LOOKS ABOUT, SITS BEFORE A MIRROR, AND DEFTLY APPLIES MAKEUP...
HA! IT FEELS GOOD TO USE MAKEUP AGAIN!
WIG

...FIRST THE WAY, THEN CLAY... WIG... AND FINALLY THE HAT AND CAPE. IN PLACE OF THE FACE OF KARLO... THE GROTESQUE ONE OF... CLAYFACE!
THE WORLD WILL ONCE AGAIN HEAR OF ME!

GOTHAM GAZETTE
KARLO "CLAYFACE" ESCAPES
A SMASHUP, WHICH STUNNED TWO PRISON GUARDS, GAVE BASIL KARLO THE CHANCE FOR ESCAPE--
KARLO GAINED FOR HIMSELF THE NAME OF CLAYFACE WHEN HE FIGURED IN THE MANY MURDERS OF
AN UNIDENTIFIED MAN YESTERDAY ATTACKED THE OWNER OF A MAKEUP STORE AND
F. MILLER ARRIVES
GEORGE

THE HOME OF BRUCE WAYNE AND HIS WARD, YOUNG DICK GRAYSON-
YOU THINK IT WAS KARLO WHO ATTACKED THAT MAKEUP STORE OWNER?
RIGHT! KARLO IS PROBABLY WEARING MAKEUP RIGHT NOW-THE MAKEUP OF CLAYFACE! DICK, GET OUT OUR WORK, CLOTHES-WE'VE GOT A JOB TO DO!
KARLO CLAYFACE ESCAPES

ONCE AGAIN, BRUCE AND DICK REVERT TO THEIR OTHER SELVES... THE BATMAN AND ROBIN, THE BOY WONDER!
DO I DETECT THE EAGER LIGHT OF BATTLE IN YOUR EYES?
YOU DO -AND HOW!

THEY PAD THROUGH THE SECRET TUNNEL BELOW THE HOUSE...

A MOMENT LATER, THE BATMOBILE ZOOMS THROUGH THE NIGHT!
GOING OVER TO ARGUS STUDIOS, AREN'T YOU?
GOOD GUESS, ROBIN. I FIGURE THAT'S THE ONE PLACE CLAYFACE WOULD BE LIKELY TO GO!

THE DYNAMIC DUO SCALES THE ARGUS STUDIO WALL AND DROPS INSIDE THE GROUNDS.

MAYBE CLAYFACE IS AROUND AND MAYBE HE'S NOT, BUT AT ANYRATE IT DOESN'T HURT TO LOOK! WE'LL SPLIT UP... BE ABLE TO COVER MORE TERRITORY THAT WAY!

WALKING ACROSS A "YACHT" SET IS A MYSTERIOUS FIGURE... CLAYFACE!
THIS STUDIO FIRED ME! ME-KARLO! I'LL DESTROY IT BY FIRE! THIS INCENDIARY BOMB SHOULD DO IT VERY NICELY!

THEN CLAYFACE SEES...
THE BATMAN! THE MAN RESPONSIBLE FOR MY CAPTURE!

CLAYFACE REACHES ON THE "YACHT" WALL AND SEIZING A FIRE HOOK, HURLS IT AT THE BATMAN!

SOME SIXTH SENSE, SOME INSTINCTIVE FEELING OF DANGER, WARNS THE BATMAN AND HE DUCKS...
WHA..?

THE BATMAN SEES HIS ENEMY AND GIVES CHASE...
CLAYFACE!

A LOW, SWEEPING TACKLE BRINGS CLAYFACE DOWN, ON A SET OF A MINIATURE CITY...
STICK AROUND CHUM!

LIKE TWO TITANS, THEY BATTLE OVER THE MINIATURE CITY...

SUDDENLY, CLAYFACE SCOOPS UP A TINY RAILROAD TRAIN AND MANAGES TO CATCH THE BATMAN ON THE SIDE OF THE HEAD...

THE BATMAN DROPS!
NOW'S MY CHANCE TO FINISH HIM OFF! ...THAT TRUCK-THAT'S THE ANSWER!

CLAYFACE SETS THE TRUCK SPEEDING AT THE BATMAN AND LEAPS OFF...
IS THE BATMAN DOOMED TO A MANGLED DEATH? WILL THE HURTLING MONSTER CLAIM THE BATMAN AS ITS VICTIM?

CLAYFACE, CERTAIN THAT THE BATMAN IS AS GOOD AS DEAD, WALKS THE STUDIO GROUNDS BENT ON MORE DESTRUCTION...
"IF THE BATMAN IS HERE, THEN THAT ROBIN BOY MUST BE AROUND! I'VE A SCORE TO SETTLE WITH HIM ALSO!"

IT IS AS IF FATE WERE DIRECTING THE SCENE, FOR ROBIN HIMSELF PASSES NEARBY.
I'M IN LUCK TONIGHT LOOK AT HIM! SO SURE OF HIMSELF! BAH! I'LL TAKE THAT OUT OF HIM!

A PIECE OF SKY SEEMS TO FALL ON ROBIN'S HEAD! A LIGHT, WHITE AND PAINFUL, FLASHES BEFORE HIS EYES-THEN ALL IS BLACKNESS!
6

CLAYFACE DRAGS THE UNCONSCIOUS BOY TO A SET CONSTRUCTED OF WOOD.
NOW THE INCENDIARY BOMB!

THERE IS A SHARP EXPLOSION, THEN-FIRE!
HA HA-BURN! -LIKE THE HATE IN MY HEART! BURN! HA HA HA!
NOW IT IS ROBIN WHOM DEATH TAPS ON THE SHOULDER! IS THIS NIGHT TO SEE THE END OF THE DYNAMIC DUO?

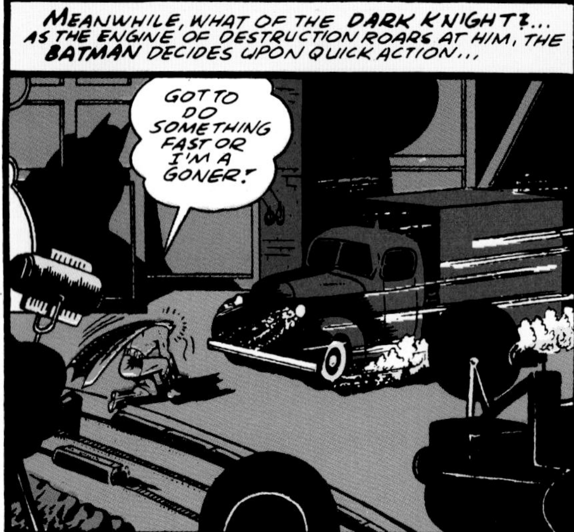
MEANWHILE, WHAT OF THE DARK KNIGHT?... AS THE ENGINE OF DESTRUCTION ROARS AT HIM, THE BATMAN DECIDES UPON QUICK ACTION...
GOT TO DO SOMETHING FAST OR I'M A GONER!

THE BATMAN DIVES INTO THE PATH OF THE TRUCK!

BUT LIES SAFE BETWEEN THE MASSIVE WHEELS!
THE BATMAN HAS MET CLAYFACE AND CHECKMATED HIS FIRST MOVE!

MEANWHILE- BACK AT THE FIRE...
IF THERE'S A BOY IN THERE, I'M AFRAID HE'S A GONER!
I TELL YOU I SEEN HIM! IT WAS CLAYFACE - AND HE LEFT A KID WITH A COSTUME ON INSIDE!
CLAYFACE!

NOT YET, HE ISN'T!
BATMAN!

THE BATMAN DOUSES HIMSELF WITH WATER...
I'M GOING IN THERE!

HE LASSOES A NEARBY PROJECTION...
YOU CAN'T GO IN THERE - IT'S SHEER SUICIDE!
LISTEN, THE BEST FRIEND I'VE GOT LIES IN THERE - GET OUT OF MY WAY! I'M GOING IN!

THE DAUNTLESS BATMAN SWINGS TOWARD THE RAGING INFERNO...

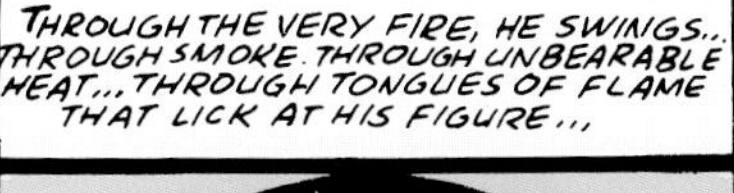
THROUGH THE VERY FIRE, HE SWINGS.. THROUGH SMOKE. THROUGH UNBEARABLE HEAT... THROUGH TONGUES OF FLAME THAT LICK AT HIS FIGURE...

-UNTIL HE DROPS INTO THE VERY MIDST OF THE ROARING FIRE... HE FIGHTS HIS WAY THROUGH LEAPING YELLOW TENDRILS, CALLING... ALWAYS CALLING...
ROBIN! ROBIN!

THEN...
ROBIN! THE FLAMES HAVEN'T REACHED HIM YET!

IT TOOK NERVE TO GO IN THERE!
MORE THAN NERVE, CHIEF-IT WAS THE LOVE FOR THAT KID!
NO SIGN OF THEM YET! IT-IT LOOKS HOPELESS!

LOOK!

THE BOY! -HOW IS HE?
HE'S ALL RIGHT! MY WET CAPE PROTECTED HIM!
DOUSING YOUR CLOTHES WITH WATER WAS A SMART STUNT-BUT YOUR GOING IN THERE WAS STILL SOMETHING I'M GOING TO REMEMBER A LONG, LONG TIME!

LATER...THE WAYNE HOME...
LOOK AT THE SIZE OF THAT EGG WHERE CLAYFACE GOT ME!
I'M GOING TO GET THAT GUY- I'M GOING TO GET HIM IF IT'S THE LAST THING I DO!

THAT NIGHT, AS PORTIA STORME RIDES HOME IN HER CAR, SHE IS STARTLED BY THE MOMENTARY GLIMPSE OF A FACE...
CLAYFACE!

...AT THE STUDIO, THE NEXT MORNING...
I TELL YOU IT WAS CLAYFACE! HE WAS WATCHING ME! I'M IN DANGER!
HE STILL HATES YOU BECAUSE HE FAILED TO KILL YOU BEFORE! HE'LL TRY AGAIN!

BUT THAT NEW PICTURE WE'RE SHOOTING...
WE'LL CONTINUE SHOOTING! IF YOU STOP NOW, YOU'LL LOSE A FORTUNE!
ATTA GIRL- JUST POST A LOT OF GUARDS AROUND, AND CLAYFACE WON'T DARE TO SHOW UP!

GABBY FEST'S LOVE FOR PUBLICITY IS TOO STRONG, AND THE NEXT DAY...
DAILY TROTTER
CLAYFACE THREATENS PORTIA STORME
BRAVE YOUNG ACTRESS TO CONTINUE WORK UNDER GUARD
STUDIO POSTS SPECIAL DETAIL ABOUT SET...
PORTIA STORME

SO THEY THINK MERE GUARDS CAN STOP ME? FOOLS! THE UTTER FOOLS!

PORTIA- THREATENED! WE'VE GOT TO DO SOMETHING!

...THAT NIGHT, PORTIA STORME HAS A VISITOR....
WHO..? -THE BATMAN!
WE MEET AGAIN! NOW LISTEN CAREFULLY- I'VE GOT SOMETHING I WANT TO SPEAK TO YOU ABOUT....

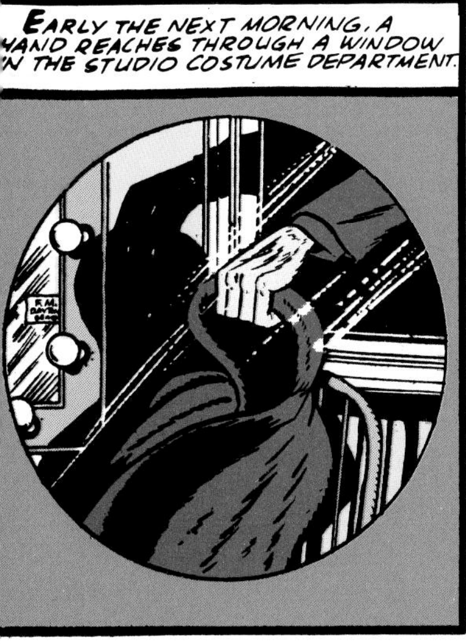
EARLY THE NEXT MORNING, A HAND REACHES THROUGH A WINDOW IN THE STUDIO COSTUME DEPARTMENT.

ANOTHER FIGURE JOINS THE MANY EXTRAS THAT STROLL PAST THE GUARDS ONTO THE SET...
NOW DON'T WORRY ABOUT A THING, PORTIA- WITH ALL THE POLICE I'VE GOT POSTED, CLAYFACE WON'T DARE TO SHOW UP!
...I'LL TRY NOT TO, MR. BENTLEY... BUT I HAVE A QUEER FEELING THAT HE WILL.

SUDDENLY, TWO MANTLED FORMS RACE TOWARD THE GUARDED SET....THEY ARE THE BATMAN AND ROBIN!
LET US THROUGH! PORTIA STORME IS IN TERRIBLE DANGER!

YEAH- FROM MASKED GUYS LIKE YOU!
LET'S GRAB 'EM, BOYS!
OKAY, BUDDY- YOU ASKED FOR IT!

I SAID, WE'RE GOING THROUGH!

...AND HE'S NOT KIDDING!

I REPEAT, GENTLEMEN- WE'RE GOING THROUGH!

ONTO THE SET RACES THE DYNAMIC DUO....
STOP THEM! STOP THEM!

I'LL STAND THESE BABIES OFF, ROBIN!

AS ROBIN DISAPPEARS WITH PORTIA STORME INTO A SMALL ALCOVE OF THE CASTLE, THE BATMAN HOLDS OFF THE ATTACKING GUARDS...
I'M AFRAID THERE'S SOME SORT OF MISTAKE, BUT I CAN'T STOP TO EXPLAIN NOW!

HOWEVER, THE NUMBER OF GUARDS PROVES TOO OVERWHELMING, AND THE DYNAMIC DUO RETREATS....

UP IN ONE OF THE TOWERS, CLAYFACE GLOATS....
THEY'RE RUNNING AWAY, LEAVING PORTIA STORME BEHIND! HA! NOW I CAN TAKE CARE OF HER WITHOUT ANY DISTURBANCE!

CLAYFACE GRIMLY PLACES AN ARROW INTO HIS GIANT BOW...DRAWS IT FULL BACK AND....
NOW... PORTIA STORME ...DIE!

THERE IS A TWANG.. A HISS...AND THE SHAFT OF DEATH BURIES ITSELF IN THE BACK OF PORTIA STORME!

THAT'S HIM - CLAYFACE!

THE BATMAN RACES UP THE STEPS LIKE A WHIRLWIND...

BUT IS MET BY CLAYFACE....

KNIFE IN HAND, CLAYFACE LEAPS....
THIS TIME YOU WILL DIE, BATMAN!

BRACING HIS BODY, THE BATMAN MEETS THE MADMAN'S CHARGE...

THE TWO LOCK IN A DEATH GRIP AND TUMBLE DOWN THE STEPS.
I'M GOING TO KILL YOU YET!
I'LL DO MY BEST TO ALTER YOUR PLANS!

THE TWO BATTLING FIGURES ROLL ACROSS THE FLOOR INTO A ROOM. CLAYFACE RISES TO HIS FEET AND UNLEASHES A TERRIBLE BLOW THAT SENDS THE BATMAN REELING.

AS CLAYFACE LIFTS A HEAVY CHAIR AND CHARGES FOR THE KILL THE BATMAN LASHES OUT WITH BOTH FEET....
I'LL...
NOW IT'S MY TURN!

THE BATMAN MOVES FORWARD WITH THE LITHE SPEED OF A TIGER. A FIST COMES UP IN A SHORT CHOPPY UPPERCUT.
HOLD THAT POSITION!

STEPPING BACK, THE BATMAN TAKES HIS MEASURE. THEN, HIS RIGHT FIST WHISTLES THROUGH THE AIR. THERE IS A SHARP CRACK LIKE THAT OF A RIFLE SHOT, AND CLAYFACE DROPS LIKE A FELLED STEER!
ROCK-A-BYE-BABY!

CLAYFACE IS TAKEN INTO POLICE CUSTODY....
PORTIA! -PORTIA! SHE'S DEAD! DEAD!
CAREFUL, BENTLEY-HER GHOST IS RISING!

SUDDENLY, THE "DEAD FIGURE RISES, WHIPS OFF PORTIA'S CLOAK AND REVEALS ROBIN.
A LIFE PRESERVER LINED WITH HEAVY CORK AND COTTON!
WE DIDN'T KNOW WHETHER HE WOULD USE A KNIFE OR NOT SO WE TOOK NO CHANCES!
YOU SEE, WE HAD IT ALL PLANNED! I HAD THE PRESERVER HIDDEN IN THE ALCOVE...

I GAVE ROBIN MY CLOAK. I ALREADY HAD ONE OF HIS COSTUMES UNDER MY DRESS! MY FACE WAS KEPT IN SHADOW BY USING THE CLOAK!
SORRY I HAD TO HIT THE GUARDS, BUT IT HAD TO LOOK GOOD SO CLAYFACE WOULDN'T GET SUSPICIOUS!
WE HAD TO MAKE CLAYFACE GIVE HIMSELF AWAY!
MY HEAD IS SPINNING! I'M DIZZY -- I'M GOING CRAZY!

WAIT I ASKED YOU ONCE BEFORE ABOUT A CAREER IN THE MOVIES! HOW ABOUT IT?
WHEN THERE'S NO MORE CRIME IN THIS WORLD, I'LL BE GLAD TO-UNTIL THEN I'M BUSY!

THAT'S THE SORT OF CAREER I WISH BRUCE WOULD PICK FOR HIMSELF! BUT I GUESS THAT'S WISHING FOR THE IMPOSSIBLE!

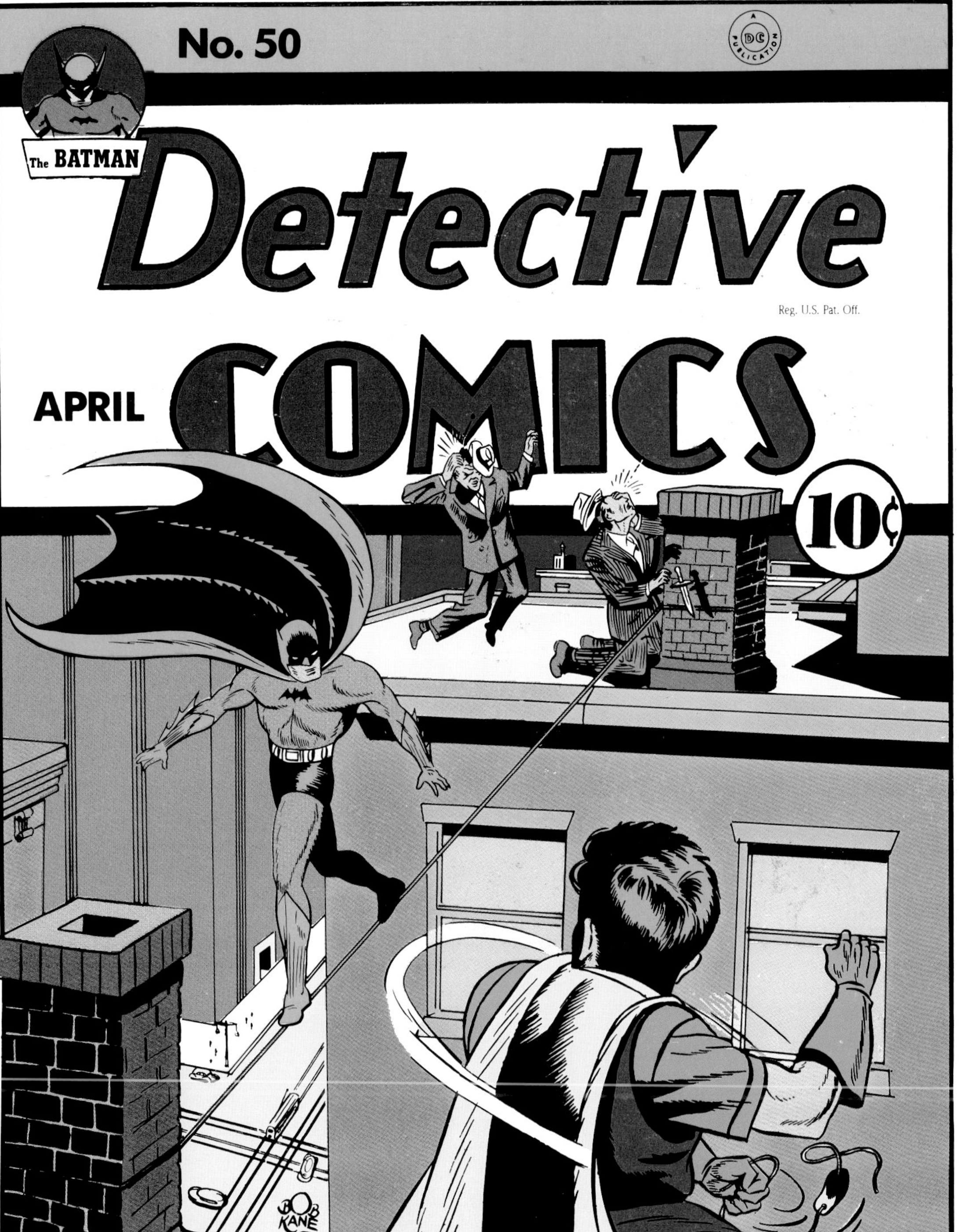
No. 50
A DC PUBLICATION
The BATMAN
Detective
Reg. U.S. Pat. Off.
APRIL
COMICS
10¢
BOB KANE

BATMAN
WITH
Robin
-THE BOY WONDER-
BY- BOB KANE
TO MANY PEOPLE, THE BATMAN IS A BEING OF MYSTERY, AN EERIE POWER. YET, HE IS A MAN-A MAN WHO HAS DEVELOPED HIS BRAIN AND HIS MUSCULAR FRAME TO THE HIGHEST DEGREE. A LIVING BEING OF THE DARKNESS; HE COMES AND GOES UNSEEN. HIS AIM IN LIFE-THE BLOTTING OUT OF ALL CRIME! ASSISTING THE BATMAN IS THAT PHENOMENAL BOY WONDER, ROBIN! IT IS THESE TWO WHO WILL SOLVE AND METE OUT JUSTICE IN.....
"THE CASE OF THE THREE DEVILS!"
ONE STILL NIGHT, AS THE BATMAN AND ROBIN GHOST OVER THE ROOFTOPS, THEY SPY THREE BIZARRE FIGURES IN FLIGHT. WITHOUT A MOMENT'S HESITATION, THE DYNAMIC DUO SWINGS DOWN TO DO BATTLE WITH THE STRANGELY-CLAD FIGURES.
AS ROBIN DROPS TO AID THE BATMAN, HE IS TACKLED IN MID-AIR BY A DEVIL-LIKE FIGURE, AND THE TWO PLUNGE TO THE ROOFTOP BELOW.....

AS ROBIN STARTS TO RISE SOMEWHAT UNSTEADILY TO HIS FEET, THE DEVIL-GARBED ATTACKER PUNISHES HIM CRUELLY WITH A WRESTLER'S TRICK....
RELAX, KID!

THEN, THE MAN SPRINGS FORWARD AND BRINGS A GUN BUTT DOWN ON THE BATMAN'S HEAD....
...AND THIS WILL TAKE CARE OF YOU, MISTER BATMAN!

THE THREE DEVILS CONTINUE THEIR FLIGHT ACROSS THE ROOFTOPS....
WHY DIDN'T YOU PLUG THE BATMAN AND GET IT OVER WITH?
SURE- AND BRING ON THE COPS? USE YOUR HEAD!

DO YOU SEE THEM?
YES- AND, IT WON'T BE LONG BEFORE WE'RE UP TO THEM.
LUCKILY, THE GUN BUTT ONLY GRAZED THE BATMAN, AND HE AND ROBIN GIVE CHASE....

AS THE THREE DEVILS PERCEIVE THEIR PURSUERS DRAWING CLOSE, ONE DIVES HEADLONG OFF THE ROOF, HIS HANDS REACHING FOR A JUTTING FLAGPOLE.....
NO! I'VE GOT A BETTER IDEA!
HEY!-THEY'RE GETTING NEARER! SHALL WE PLUG 'EM?

WHEN HE GAINS THE FLAGPOLE, HE HOOKS HIS LEGS AROUND IT AND DANGLES HEAD DOWN.....
LET'S GO!

A DARING PLUNGE BY THE SECOND DEVIL.....
ALLEY OOP!

.....A GIANT SWING THROUGH EMPTY SPACE, HE GRASPS THE HANDS OF THE FIRST DEVIL.....

...DOES A SOMERSAULT IN MID-AIR AND STREAKS TOWARD A FIRE-ESCAPE RUNG ON THE NEXT BUILDING.....

THE SCENE IS REPEATED BY THE LAST THIEF.....

....AND THE THIRD DEVIL IS CAUGHT BY THE SECOND DEVIL......
GOT YOU!

......THEN THE FIRST MAN LEAVES THE FLAGPOLE AND DIVES TOWARD HIS COMPANION, WHOSE DANGLING FORM SWINGS OUT TO MEET HIM...

THE THREE, THEN, SCRAMBLE UP THE LADDER AND CONTINUE THEIR SUCCESSFUL FLIGHT!
OKAY! STEP ON IT!

THE BATMAN AND ROBIN ARRIVE TOO LATE!
BOY, DID YOU SEE HOW THEY GOT AWAY?
YES- AND VERY NEATLY DONE, ROBIN. LOOKS LIKE WE'RE IN FOR SOME STIFF COMPETITION! THOSE DEVILS ARE DARE-DEVILS!

IN THE ENSUING WEEKS, THE NAME OF THE "THREE DEVILS" BECOMES WELL KNOWN- TOO WELL KNOWN FOR COMFORT!
RECORD
THREE DEVILS LOOT JEWELRY STORE
NEWS
THREE DEVILS M
DARING ESCAPE
AFTER HOLDUP
VILS STEAL
FAMOUS
'S RUBY...

WELL, CAN YOU TELL ME WHY YOU DIDN'T CATCH THE THREE DEVILS THIS TIME?
CATCH THEM? WE CAN'T EVEN GET CLOSE TO THEM!
THEY HOP AROUND LIKE MEXICAN JUMPING BEANS!

AT HIS HOME, BRUCE WAYNE CHATS WITH HIS YOUNG WARD, DICK GRAYSON...
THOSE THREE DEVILS SEEM TO BE GIVING THE POLICE A VERY DEVIL OF A TIME! A BAD PUN, DICK, BUT QUITE TRUE, NEVERTHELESS!

DICK, WHAT DO YOU THINK THE THREE DEVILS DO WITH ALL THE JEWELS THEY'VE STOLEN?
WHY- WHY, THEY SELL THEM FOR MONEY, OF COURSE!

BUT WAIT- THEY CAN'T SELL THEM TO JEWELRY STORES.
EXACTLY! THEY MUST SELL THE STUFF TO A "FENCE"! - A MAN WHO BUYS STOLEN DIAMONDS!

THERE ARE ONLY TWO FENCES IN THE CITY BIG ENOUGH TO BUY AND CUT UP THE DIAMONDS THE DEVILS HAVE STOLEN!
I SEE- AND WE'RE GOING TO KEEP AN EYE ON THE TWO FENCES! HERE WE GO AGAIN!

THE TWO DON STRANGE GARB..... AND ONCE AGAIN BECOME THEIR OTHER, STRANGER SELVES.....
I'M ALL SET... LET'S GO!
.....THE BATMAN AND ROBIN, THE BOY WONDER, ARE READY TO DO BATTLE WITH THE THREE DEVILS!

TAKING ALONG THOSE NEW ROCKET-ROLLER SKATES WE DEVELOPED?
YES, I FIGURE THEY MIGHT COME IN HANDY!

NIGHTFALL! THE MOON IS LIKE AN UNWINKING EYE AS IT LOOKS DOWN AT THE TWO MANTLED FIGURES WHO SLINK SILENTLY IN THE SHADOWS ACROSS THE GREY CITY STREETS....

THE DENS OF THE TWO NOTORIOUS FENCES ARE WATCHED.....

NOTHING YET! WE'LL JUST HAVE TO KEEP WATCHING.

NIGHT AFTER NIGHT, THE DYNAMIC DUO MOVES DEEP IN DARKNESS, KEEPING THEIR CONSTANT VIGIL.
NO SIGN OF THEM!
IT LOOKS LIKE MY SCHEME HAS LAID AN EGG - AND A LARGE EGG AT THAT!

THEN....
NOT YET IT HASN'T -LOOK!
THE THREE DEVILS! ACTION AT LAST!

INSIDE THE DEN OF FRANKIE THE FENCE...
HERE'S SOME MORE STUFF FOR YOU, FRANKIE!
LET'S TAKE A LOOK AT IT!

NOT BAD-NOT BAD!
WHAT DO YA MEAN NOT BAD? THAT STUFF WAS TAKEN FROM THE VAN DEEKES' SAFE!

-AND IT'S GOING RIGHT BACK AGAIN!
THE BATMAN!

WITH ONE LIGHTNING MOVE, THE BATMAN WHEELS ACROSS THE ROOM-HIS MUSCULAR FRAME RAMS INTO THE THREE DEVILS!...

THE BOY WONDER BRINGS HIS LITHE BODY INTO PLAY....
HELP! MIKE! TRIGGER! JOE!
ME FOR YOU!

A SIDE DOOR BANGS OPEN AND THREE THUGS BURST INTO THE ROOM.....
WHAT...? WHAT'S GOIN' ON-A RIOT?
THE BATMAN! NOW'S OUR CHANCE TO GET THAT GUY!
LOOK -THE BATMAN!

A THUG HURLS HIMSELF AT THE BATMAN. BUT FINDS HIMSELF TACKLING EMPTY AIR!
GETTING ME IS NOT GOING TO BE SO EASY!

THAT'S WHAT I WANT! OOPS... PARDON ME!

THE BATMAN AND ROBIN HOLD THEIR OWN AGAINST ODDS!
NICE LITTLE RIOT WE STARTED, EH, ROBIN?
IT'S NOT SO BAD!
I'D BE SAFER FIGHTING A TIGER THAN THE BATMAN, WOW!?

FRANKIE WHIPS OUT A GLEAMING KNIFE, AND CIRCLING BEHIND THE BATMAN, RAISES IT ALOFT FOR THE PLUNGE.....

I DON'T KNOW HOW THIS BOOK GOT MIXED UP IN YOUR PLACE, BUT IT'S A CINCH YOU NEVER READ IT!
CRIME DOES NOT PAY!
AWK!
BONK!
7

TRIGGER GETS DESPERATE AND LIVES UP TO HIS NAME..... AVOIDING THE WHINING BULLETS, THE BATMAN GRAZES HIS HEAD ON THE EDGE OF THE TABLE!
I'LL STOP YA!

YOU FOOL! THAT SHOT WILL BRING THE POLICE!
I FORGOT!
THIS SIDE DOOR- HURRY! IT LEADS TO THE STREET!

WHAT'S THE IDEA OF THE CAR?
GET IN! THE STREET WILL BE ALIVE WITH POLICE! WE CAN'T LET OURSELVES BE SEEN WITH OUR COSTUMES ON!

AS THE CAR BOLTS FROM THE CURB, A FIGURE LOOKS AFTER IT.... ROBIN, THE BOY WONDER!
THE BATMAN WILL BE ALL RIGHT. I'VE GOT TO FOLLOW THE DEVILS! NOW FOR MY ROCKET-SKATES!

ON GO THE STRANGE ROLLER SKATES. A LEVER IS PUSHED ON EACH, AND ROBIN IS WHIZZING AFTER THE CAR!
BOY- THESE THINGS CAN TRAVEL!
Thrifty

THE BOY WONDER LEANS FORWARD TO KEEP HIS BALANCE AS HE STREAKS LIKE A FLASH OVER THE PAVED STREET....
ROBIN'S ROCKET-SKATES! NOT A BAD NAME!

MEANWHILE, WHAT OF THE BATMAN? ....AS HE RISES TO HIS FEET, A BLUE-UNIFORMED FIGURE CONFRONTS HIM......
THE LAW!
WHA....THE BATMAN! I'VE GOT THE BATMAN!

COULD YOU BE TELLIN' ME WHAT'S BEEN GOIN' ON HERE?
THAT'S EASY! THE THREE DEVILS HAVE BEEN DISPOSING OF THEIR LOOT BY WAY OF FRANKIE THE FENCE! I TRIED TO BREAK UP THE COMBINATION- BUT THEY GOT AWAY!

IF I EVER MEET THEM AGAIN THEY WON'T GET AWAY!
I'M SURE THEY WON'T. 'TIS A FUNNY THING, MR. BATMAN, BUT I HAVE A LOT OF RESPECT FOR YE- EVEN THOUGH YOUR METHODS AIN'T EXACTLY PEACEFUL!

YE KNOW, IF YOU WAS TA BE HITTIN' ME ONCE, I GUESS THEN I COULDN'T HOLD YE - AND I'D STILL BE CARRYIN' OUT ME DOOTY!
SAY, YOU'RE OKAY!

SOCK AWAY!
AS LONG AS YOU SAY SO - HERE IT IS!

...AND WHEN OTHER POLICE BREAK IN....
IT'S RILEY! HE'S UNCONSCIOUS!
...AND WILL YOU LOOK AT THE MAN... HE-HE LOOKS LIKE HE WAS GRINNING AT SOMETHING!

IN THE MEANTIME, ROBIN HAS TRAILED THE DEVILS TO THE EDGE OF TOWN....
THEY'RE GOING INTO THAT TUNNEL!

ROBIN FOLLOWS...
WHY-WHY, THIS IS THE ABANDONED TUNNEL THAT CONNECTS WITH THE SUBWAY!

AS THE THREE DEVILS TURN A CORNER, ROBIN IS CLOSE BEHIND, WHEN SUDDENLY SOMETHING LANDS ON HIS HEAD WITH A PARALYZING THUD!

I'LL PLUG THE KID AND GET IT OVER WITH!
NO! IF HIS BODY IS DISCOVERED WITH A SLUG IN IT, THE COPS WILL INVESTIGATE AND MAYBE FIND OUR HIDEOUT!
LET'S SHOVE HIM ON THE SUBWAY TRACK. THE TRAIN WILL FINISH HIM AND IT WILL LOOK LIKE AN ACCIDENT -LOOK LIKE HE FELL OFF THE STATION.

A MOMENT LATER, ROBIN'S INERT FORM IS LYING ACROSS A SUBWAY EXPRESS TRACK.....IN THE DISTANCE, THE WAIL OF A TRAIN WHISTLE IS HEARD....
WOOOO

AS ROBIN GAINS CONSCIOUSNESS, HE IS AWARE OF A THROBBING NOISE... THE GROUND SHIVERS... A SUBWAY TRAIN IS APPROACHING!!

DEATH- CRUSHING DEATH IS HURTLING AT HIM AS THE TRAIN ROARS OUT OF THE TUNNEL...
TRAIN-- GROGGY- CAN'T MOVE- GOT NO STRENGTH!

THE TERRIBLE BLOW ON THE HEAD HAS LEFT ROBIN STILL DIZZY AND WEAK! THE TRAIN LEAPS AT HIM AT A TERRIFYING SPEED...
GOT TO MOVE- GOT TO.....
IT POUNDS OVER THE RAILS, ITS WHEELS SCREAMING LIKE TORTURED BEASTS....

SUDDENLY, AS THE TRAIN RUSHES AT HIM LIKE A GIGANTIC MONSTER OF STEEL, ROBIN MAKES A DESPERATE TRY... ROLLS AND SLIPS DOWN IN THE GRAVEL PIT THAT RUNS BETWEEN THE TRACKS....

HE IS NOT A SECOND TOO SOON, FOR AN INSTANT LATER THE TRAIN IS DASHING OVER HIM AT BULLET SPEED!

LATER, WHEN HE IS ABLE, ROBIN RACES HOME TO RELATE EVERYTHING TO THE BATMAN....
...SO I'M ALL RIGHT NOW. ANYWAY, WE KNOW WHERE THE HIDEOUT OF THE THREE DEVILS IS!
APPROPRIATE THAT THE DEVILS SHOULD HAVE A HIDEOUT UNDERGROUND -SORT OF IN KEEPING WITH THEIR CHARACTER! WE'LL TAKE A LOOK TOMORROW AFTER YOU'VE RESTED!

THE NEXT NIGHT, THE DYNAMIC DUO RETRACE ROBIN'S STEPS AND ENTER THE HIDDEN ABODE OF THE THREE DEVILS!
THEY'RE GONE!
PROBABLY OUT PULLING ONE OF THEIR JOBS!

THE BATMAN IDLY INSPECTS THE BOOK ON THE TABLE.
A BOOK FULL OF NEWSPAPER CLIPPINGS - ALL ABOUT CIRCUS ACROBATS! NOW I'VE GOT IT-THE THREE DEVILS ARE FORMER CIRCUS ACROBATS!
NO WONDER THEY WERE ABLE TO HOP AROUND LIKE THEY DID!

LOOK-THIS ARTICLE TELLING ABOUT A JEWELRY CONCERN OPENING ON THE TOP FLOOR OF THE CAPITOL STATE BUILDING-IT'S UNDERLINED!
THAT MEANS THEY'VE GONE TO LOOT THE PLACE! C'MON-THERE'S NOT A MOMENT TO LOSE!

ATOP THE OBSERVATION TOWER OF THE CAPITOL STATE BUILDING....
OKAY-I'LL LOWER YOU DOWN TO THE WINDOW!
RIGHT! THIS WILL BE A CINCH FOR US!

SUDDENLY, TWO FIGHTING WHIRLWINDS FLASH IN THEIR MIDST...
THE BATMAN! HE KNOWS ABOUT US!
I'LL MAKE YOU REGRET YOU LEFT THE CIRCUS TO BECOME CROOKS!
THAT KID- HE'S STILL ALIVE!

OVER THE ROOF TOP THEY BATTLE, WHEN SUDDENLY A DEVIL MANAGES TO HIT ROBIN A TERRIBLE BLOW...
HAH!
UGH!

THE BOY TUMBLES BACK OVER THE BALUSTRADE AND PLUNGES DOWN!....

AS THE BOY'S TWISTING BODY FLASHES PAST THE NEARBY BUILDING, HIS MANTLE BILLOWS OUT, CATCHES HOLD ON THE HOUR HAND OF THE GIANT CLOCK ON THE BUILDING FACE....

...AND ROBIN DANGLES IN MID AIR!
WHEW! SAVED IN THE NICK OF "TIME"!

THE BATMAN MAKES A DESPERATE LEAP FOR THE BELFRY TOWER....
THAT CAPE WON'T STAND THE STRAIN VERY LONG! I'VE GOT TO HELP! THAT BELFRY TOWER... I MAY BE ABLE TO REACH HIM FROM THERE!

THE THREE DEVILS SPRING AFTER THE BATMAN!
HE'S THE ONLY ONE WHO KNOWS WHO WE ARE!
WE'VE GOT TO KILL HIM TO PROTECT OURSELVES!

HIGH UP ON THE BELL TOWER CROSS-BEAMS, THERE IS A TITANIC STRUGGLE...

MEANWHILE, AS ROBIN DANGLES PERILOUSLY IN SPACE, A MURDEROUS DEVIL LEVELS A GUN AT HIS HELPLESS FIGURE...
NOW'S MY CHANCE TO GET THAT KID-- I CAN'T MISS...

A CREAKING BOARD WARNS ROBIN, WHOSE HAND DARTS IN HIS JERKIN AND PRODUCES THE SLING-SHOT!
NOT A SECOND TO LOSE...

EVEN FROM HIS DIFFICULT POSITION, ROBIN'S AIM IS TRUE! THE DEVIL TOPPLES FROM HIS PERCH AS THE STEEL PELLET CATCHES HIM SQUARELY IN THE FOREHEAD!
YAAAAAA
Z..I..N..G..
13

SUDDENLY, THE CLOCK INDICATES NINE O'CLOCK! UP IN THE BELFRY, MACHINERY SETS THE BELL IN MOTION TO TOLL THE HOUR...
THE HOUR-- NOW'S MY CHANCE!

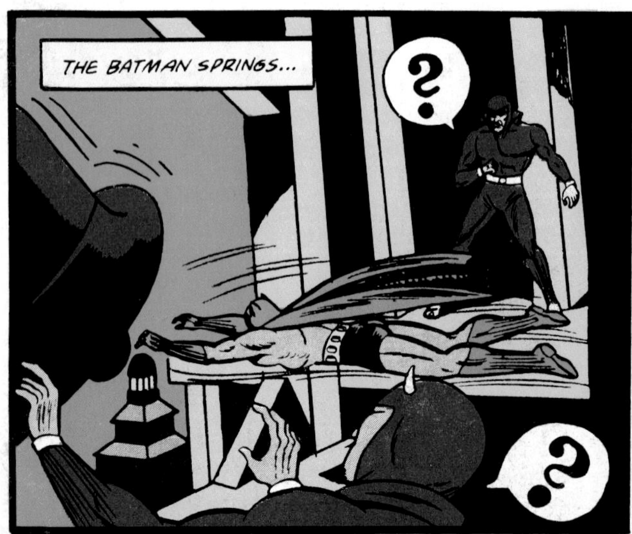
THE BATMAN SPRINGS...
?
?

AS THE BATMAN CATCHES THE CLAPPER, THE BELL SWINGS OUT...
RING!
RING OUT, WILD BELLS!
RING!
RING!

...THEN AS IT SWINGS BACK AGAIN INTO THE BELFRY, THE BATMAN LASHES OUT WITH BOTH FEET!
...AND HERE'S WHERE I RING THE BELL WITH YOU FELLOWS!

...THE MURDERING DEVILS TOPPLE TO THE FLOOR BELOW!

WITH THE AID OF HIS SILK ROPE, THE BATMAN RESCUES ROBIN!

LATER...
WHEW! I'VE HAD ENOUGH EXCITEMENT TO DO ME FOR A LONG TIME!
THOSE DEVILS DID GIVE US A BIT OF TROUBLE, DIDN'T THEY?
BOB KANE

THEY WOULD HAVE BEEN MUCH BETTER OFF IF THEY HAD STAYED WITH THE CIRCUS.
LIKE A LOT OF OTHER PEOPLE, THEY THOUGHT THEY COULD PICK UP WEALTH THE EASY WAY. THEY SHOULD HAVE REALIZED THAT'S THE HARDEST WAY —WHICH ONCE AGAIN PROVES THAT CRIME DOESN'T PAY!